TEACHER'S GUIDE

GRADE 3

Authors

Ruth Nathan
Laura Robb

Great Source Education Group

a Houghton Mifflin Company
Wilmington, Massachusetts
www.greatsource.com

Authors

Ruth Nathan, one of the authors of *Writers Express* and *Write Away*, is the author of many professional books and articles on literacy. She earned a Ph.D. in reading from Oakland University in Rochester, Michigan, where she co-headed their reading research laboratory for several years. She currently teaches in third grade, as well as consults with numerous schools and organizations on reading.

Laura Robb, author of *Reading Strategies That Work* and *Teaching Reading in the Middle School*, has taught language arts at Powhatan School in Boyce, Virginia, for more than thirty years. She also mentors and coaches teachers in Virginia public schools and speaks at conferences throughout the country.

Great Source® is a registered trademark of Houghton Mifflin Company.

Printed in the United States of America.

International Standard Book Number: 0-669-48441-5

1 2 3 4 5 6 7 8 9 10 POO 06 05 04 03 02 01 00

Readers and Reviewers

Judy Backlund
Mt. Stuart School
Ellensburg, WA

Pam Baglien
Sunnyside Elementary
New Brighton, MN

Jackie Bledsoe
Jamieson Elementary
Detroit, MI

Diane Brown
Island Lake School
Shoreview, MN

Nan Bryant
Apple Pie Ridge Elementary
Winchester, VA

Sara Cerniglia
Creek Valley Elementary
Edina, MN

Carol Chapman
Powhatan School
Boyce, VA

Janet DeBoer
Stonewall Magnet School
Lexington, KY

Helen Dorothy
Little Village Academy
Chicago, IL

Rosalee Fructer
Dickson Elementary
Chicago, IL

Kathy Hawkins
Sydney Glen Elementary
Port Orchard, WA

Candy Hernandez
Dike-Newell School
Bath, ME

Judy Jacobsen
Bel Air Elementary
New Brighton, MN

Lois Johnson
Cedar Grove Elementary School
Panama City, FL

Debbie King
Augustus Burly Elementary
Chicago, IL

Diane Kraft
Apple Creek School
Bismark, ND

Deb Larson
Berryton Elementary School
Berryton, KS

Emily N. Luke
Patronis Elementary School
Panama City, FL

Judith McAllister
Fisher Mitchell Elementary School
Bath, ME

Kim Prater
Cedar Grove Elementary School
Panama City, FL

Barbara (Dee) Pringle
South School
Londonderry, NH

Nancy Roche
Powhatan School
Boyce, VA

Sheri Sayers
LA Unified School District

Beth Schmar
Emporia State University
Emporia, Kansas

Jean Smith
Depaul University
Chicago, IL

Lucy W. Smith
Patronis Elementary School
Panama City, FL

Louis Soria
Augustus Burly Elementary
Chicago, IL

Jane Suminski
Luther-Burbank Elementary
Milwaukee, WI

Jana Svendsen
Lincoln Elementary School
Mt. Vernon, WA

Janet Thompson

Lisa Vance
Echo Horizon School
Culver City, CA

Dr. Carol Warmuth
Washington Rose Elementary
Roosevelt, NY

Charon P. Wood
Templeton Elementary
Riverdale, MD

Table of Contents

Introduction to Program

Strategy Handbook

Table of Contents

LEXILE / GRADE LEVEL

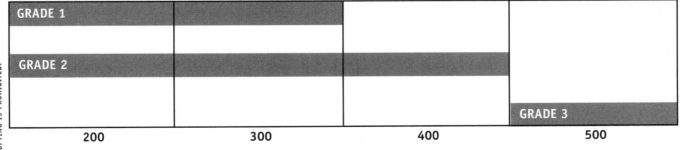

PUPIL'S EDITION SKILLS AND STRATEGIES

The chart below identifies the strategies for each part of each pupil's edition lesson.

Selection	I. Prereading	II. Response Notes	Comprehension	Word Work
1. Play Ball, Amelia Bedelia (fiction)	predict	question	retell	suffixes
2. Poems about the Weather (poetry)	word web	draw	double-entry journal	building new words
3. Frogs (nonfiction)	anticipation guide	make clear	directed reading	compound words
4. I'll Catch the Moon (fiction)	word web	draw	directed reading	building new words
5. Volcanoes: Mountains That Blow Their Tops (nonfiction)	preview	make clear	directed reading	silent e and word endings
6. Cave People (nonfiction)	K-W-L chart	make clear	directed reading	syllables
7. Look at Your Eyes (nonfiction)	preview	question	cause and effect chart	prefixes and suffixes
8. Just a Few Words, Mr. Lincoln (nonfiction)	think-pair-and-share	connect	directed reading	base words
9. Why I Sneeze, Shiver, Hiccup, and Yawn (nonfiction)	K-W-L chart	make clear	directed reading	dividing words by their syllables
10. Marvin Redpost: Alone in His Teacher's House (fiction)	think-pair-and-share	connect	double-entry journal	silent e and word endings
11. Hungry, Hungry Sharks (nonfiction)	preview	make clear	directed reading	building new words
12. Buffalo Bill and the Pony Express (nonfiction)	anticipation guide	question	story frame	base words
13. Tomás and the Library Lady (fiction)	think-pair-and-share	draw	double-entry journal	compound words
14. Going Home (fiction)	predict	connect	story chart	silent e words and words ending in two consonants
15. Fox and Crane (fiction)	think-pair-and-share	question	retell	base words
16. Abuela (fiction)	word web	draw	double-entry journal	prefixes and suffixes

III. Prewriting	IV. Writing	Grammar/Usage	V. Assessment
brainstorm	letter	commas	enjoyment
brainstorm	poem	spelling	ease
narrowing a topic	expository paragraph	initial capitalization	meaning
web/topic sentence	descriptive paragraph	commas in a series	ease
main idea/detail chart	expository paragraph	initial capitalization	enjoyment
5Ws chart	news story	end punctuation	understanding
narrowing a topic	expository paragraph	commas in compound sentences	meaning
clustering	journal entry	commas in a series	understanding
a) main idea and details b) closing sentence	expository paragraph	capitalization	enjoyment
character cluster	journal entry	apostrophes and contractions	understanding
web	descriptive paragraph	spelling	meaning
character map	letter	commas in headings and dates	ease
story chart	story ending	apostrophes in singular possessives	enjoyment
brainstorm	poem	apostrophes in plural possessives	ease
story chart	story ending	apostrophes in plural possessives	understanding
character map	descriptive paragraph	capitalization	meaning

TEACHER'S GUIDE SKILLS AND STRATEGIES

The chart below identifies the strategies for each part of each teacher's edition lesson.

Selection	Vocabulary	Prereading	Comprehension
1. Play Ball, Amelia Bedelia (fiction)	context clues	a) prediction b) picture walk	retelling
2. Poems about the Weather (poetry)	context clues	a) word web b) graphic organizer	double-entry journal
3. Frogs (nonfiction)	context clues	a) anticipation guide b) think-pair-and-share	stop and think questions
4. I'll Catch the Moon (fiction)	context clues	a) word web b) picture walk	stop and think questions
5. Volcanoes: Mountains That Blow Their Tops (nonfiction)	context clues	a) preview b) K-W-L	stop and think questions
6. Cave People (nonfiction)	context clues	a) K-W-L b) quickwrite	stop and think questions
7. Look at Your Eyes (nonfiction)	context clues	a) preview b) skim	cause-effect interrupter
8. Just a Few Words, Mr. Lincoln (nonfiction)	context clues	a) think-pair-and-share b) clustering	stop and think questions
9. Why I Sneeze, Shiver, Hiccup, and Yawn (nonfiction)	context clues	a) K-W-L b) anticipation guide	stop and think questions
10. Marvin Redpost: Alone in His Teacher's House (fiction)	context clues	a) think-pair-and-share b) web	double-entry journal
11. Hungry, Hungry Sharks (nonfiction)	synonyms	a) preview b) quickwrite	stop and think questions
12. Buffalo Bill and the Pony Express (nonfiction)	context clues	a) anticipation guide b) prediction	story frames
13. Tomás and the Library Lady (fiction)	context clues	a) think-pair-and-share b) preview	double-entry journal
14. Going Home (fiction)	context clues	a) predictions b) anticipation guide	story chart
15. Fox and Crane (fiction)	synonyms	a) think-pair-and-share b) story impression	retell
16. Abuela (fiction)	context clues	a) word web b) picture walk	double-entry journal

Questions	Prewriting	Assessment
a) comprehension b) critical thinking	brainstorm	multiple-choice test
a) comprehension b) critical thinking	brainstorm	multiple-choice test
a) comprehension b) critical thinking	narrowing a topic	multiple-choice test
a) comprehension b) critical thinking	web/topic sentence	multiple-choice test
a) comprehension b) critical thinking	main idea and supporting details	multiple-choice test
a) comprehension b) critical thinking	5Ws chart	multiple-choice test
a) comprehension b) critical thinking	narrowing a topic	multiple-choice test
a) comprehension b) critical thinking	brainstorm	multiple-choice test
a) comprehension b) critical thinking	main idea and supporting details	multiple-choice test
a) comprehension b) critical thinking	character map	multiple-choice test
a) comprehension b) critical thinking	web	multiple-choice test
a) comprehension b) critical thinking	character map	multiple-choice test
a) comprehension b) critical thinking	story chart	multiple-choice test
a) comprehension b) critical thinking	brainstorm/ web	multiple-choice test
a) comprehension b) critical thinking	story chart	multiple-choice test
a) comprehension b) critical thinking	character map	multiple-choice test

CORRELATION TO *WRITE AWAY* AND *WRITE ON TRACK*

Like the *Write Away* and *Write on Track* handbooks, the *Sourcebook* will appeal to teachers who believe that writing is a way of learning. This *Sourcebook*, like *Write Away*, is a book to "grow in." Here students read a series of carefully sequenced selections and respond to them. They jot notes, create organizers, plan and brainstorm compositions, and write drafts of their work. The *Sourcebook* is one way for students to read and write weekly if not daily.

After students write, they are asked to look again at their compositions in a feature called **Writers' Checklist**. This feature in **Part IV Write** highlights two or three key points of Grammar, Usage, and Mechanics. These features are brief mini-lessons. They invite students to look back at their writing and apply some aspect of Grammar, Usage, or Mechanics to it.

In the *Sourcebooks*, both the kinds of writing and the mini-lessons on Grammar, Usage, and Mechanics afford the best opportunities to use the *Write Away* or *Write on Track* handbooks as a reference. To make this convenient, the writing activities are correlated to the handbooks below, and the mini-lessons are correlated on the following page.

For Writing Activity

Selection Title	Writing Activity	*Write Away* © 2000 (pages)	*Write on Track* (pages)
1. *Play Ball, Amelia Bedelia*	letter	72–75, 96–101	92–95, 122–129, 297
2. Poems about the Weather	poem	124–125, 151–167	177–189
3. *Frogs*	expository paragraph	54–61	60
4. *I'll Catch the Moon*	descriptive paragraph	54–61	59
5. *Volcanoes: Mountains That Blow Their Tops*	expository paragraph	54–61	60
6. *Cave People*	news story	92–95	110–115
7. *Look at Your Eyes*	expository paragraph	54–61	60
8. *Just a Few Words, Mr. Lincoln*	journal entry	27–29, 65–67	77–81
9. *Why I Sneeze, Shiver, Hiccup, and Yawn*	expository paragraph	54–61	60
10. *Marvin Redpost: Alone in His Teacher's House*	journal entry	27–29, 65–67	77–81
11. *Hungry, Hungry Sharks*	descriptive paragraph	54–61	59
12. *Buffalo Bill and the Pony Express*	letter	72–75, 96–101	92–95, 122–129, 297
13. *Tomás and the Library Lady*	story ending	131–149	159–169
14. *Going Home*	poem	124–125, 151–167	177–189
15. "Fox and Crane"	story ending	131–149	159–169
16. *Abuela*	descriptive paragraph	54–61	59

CORRELATION TO *WRITE AWAY* AND *WRITE ON TRACK*

For Writing Mini-Lesson

Selection Title	Writing Mini-Lesson	*Write Away* © 2000 (pages)	*Write On Track* (pages)
1. *Play Ball, Amelia Bedelia*	commas in greetings and closings	250–251	297
2. Poems About the Weather	spelling	266–267, 260–265	224–227, 314–317
3. *Frogs*	initial capitalization	255–256	307–309
4. *I'll Catch the Moon*	commas in a series	250–251	297
5. *Volcanoes: Mountains That Blow Their Tops*	capitalization	255–256	307–309
6. *Cave People*	end punctuation	248–249	296, 303–304
7. *Look at Your Eyes*	commas in compound sentences	250–251	298
8. *Just a Few Words, Mr. Lincoln*	commas	250–251	297–299
9. *Why I Sneeze, Shiver, Hiccup, and Yawn*	capitalization	255–256	307–309
10. *Marvin Redpost: Alone in His Teacher's House*	apostrophes in contractions	202–203, 252	301
11. *Hungry, Hungry Sharks*	spelling	266–267, 260–265	224–227, 314–317
12. *Buffalo Bill and the Pony Express*	commas	250–251	297–299
13. *Tomás and the Library Lady*	apostrophes in singular possessives	252	301
14. *Going Home*	apostrophes in plural possessives	252	301
15. *"Fox and Crane"*	apostrophes in plural possessives	252	301
16. *Abuela*	capitalization	255–256	307–309

OVERVIEW

This **Sourcebook** targets struggling readers. In grades 3–5, these students need to be matched with quality literature that they can actually read. They need to be motivated, and they need good instruction in strategies that will help them learn how to transform sentences into a comprehensible text. They also need help with getting ready to write, help with grammar, usage, and mechanics; and they need help with writing different kinds of texts—letters, journal entries, descriptive paragraphs, and so forth.

A Comprehensive Approach

Because struggling readers have so many different needs, they often receive a number of small, separate activities—work on main idea and details, a list of spelling rules, some word work on prefixes, practice writing a topic sentence, and comma rules. But it seldom adds up to a coherent whole for students.

That's where this **Sourcebook** comes in. The **Sourcebook** takes a holistic approach, not a piecemeal one. Through a comprehensive 5-part lesson, each **Sourcebook** lesson walks the students through the steps needed to read a text at their reading level and write about it. The lessons pull it all together for students, weaving together many different skills into a coherent whole.

The 5-part lesson plan is:

   I. BEFORE YOU READ (prereading)

  II. READ (active reading and comprehension)

 III. GET READY TO WRITE (prewriting)

  IV. WRITE (writing, revising, grammar, usage, and mechanics)

   V. LOOK BACK (reflecting and self-assessment)

With this comprehensive approach, students can see the whole process of reading and writing. By following a consistent pattern, students can internalize key aspects of the reading and the writing process. These patterns will help students build the habits they need to become successful readers and writers. See also the Book and Lesson Organization overviews on pages 18–24.

A Strategy-Intensive Approach

The **Sourcebook** also uses a strategy-intensive approach. Each **Sourcebook** builds students' repertoire of reading strategies in at least three areas.

1. To build motivation and background, prereading strategies are used to get students ready to read and to help them see the prior knowledge they already bring to their reading experiences.

2. To build active readers, each **Sourcebook** begins with an overview called "Be an Active Reader," showing students ways to mark up texts and respond to them. Then, at least one of these strategies is used in each lesson.

3. To build comprehension, each **Sourcebook** uses 3–5 different comprehension strategies, such as Double-entry journals, retelling, using graphic organizers, and so on. By embedding these strategies in the literature, the **Sourcebook** shows students exactly which strategies to use and when to use them, building the habits of good readers. Then, after students finish reading, they are directed to go back and reread.

A Literature-Based Approach

Above all, the *Sourcebook* takes a literature-based approach. It presents 16 selections of quality literature of various genres by a wide range of authors. These selections are leveled in difficulty, starting with the easiest selection and progressing to more difficult ones. This leveling of the selections makes it easy to match students to literature they can actually read.

An Interactive Approach

The *Sourcebook* is an interactive book. It is intended to be a journal for students, in which they can write out their ideas about selections, plan and write out compositions, and record their progress throughout the year. Students should "own" their *Sourcebooks*, carrying them, reading in them, marking in them, and writing in them. They should become a record of their progress and accomplishments. Students will take pride in "their" *Sourcebook*.

Lesson Planning

A single *Sourcebook* lesson can be taught in approximately 8–10 class periods, whether that is over two, three, or even four weeks.

DAY 1 Build background and discuss the selection.

DAY 2 Read the introduction. Do the prereading activity.

DAY 3 Introduce the selection. Discuss how to respond to the selection and the example. Then read the selection the first time.

DAY 4 Finish reading the selection. Then encourage students to read the selection again, this time writing in the Response Notes.

DAY 5 Finish reading. Reread the selection again, as necessary, and respond to the comprehension activities in selection.

DAY 6 Do Word Work and point out the Reading Reminder.

DAY 7 Begin Get Ready to Write.

DAY 8 Begin Writing Activity.

DAY 9 Finish writing. Talk about the Writers' Checklist mini-lesson, and revise writing.

DAY 10 Reflect on the selection and what was learned.

Assessment

Each *Sourcebook* lesson includes a multiple-choice test for assessment, as well as a more holistic self-assessment in the pupil's book in **Part V Look Back**. Both are useful gauges of student progress. Teachers need to demonstrate the progress their students have made throughout the year. The best measure of that progress will be a student's marked-up *Sourcebook* and the greater confidence and fluency with which students will be reading by the end of the year. For additional assessment ideas, see the **Strategy Handbook** in this *Teacher's Guide*.

MATCHING READERS WITH SELECTIONS

Probably one of the greatest challenges nowadays for teachers is matching readers with the right texts. The range of reading abilities in classrooms often spans four or even five grade levels. Some students read two grade levels below, and some read two or more grade levels above grade level. The teacher's job is to match each of his or her students (usually 25 to 35 children) to the exact reading level, day in and day out. It is a large order.

What Level Is It?

To help match students to the appropriate books, educators have relied on "readability formulas" and levels. None of these measures is perfectly reliable. They are crucial, however, because you cannot read every book before matching it to each student in class.

The solution adopted in the *Sourcebooks* for grades 3–5 has been to begin with selections approximately two years below the student's actual grade level. That means that *Sourcebook*, grade 3, begins with what are normally considered grade 1 selections. Then, by the end of each book, the last few selections are approximately on grade level.

How Are Selections Leveled?

The selections in each *Sourcebook* are leveled, starting with the easiest and progressing to the most difficult. The measure relied upon to order them in the *Sourcebooks* is Lexile levels. They are readability measurements that place readings on a common scale, beginning at 100 and going up to 1700. Reading programs, reading specialists, and the authors of this series all have used this readability measurement and found it useful. For the purposes in the *Sourcebooks*, the Lexile Framework provided a standard way to assess the relative difficulty of selections and a convenient measure to gauge which selections might be appropriate for students who are reading two or more years below their grade level.

How Does This Help?

Because the selections in each *Sourcebook* are leveled, you can start groups of students at the beginning, middle, or end of the book. Begin with selections that are easy for students to build their confidence. Then gradually work toward more challenging ones.

At the same time, use the additional books by the author and those on the same theme suggested in this *Teacher's Guide*. Each *Sourcebook* lesson begins with recommendations of more books that are at or around the same Lexile level as the selection in the *Sourcebook*. The benefit of this plan is that it helps you quickly locate a lot of books you can use. You can also keep track when students begin to read harder books, challenging and also supporting them.

The *Sourcebooks* will help you spend more time guiding students' learning than searching for the appropriate books. That part, at least, has already been done.

HOW TO USE THIS BOOK

Guiding Struggling Learners

Frequently schools have classes with students of all ability levels, from a few grade levels below to one or two grade levels above. Then, "average" students in one school district vary greatly from "average" students in a neighboring one. The *Sourcebook* series aims at those students who consistently rank in the lower 50 percent of text scores and national averages.

The *Sourcebook* offers a comprehensive program of student-appropriate literature, strategy-building, writing, revising, and reflecting. The approach is a holistic one. Rather than assigning a worksheet to attack a specific problem—say, comprehension—the *Sourcebook* addresses the broader problems as well.

Each *Sourcebook* weaves together a comprehensive network of skills (see pages 6–9) that brings together the appropriate literature, reading strategies for that literature, and prewriting, writing, and revising activities. Students who work through even two or three entire selections will benefit greatly by seeing the whole picture of reading actively and writing about the text. They will also benefit from the sense of accomplishment that comes through completion of a whole task and that results in creative, original work of their own—perhaps some of the first they have accomplished.

Working with Students in Groups

Students who are reading at the same level are often grouped together. Some students are often pulled out for special tutoring with trained reading tutors. Those students reading below grade level are placed in another group, those reading on level in still another group, and those reading above level in one or more other groups. For you as the teacher, the effort becomes how to juggle the various groups and keep them all on task.

That's where the *Sourcebook* comes in. Each lesson presents a sustained, meaningful assignment that can be targeted at specific groups in your class. Students show reluctance to read when a selection is too difficult or frustrating for them to read independently. With the *Sourcebook*, you can match the group to a selection at a Lexile level that is just right. Then you have a sustained, meaningful lesson to guide them through as well as a number of additional books for the group to read at the same level.

Integrating Lessons with Other Activities

Because *Sourcebook* lessons are comprehensive, you can integrate read-alouds, strategy lessons on comprehension, word work on prefixes, suffixes, and base words, and writing mini-lessons. Each lesson affords you any number of opportunities to intervene at the right moment to guide students' learning.

Students can read selections silently to themselves and then work independently in one group while you are giving a strategy lesson with another group. Or, students may be reading independently any number of books on the same subject or theme.

Pulling Everything Together

The benefit of the *Sourcebook* comes in having everything pulled together in one place—for you and the student. You have 16 integrated units to choose from. Students have a book of their own, one they "own," that keeps them on track, guiding their learning and recording their progress. So, if you have interruptions because of holidays, field trips, or simply scheduling challenges, the *Sourcebook* holds the lesson together, allowing you and the students to double back if necessary and remember where they have been and where they are going.

Summary

The *Sourcebook* will not fix every learning problem for every student, but it will be helpful for struggling readers, especially those who are reading one or two years below their academic grade. Reading and writing deficits are hard, almost intractable problems for students and require a great amount of effort—on the part of the teacher and the student—to make any real improvement. The *Sourcebook* is one helpful tool in helping you create better readers and writers.

FREQUENTLY ASKED QUESTIONS

Because the *Sourcebooks* were extensively reviewed by teachers, a number of commonly asked questions have surfaced already, and the answers to them might be helpful in using the program.

1. Why is it called a *Sourcebook*?

The word *Sourcebook* captures a number of connotations and associations that seemed just right. For one, it is published by Great Source Education. The word *source* also had the right connotation of "place to go for a real, complete solution," as opposed to the other products that helped in only a limited area, such as "main idea" or "analogies." And, lastly, the term *Sourcebook* fit nicely alongside *Daybook*, another series also published by Great Source that targets better readers and writers who need help in critical reading, as opposed to this series that targets struggling readers.

2. Can students write in the *Sourcebook*?

Absolutely. Only by physically marking the text will students become truly active readers. To interact with a text and truly read as an active reader, students must write in the *Sourcebook*. The immediacy of reading and responding right there on the page is integral to the whole idea of the *Sourcebook*. By writing in the text, students build a sense of ownership about their work that is impossible to match through worksheets handed out week after week. The *Sourcebook* also serves, in a sense, like the student's portfolio and can become one of the most tangible ways of demonstrating a student's progress throughout the year.

3. Can I photocopy these lessons?

No, you cannot. Each page of the pupil's book carries a notice that explicitly states "copying is prohibited." To copy them illegally infringes on the rights of the authors of the selections and the publishers of the book. Writers such as Patricia McKissack, Arthur Dorros, Byrd Baylor, and others have granted permission to use their work in the *Sourcebook*, but not the right to copy it.

You can, however, copy the blackline masters in this *Teacher's Guide.* These pages are intended for you to photocopy and use in the classroom and are marked clearly on each page.

4. Can I skip around in the *Sourcebook*?

Teachers will often want to skip around and adjust the *Sourcebook* to their curriculum. But, in *Sourcebooks* 3–5, the selections are sequenced in the order of the reading difficulty. Selections in grade 3 progress from a Lexile reading level of 220 to 510. A similar progression exists at the other grade levels. The benefit comes in having selections you know will be appropriate for students and in having skills that are carefully sequenced. The writing expected of students progresses in difficulty, just as the readability does, moving from easiest to hardest. Further, the Word Work skills build off one another, so that terms such as "base word" and "consonant cluster" are assumed in later lessons after being introduced in earlier ones.

5. Where did the strategies used throughout the book come from?

Most of the reading strategies used are commonplace in elementary classrooms throughout the country. Reading textbooks as well as teacher resource books and in-services all describe the prereading and comprehension strategies used in the *Sourcebooks*. What is unusual in the *Sourcebooks* is the way these strategies have been woven together and applied to high-quality, appropriate literature.

6. Why do you direct students to read and reread the selection?

One suggestion from reviewers was to help struggling readers by asking them to do one thing at a time. Teachers suggested it was easier to read a selection once just to get a sense of it, a second time to respond to it in the Response Notes, and a third time to respond to the comprehension activities embedded in the selection. Rather than ask students to do three things at once, the lessons progress in manageable steps. It reduces frustration and increases chances of success. Plus, additional readings of a selection increase reading fluency and help improve comprehension.

7. Why do the *Sourcebooks* rely on Lexile measurements of readability?

The benefit of Lexile measurements are that they provide small increments of readability—say, from 220 to 240—and they are in wide use. The Lexile Framework for Reading has an easily accessed website (www.lexile.com) that allows you to search for authors and titles at specific readability levels. The website already has measured a huge selection of books and lexiled them. As a result, this measurement provided a public standard by which to assess readability and an ongoing tool for teachers.

8. How were the selections chosen and what is their readability?

Each selection in the *Sourcebooks* met numerous criteria: quality of the selection, readability, balance of fiction vs. nonfiction, as well as sex and ethnicity of the authors.

None of the criteria mattered if the selection did not hold the interest of students and didn't seem to be on a worthwhile subject or topic. But it is worth noting that nearly 50 percent of the selections in the *Sourcebooks* are nonfiction, at the request of teachers who wanted more help with this genre.

9. How can I know if my students can read this literature?

You have a number of ways to know how well your students can read the selections. First, you can simply try out a lesson or two with students.

Second, you can use a 10- or 15-word vocabulary pretest as a quick indicator. Choose 10 words randomly from each selection. Ask students to circle the ones they know and underline the ones they don't know. If students know only 1–5 words, then the selection will probably be frustrating for them. Spend some time preteaching the key vocabulary.

Third, ask students to read a selection aloud. By listening to the kind of miscues students make, you can gauge whether a selection is at, below, or above his or her reading level.

10. What if my students need even more help than what's in the *Sourcebook*?

This *Teacher's Guide* has been designed as the next level of support. Extra activities and blackline masters on vocabulary, comprehension, prewriting, and assessment are included here so that they can be used at the teacher's discretion. These aids can help scaffold individual parts of lessons, giving more help with Vocabulary, Word Work, or Prewriting. But let students work through the lessons. Even if they make mistakes, they still may be making progress and may need only a little patience and encouragement. The *Sourcebooks* offer a good foundation for your curriculum.

ORGANIZATION

Book Organization

Each *Sourcebook* has 16 selections organized sequentially from the easiest readability to the hardest. The first lesson begins with a selection at approximately two grade levels below the academic level. That is, *Sourcebook*, grade 3 begins with a selection at Lexile 220, which is approximately the middle of first grade.

Lesson Organization

Each lesson in the *Sourcebook* starts with an introduction that draws students into the selection, often by asking a provocative question or making a strong statement. The purpose of this introduction is to stimulate students' prior knowledge and build interest.

Opener

- Each selection begins with an introduction to create motivation for reading.

I. Before You Read

- Each lesson has five parts.

- The prereading step—the critical first step—builds background and further helps students access prior knowledge. Among the prereading strategies included in **Part I** of this *Sourcebook* are:

  - Think-Pair-and-Share
  - Anticipation Guide
  - Previewing
  - Word Web
  - K-W-L

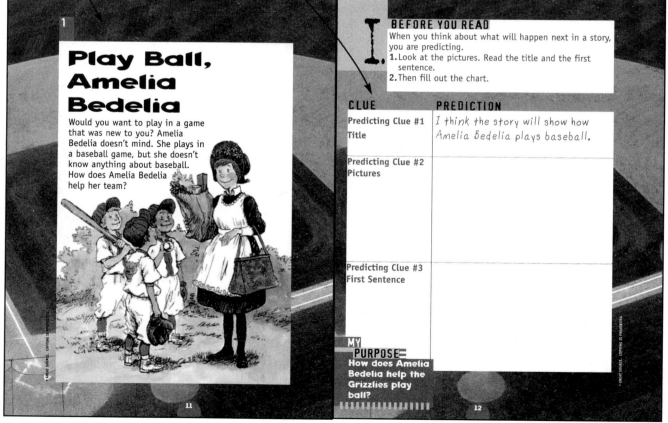

1

Play Ball, Amelia Bedelia

Would you want to play in a game that was new to you? Amelia Bedelia doesn't mind. She plays in a baseball game, but she doesn't know anything about baseball. How does Amelia Bedelia help her team?

11

I. BEFORE YOU READ

When you think about what will happen next in a story, you are predicting.

1. Look at the pictures. Read the title and the first sentence.
2. Then fill out the chart.

CLUE	PREDICTION
Predicting Clue #1 Title	*I think the story will show how Amelia Bedelia plays baseball.*
Predicting Clue #2 Pictures	
Predicting Clue #3 First Sentence	

MY PURPOSE
How does Amelia Bedelia help the Grizzlies play ball?

12

II. Read

- The reading step begins by telling students what they are to read and then details how they are to read the selection. The first step tells students how to mark the text. The second step reminds them to write their reactions or responses in the Response Notes. An example of an acceptable response is always provided.

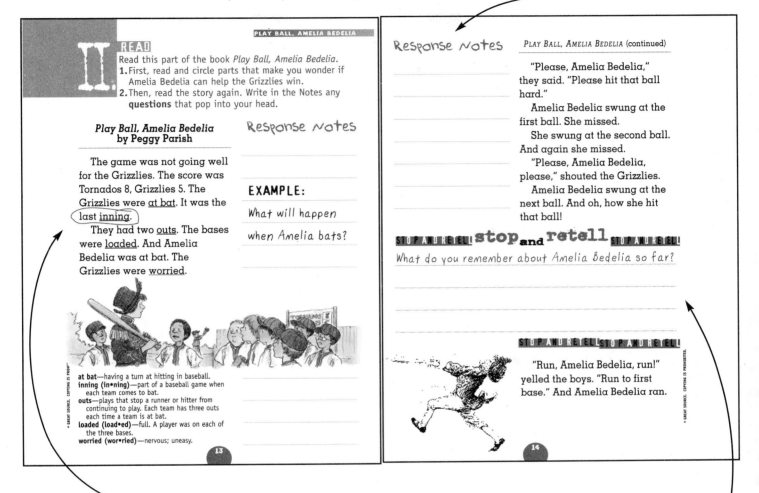

- The selection follows, with the challenging vocabulary highlighted throughout the selection. Vocabulary is defined at the bottom of the page. Each word is broken into syllables to make it easier for students to pronounce, with the stressed syllable highlighted in bold.

- Then, within each selection, a powerful comprehension strategy is embedded to help build in students the habits of good readers. Among the comprehension strategies included in **Part II** of this *Sourcebook* are:

  - Predict

  - Stop and Think (directed reading)

  - Storyboards (using graphic organizers)

  - Double-entry Journals

  - Retelling

- Then, at the end of each selection, students take time for Word Work to develop their word attack skills. Students who struggle to read in the early grades need help in breaking apart words to improve their reading fluency. The purpose of these activities is to help students know how to handle longer words. Among the Word Work activities in this *Sourcebook* are:

  - consonant clusters

  - prefixes and suffixes

  - compound words

  - syllables

  - contractions

  - word stems

  - adding endings

PLAY BALL, AMELIA BEDELIA

WORD WORK

Missed, *missing*, and *misses* have something in common. Each word has a **base word** (*miss*) and an **ending** (*-ed, -ing, -es*). An ending added to a base word is called a **suffix** (suh-fix).

> Amelia *missed* the ball!
> Amelia is *missing* the ball!
> Amelia *misses* the ball!

One way to add a suffix to a base word is just to add it.

miss + ed = *missed*
miss + ing = *missing*
miss + es = *misses*

A suffix is a great tool for making new words. Add the suffixes to the words below to make new words.

jump + ing =

leap + ed =

read + ing =

mix + es =

spend + ing =

wait + ing =

smell + ed=

READING REMINDER

Stories show what characters are like by what they say and do.

17

- At the bottom of the page, students will see a "Reading Reminder" that gives a critical reading tip. The "reminders" attempt to make explicit the strategies good readers use.

III. Get Ready to Write

- The prewriting step helps get students ready to write. Through one or two carefully sequenced activities, the prewriting step helps students prepare to write. Students generate ideas, choose and narrow a subject, and create supporting details. Often the prewriting activities will include one or more models. Among the prewriting activities are:

  - Main Idea and Supporting Details

  - Brainstorming

  - Writing a Topic Sentence

  - Word Web

  - Character Map

  - Story Chart

  - Narrowing a Topic

III GET READY TO WRITE

A. MAKE A LIST
Pretend you are writing a letter to a friend. Tell your friend about the funny things Amelia Bedelia did. Brainstorm a list of what you want to include below. One idea is on the list. You fill in the rest.

1. She took the first base.

2.

3.

4.

B. LOOK AT A MODEL
Look at these 5 parts of a friendly letter.

1. date → September 10, 2000

2. greeting — Dear Jim,

3. body — Today I saw a strange ball game. Amelia Bedelia played in it, and she was funny.

4. closing → Your friend,

5. signature → Jill

18

IV. Write

- The writing step begins with step-by-step instructions for building a writing assignment. Taken together, these instructions form the writing rubric for students to use in building the assignment. Among the writing assignments students are asked to write are:

  - Paragraph with topic sentence
  - Narrative paragraph
  - Expository paragraph
  - Journal entry
  - Descriptive paragraph
  - Letter
  - News Article

- Each **Part IV Write** also includes a **Writers' Checklist**. Each one is a brief mini-lesson on a relevant aspect of grammar, usage, or mechanics. The intent of the **Writers' Checklist** is to ask students appropriate questions after they write, instilling the habit of going back into their work to revise, edit, and proofread. The **Writers' Checklist** also affords teachers the opportunity to teach relevant grammar, usage, and mechanics skills at a teachable moment.

PLAY BALL, AMELIA BEDELIA

IV. WRITE

Now you are ready to write your own **letter**.
1. Use the ideas from your brainstorming list on page 18.
2. First, check the 3 ideas you want to include.
3. Follow the 5 parts of a friendly letter.
4. Use the Writers' Checklist to edit your work.

Continue your letter on the next page.

19

Continue your letter.

WRITERS' CHECKLIST

Commas

☐ Did you use commas correctly in the heading, greeting, and closing?
EXAMPLES:
Bedford, Iowa
Dear Susan,
Your friend,

V. Look Back

- The last step of each lesson asks students to monitor their own reading and reflect. Students are asked a question about their reading and writing experience from the **Readers' Checklist**. This "looking back" is intended to help students see what they learned in the lesson. They are intentionally asked more than simply, "Did you understand?"

For good readers, reading is much, much more than "Did you get it?" Good readers read for pleasure, for information, for the pure enjoyment of reading artfully written material, for personal curiosity, for a desire to learn more, and countless other reasons. For students to see that reading is worthwhile to them, they need to believe the payoff is more than "Did you get it?" on a five-question multiple-choice test.

The *Sourcebook* attempts with **Part V Look Back** to help students ask the questions good readers ask of themselves when they read. It attempts to broaden the reasons for reading by asking students to consider four reasons for reading:

- Enjoyment

- Understanding

- Ease

- Meaning

Continue your letter.

WRITERS' CHECKLIST

Commas

☐ **Did you use commas correctly in the heading, greeting, and closing?**
EXAMPLES:
Bedford Iowa
Dear Susan
Your friend

V. LOOK BACK
Write an answer to this question. What part of the story about Amelia Bedelia did you enjoy the most?

Think about Your Reading
READERS' CHECKLIST
Enjoyment
■ **Did you like the reading?**
■ **Would you recommend the reading to a friend?**

20

© GREAT SOURCE. COPYING IS PROHIBITED.

The *Sourcebook* is color coded for both aesthetic and organizational purposes. The color red is used for instructions. Black indicates literature, footnotes, and examples. Blue means the student will complete an activity.

How to Read a Lesson

Here are 3 easy steps to help you get the most out of the readings in this book.

1. For each reading, **read it once** and just circle or underline the important parts.

2. Then **read it again.** On the second reading, write questions or comments in the Notes.

3. Then, at the end of each reading, you will find a part called **Reread.** This part asks you to go back one more time and be sure you have answered all the questions.

Red=Follow Directions

Blue=Write Here

Black=Read This

PLAY BALL, AMELIA BEDELIA

READ

Read this part of the book *Play Ball, Amelia Bedelia.*
1. First, read and circle parts that make you wonder if Amelia Bedelia can help the Grizzlies win.
2. Then, read the story again. Write in the Notes any **questions** that pop into your head.

Play Ball, Amelia Bedelia
by Peggy Parish

The game was not going well for the Grizzlies. The score was Tornados 8, Grizzlies 5. The Grizzlies were at bat. It was the last inning.
They had two outs. The bases were loaded. And Amelia Bedelia was at bat. The Grizzlies were worried.

Response Notes

EXAMPLE:

What will happen when Amelia bats?

at bat—having a turn at hitting in baseball.
inning (in•ning)—part of a baseball game when each team comes to bat.
outs—plays that stop a runner or hitter from continuing to play. Each team has three outs each time a team is at bat.
loaded (load•ed)—full. A player was on each of the three bases.
worried (wor•ried)—nervous; uneasy.

1

By reading and rereading, you will do what good readers do.

←←← **reread** →→→

Read the story again. Look for details that help you understand how Amelia Bedelia helped her team. Be sure you answered the **Stop and Retell** questions.

10

Organization

TEACHER'S LESSON PLANS

Each lesson plan for the teacher of the *Sourcebook* has **twelve** pages:

PAGE 1 **Background and Bibliography**

- The lesson begins with background on the author and selection, and gives at least three additional titles by this author or on this same subject.

- The additional titles in the bibliography are included both for read-alongs and as independent reading, giving you ways to introduce the author, selection, and general subject.

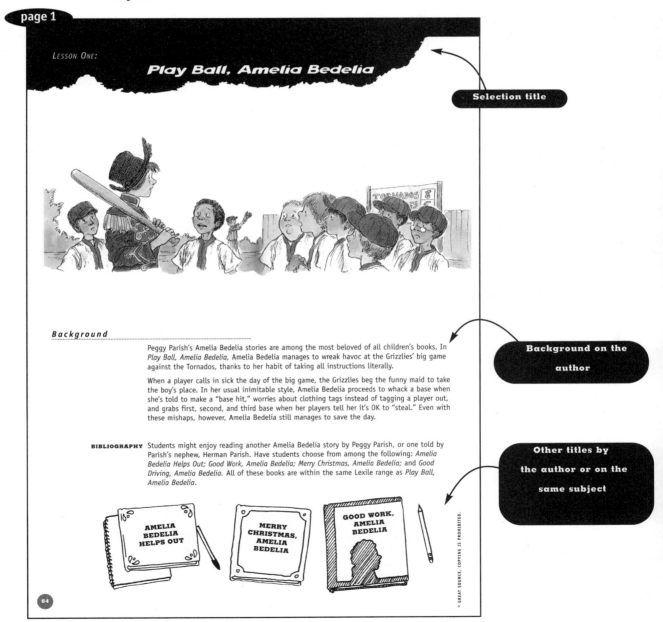

page 1

LESSON ONE:

Play Ball, Amelia Bedelia

Selection title

Background

Peggy Parish's Amelia Bedelia stories are among the most beloved of all children's books. In *Play Ball, Amelia Bedelia*, Amelia Bedelia manages to wreak havoc at the Grizzlies' big game against the Tornados, thanks to her habit of taking all instructions literally.

When a player calls in sick the day of the big game, the Grizzlies beg the funny maid to take the boy's place. In her usual inimitable style, Amelia Bedelia proceeds to whack a base when she's told to make a "base hit," worries about clothing tags instead of tagging a player out, and grabs first, second, and third base when her players tell her it's OK to "steal." Even with these mishaps, however, Amelia Bedelia still manages to save the day.

BIBLIOGRAPHY Students might enjoy reading another Amelia Bedelia story by Peggy Parish, or one told by Parish's nephew, Herman Parish. Have students choose from among the following: *Amelia Bedelia Helps Out; Good Work, Amelia Bedelia; Merry Christmas, Amelia Bedelia;* and *Good Driving, Amelia Bedelia*. All of these books are within the same Lexile range as *Play Ball, Amelia Bedelia*.

Background on the author

Other titles by the author or on the same subject

AMELIA BEDELIA HELPS OUT

MERRY CHRISTMAS, AMELIA BEDELIA

GOOD WORK, AMELIA BEDELIA

64

PAGE 2 **How to Introduce the Reading**

- The next page of the teacher's plan introduces the selection and gives teachers a way to motivate students to read. In most cases, the introduction serves as a way to create a sense of expectation in students and to provide some initial background for the reading.

Other Reading

- Three more titles written at the same readability level are included in "Other Reading." The purpose is to suggest to teachers titles at this same reading level, so students can go beyond the selection in the text to other appropriate titles.

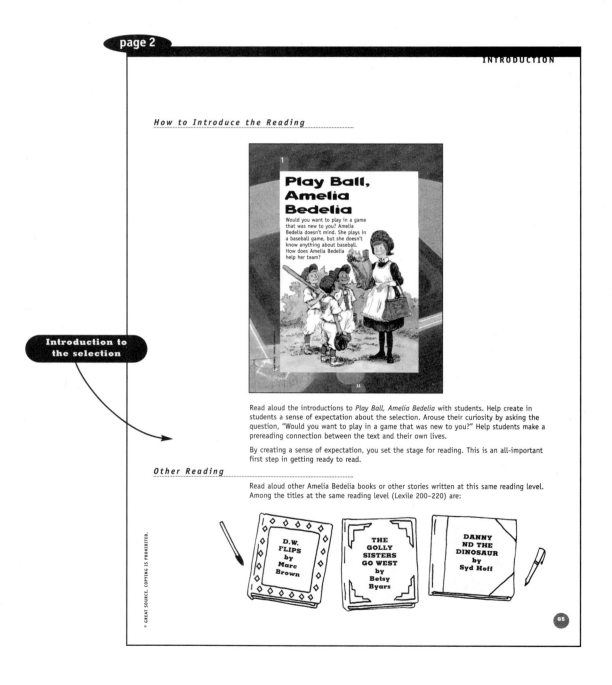

page 2

INTRODUCTION

How to Introduce the Reading

Play Ball, Amelia Bedelia

Would you want to play in a game that was new to you? Amelia Bedelia doesn't mind. She plays in a baseball game, but she doesn't know anything about baseball. How does Amelia Bedelia help her team?

Introduction to the selection

Read aloud the introductions to *Play Ball, Amelia Bedelia* with students. Help create in students a sense of expectation about the selection. Arouse their curiosity by asking the question, "Would you want to play in a game that was new to you?" Help students make a prereading connection between the text and their own lives.

By creating a sense of expectation, you set the stage for reading. This is an all-important first step in getting ready to read.

Other Reading

Read aloud other Amelia Bedelia books or other stories written at this same reading level. Among the titles at the same reading level (Lexile 200–220) are:

D.W. FLIPS by Marc Brown

THE GOLLY SISTERS GO WEST by Betsy Byars

DANNY ND THE DINOSAUR by Syd Hoff

© GREAT SOURCE. COPYING IS PROHIBITED.

65

PAGE 3 Skills and Strategies Overview

Each lesson plan in the *Sourcebook* begins with a chart giving an overview of the skills covered in the lesson. The purpose is to give teachers an at-a-glance picture of the lesson.

Note in the chart the vocabulary words that are highlighted. These words from the selection are presented in the **Vocabulary** blackline master to help familiarize students with key words in the selection.

Other Resources

Each lesson in the *Sourcebook* contains a wealth of additional resources to support you and your students. In all, six blackline masters provide additional scaffolding for you at critical parts of the lesson: Vocabulary, Prereading, Comprehension, Word Work, Prewriting, and Assessment.

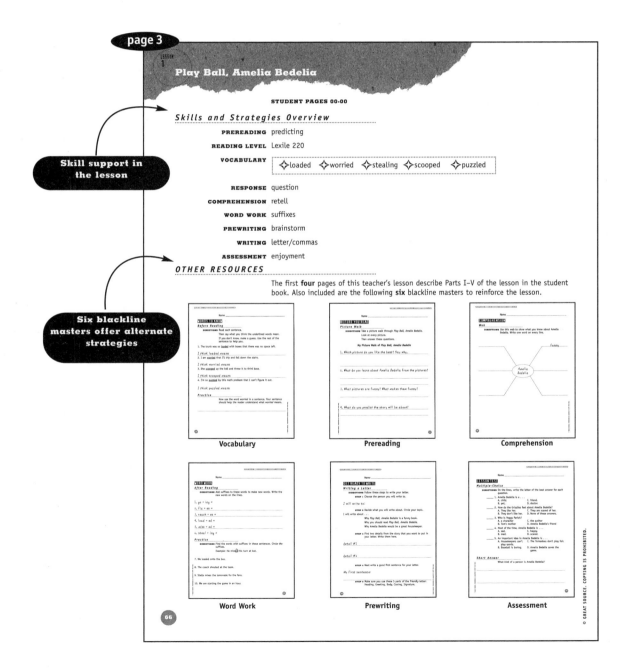

PAGE 4 **Before You Read**

- The *Teacher's Guide* walks through each lesson in the *Sourcebook*, following the five-step lesson plan and explaining how to teach each part.

- At each part, the appropriate additional blackline masters are cross-referenced.

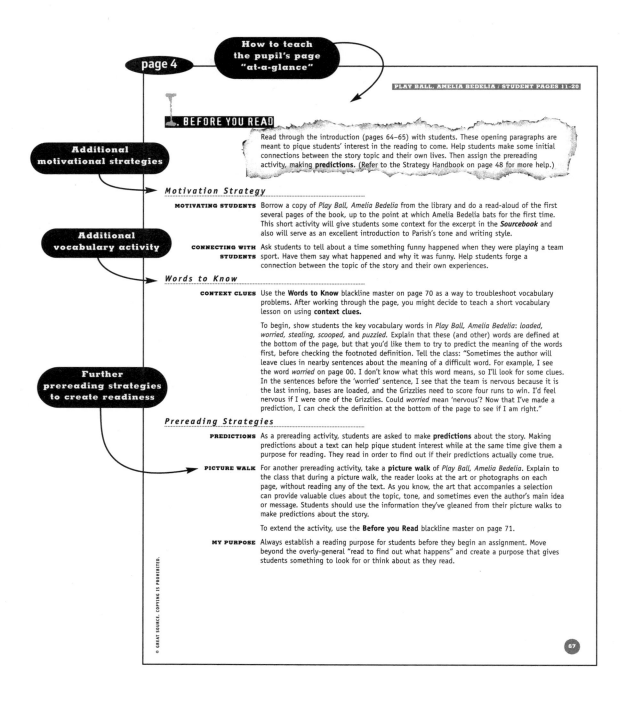

How to teach the pupil's page "at-a-glance"

page 4

PLAY BALL, AMELIA BEDELIA / STUDENT PAGES 11-20

I. BEFORE YOU READ

Read through the introduction (pages 64–65) with students. These opening paragraphs are meant to pique students' interest in the reading to come. Help students make some initial connections between the story topic and their own lives. Then assign the prereading activity, making **predictions**. (Refer to the Strategy Handbook on page 48 for more help.)

Additional motivational strategies

Motivation Strategy

MOTIVATING STUDENTS Borrow a copy of *Play Ball, Amelia Bedelia* from the library and do a read-aloud of the first several pages of the book, up to the point at which Amelia Bedelia bats for the first time. This short activity will give students some context for the excerpt in the *Sourcebook* and also will serve as an excellent introduction to Parish's tone and writing style.

Additional vocabulary activity

CONNECTING WITH STUDENTS Ask students to tell about a time something funny happened when they were playing a team sport. Have them say what happened and why it was funny. Help students forge a connection between the topic of the story and their own experiences.

Words to Know

CONTEXT CLUES Use the **Words to Know** blackline master on page 70 as a way to troubleshoot vocabulary problems. After working through the page, you might decide to teach a short vocabulary lesson on using **context clues.**

To begin, show students the key vocabulary words in *Play Ball, Amelia Bedelia*: *loaded, worried, stealing, scooped,* and *puzzled.* Explain that these (and other) words are defined at the bottom of the page, but that you'd like them to try to predict the meaning of the words first, before checking the footnoted definition. Tell the class: "Sometimes the author will leave clues in nearby sentences about the meaning of a difficult word. For example, I see the word *worried* on page 00. I don't know what this word means, so I'll look for some clues. In the sentences before the 'worried' sentence, I see that the team is nervous because it is the last inning, bases are loaded, and the Grizzlies need to score four runs to win. I'd feel nervous if I were one of the Grizzlies. Could *worried* mean 'nervous'? Now that I've made a prediction, I can check the definition at the bottom of the page to see if I am right."

Further prereading strategies to create readiness

Prereading Strategies

PREDICTIONS As a prereading activity, students are asked to make **predictions** about the story. Making predictions about a text can help pique student interest while at the same time give them a purpose for reading. They read in order to find out if their predictions actually come true.

PICTURE WALK For another prereading activity, take a **picture walk** of *Play Ball, Amelia Bedelia*. Explain to the class that during a picture walk, the reader looks at the art or photographs on each page, without reading any of the text. As you know, the art that accompanies a selection can provide valuable clues about the topic, tone, and sometimes even the author's main idea or message. Students should use the information they've gleaned from their picture walks to make predictions about the story.

To extend the activity, use the **Before you Read** blackline master on page 71.

MY PURPOSE Always establish a reading purpose for students before they begin an assignment. Move beyond the overly-general "read to find out what happens" and create a purpose that gives students something to look for or think about as they read.

67

PAGE 5 **Read**

- In **Part II, Read**, students are directed to read the selection and are given an active reading strategy.

- Each **Part II** instructs students to read the selection once with an active reading strategy, and then read it again and write their thoughts or comments in the **Response Notes**.

- **Reread** asks students to go back to the selection a third time to be sure they have answered all of the questions in the comprehension activity.

- Word Work explains the decoding skill taught in the lesson and why the skill is important for developing readers. A blackline master with additional work in this same word skill is also cross-referenced here.

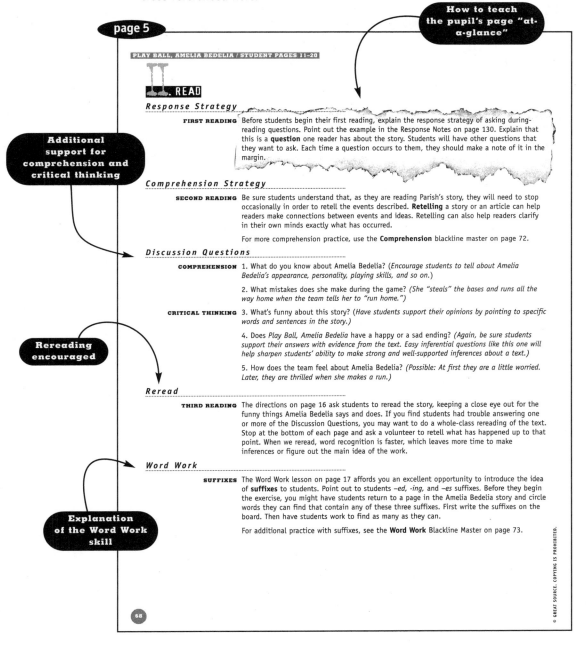

page 5

How to teach the pupil's page "at-a-glance"

PLAY BALL, AMELIA BEDELIA / STUDENT PAGES 11–20

II. READ

Response Strategy

Additional support for comprehension and critical thinking

FIRST READING Before students begin their first reading, explain the response strategy of asking during-reading questions. Point out the example in the Response Notes on page 130. Explain that this is a **question** one reader has about the story. Students will have other questions that they want to ask. Each time a question occurs to them, they should make a note of it in the margin.

Comprehension Strategy

SECOND READING Be sure students understand that, as they are reading Parish's story, they will need to stop occasionally in order to retell the events described. **Retelling** a story or an article can help readers make connections between events and ideas. Retelling can also help readers clarify in their own minds exactly what has occurred.

For more comprehension practice, use the **Comprehension** blackline master on page 72.

Discussion Questions

COMPREHENSION 1. What do you know about Amelia Bedelia? *(Encourage students to tell about Amelia Bedelia's appearance, personality, playing skills, and so on.)*

2. What mistakes does she make during the game? *(She "steals" the bases and runs all the way home when the team tells her to "run home.")*

CRITICAL THINKING 3. What's funny about this story? *(Have students support their opinions by pointing to specific words and sentences in the story.)*

Rereading encouraged

4. Does *Play Ball, Amelia Bedelia* have a happy or a sad ending? *(Again, be sure students support their answers with evidence from the text. Easy inferential questions like this one will help sharpen students' ability to make strong and well-supported inferences about a text.)*

5. How does the team feel about Amelia Bedelia? *(Possible: At first they are a little worried. Later, they are thrilled when she makes a run.)*

Reread

THIRD READING The directions on page 16 ask students to reread the story, keeping a close eye out for the funny things Amelia Bedelia says and does. If you find students had trouble answering one or more of the Discussion Questions, you may want to do a whole-class rereading of the text. Stop at the bottom of each page and ask a volunteer to retell what has happened up to that point. When we reread, word recognition is faster, which leaves more time to make inferences or figure out the main idea of the work.

Word Work

SUFFIXES The Word Work lesson on page 17 affords you an excellent opportunity to introduce the idea of **suffixes** to students. Point out to students *–ed, -ing,* and *–es* suffixes. Before they begin the exercise, you might have students return to a page in the Amelia Bedelia story and circle words they can find that contain any of these three suffixes. First write the suffixes on the board. Then have students work to find as many as they can.

Explanation of the Word Work skill

For additional practice with suffixes, see the **Word Work** Blackline Master on page 73.

68

© GREAT SOURCE. COPYING IS PROHIBITED.

PAGE 6 Get Ready to Write, Write, and Look Back

- The page begins with additional help with prewriting and references another blackline master that offers additional support.

- Next, the students write. Explicit instructions on the assignment are included in the pupil's text. But here students are also introduced to the **Writers' Checklist**, which gives the Grammar, Usage, and Mechanics mini-lesson.

- The Writing Rubric gives teachers a way to evaluate students' writing.

- The lesson ends by encouraging students to look back and reflect on what they have read and references a **Readers' Checklist**. The Assessment blackline master is also cross-referenced here.

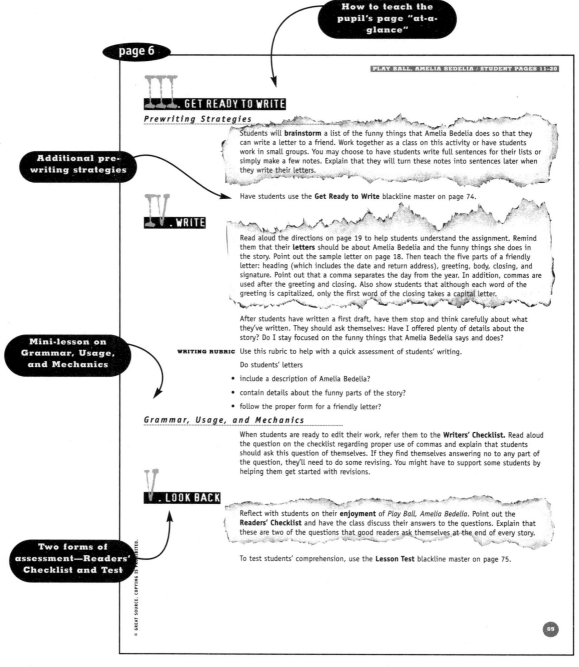

How to teach the pupil's page "at-a-glance"

page 6

PLAY BALL, AMELIA BEDELIA / STUDENT PAGES 11-20

III. GET READY TO WRITE

Prewriting Strategies

Additional pre-writing strategies

Students will **brainstorm** a list of the funny things that Amelia Bedelia does so that they can write a letter to a friend. Work together as a class on this activity or have students work in small groups. You may choose to have students write full sentences for their lists or simply make a few notes. Explain that they will turn these notes into sentences later when they write their letters.

Have students use the **Get Ready to Write** blackline master on page 74.

IV. WRITE

Read aloud the directions on page 19 to help students understand the assignment. Remind them that their **letters** should be about Amelia Bedelia and the funny things she does in the story. Point out the sample letter on page 18. Then teach the five parts of a friendly letter: heading (which includes the date and return address), greeting, body, closing, and signature. Point out that a comma separates the day from the year. In addition, commas are used after the greeting and closing. Also show students that although each word of the greeting is capitalized, only the first word of the closing takes a capital letter.

After students have written a first draft, have them stop and think carefully about what they've written. They should ask themselves: Have I offered plenty of details about the story? Do I stay focused on the funny things that Amelia Bedelia says and does?

WRITING RUBRIC Use this rubric to help with a quick assessment of students' writing.

Do students' letters

- include a description of Amelia Bedelia?
- contain details about the funny parts of the story?
- follow the proper form for a friendly letter?

Mini-lesson on Grammar, Usage, and Mechanics

Grammar, Usage, and Mechanics

When students are ready to edit their work, refer them to the **Writers' Checklist.** Read aloud the question on the checklist regarding proper use of commas and explain that students should ask this question of themselves. If they find themselves answering no to any part of the question, they'll need to do some revising. You might have to support some students by helping them get started with revisions.

V. LOOK BACK

Reflect with students on their **enjoyment** of *Play Ball, Amelia Bedelia*. Point out the **Readers' Checklist** and have the class discuss their answers to the questions. Explain that these are two of the questions that good readers ask themselves at the end of every story.

Two forms of assessment—Readers' Checklist and Test

To test students' comprehension, use the **Lesson Test** blackline master on page 75.

69

Each lesson plan in the *Sourcebook Teacher's Guide* has six blackline masters for additional levels of support for key skill areas.

PAGE 7 **Words to Know**

- Each **Words to Know** blackline master helps students learn the meanings of five words from the selection. The purpose of this blackline master is to expose students to the meanings of five key words in the selection, giving them readiness before they read.

Meanings from five words from the selection are taught

page 7

PLAY BALL, AMELIA BEDELIA / STUDENT PAGES 11–20

Name _____

WORDS TO KNOW

Before Reading

DIRECTIONS Read each sentence.

Then say what you think the underlined words mean.

If you don't know, make a guess. Use the rest of the sentence to help you.

1. The trunk was so <u>loaded</u> with boxes that there was no space left.

I think loaded means _____

2. I am <u>worried</u> that I'll trip and fall down the stairs.

I think worried means _____

3. She <u>scooped</u> up the ball and threw it to third base.

I think scooped means _____

4. I'm so <u>puzzled</u> by this math problem that I can't figure it out.

I think puzzled means _____

Practice

Now use the word *worried* in a sentence. Your sentence should help the reader understand what *worried* means.

_____

_____

Vocabulary pre-teaches important words from the selection

70

© GREAT SOURCE. PERMISSION IS GRANTED TO COPY THIS PAGE.

PAGE 8 Before You Read

- An additional Prereading activity is included to ensure students have sufficient background for reading the selection. Generally the purpose of the activities is to activate students' prior knowledge about a subject and help them predict what the selection is about.

page 8

Name _____

BEFORE YOU READ

Picture Walk

DIRECTIONS Take a picture walk through *Play Ball, Amelia Bedelia*.
Look at every picture.
Then answer these questions.

My Picture Walk of *Play Ball, Amelia Bedelia*

1. Which picture do you like the best? Say why.

_____

_____

2. What do you learn about Amelia Bedelia from the pictures?

_____

_____

3. What pictures are funny? What makes them funny?

_____

_____

4. What do you predict the story will be about?

_____

_____

Additional prereading activity builds background and activates students' prior knowledge

71

PAGE 9 Comprehension

- Each **Comprehension** blackline master affords teachers still another way to build students' understanding of the selection, using a different strategy from the one found in the *Sourcebook*.

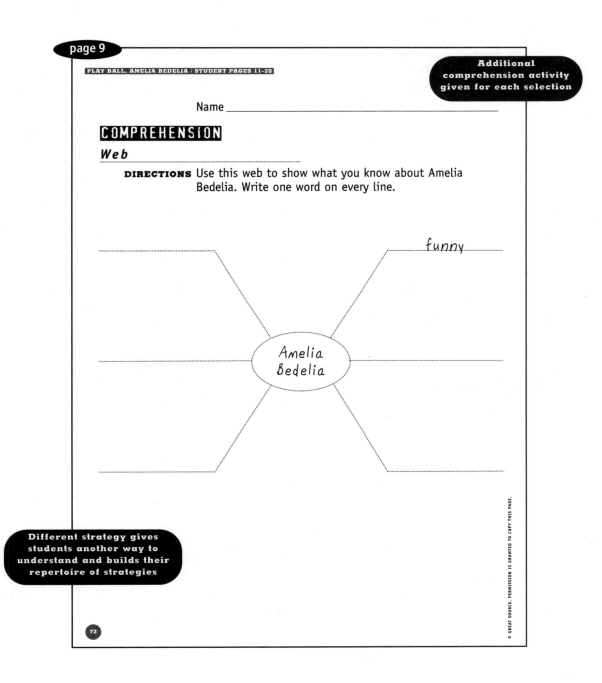

page 9

Additional comprehension activity given for each selection

PLAY BALL, AMELIA BEDELIA / STUDENT PAGES 11-20

Name _____

COMPREHENSION

Web

DIRECTIONS Use this web to show what you know about Amelia Bedelia. Write one word on every line.

funny

Amelia Bedelia

Different strategy gives students another way to understand and builds their repertoire of strategies

© GREAT SOURCE. PERMISSION IS GRANTED TO COPY THIS PAGE.

72

PAGE 10 Word Work

- Each **Word Work** activity offers additional practice on the skills shown in the pupil's book. Often students will need repeated practice on a skill before they internalize it.

---

page 10

Extra practice on Word Work skill

Name _____

WORD WORK

After Reading

DIRECTIONS Add suffixes to these words to make new words. Write the new words on the lines.

1. go + ing = _____
2. fix + es = _____
3. reach + es = _____
4. load + ed = _____
5. miss + ed = _____
6. steal + ing = _____

Practice

Repeated practice helps students remember the skill

DIRECTIONS Find the words with suffixes in these sentences. Circle the suffixes.

Example: He miss(ed) his turn at bat.

7. We loaded onto the bus.

8. The coach shouted at the team.

9. Stella mixes the lemonade for the fans.

10. We are starting the game in an hour.

73

PAGE 11 **Prewriting**

- Often some students will need even more scaffolding than appears in the pupil's lesson as they prepare for the writing assignment.

- The "extra step" in preparing to write is the focus of the prewriting blackline master.

page 11

Additional support for the writing assignment

PLAY BALL, AMELIA BEDELIA / STUDENT PAGES 11–20

Name _____

GET READY TO WRITE
Writing a Letter

DIRECTIONS Follow these steps to write your letter.

STEP 1 Choose the person you will write to.

I will write to: _____

STEP 2 Decide what you will write about. Circle your topic.

I will write about . . .

> Why *Play Ball, Amelia Bedelia* is a funny book.
> Why you should read *Play Ball, Amelia Bedelia*.
> Why Amelia Bedelia would be a great housekeeper.

STEP 3 Find two details from the story that you want to put in your letter. Write them here.

detail #1 _____

_____

detail #2 _____

_____

STEP 4 Next write a good first sentence for your letter.

My first sentence: _____

_____

STEP 5 Make sure you use these 5 parts of the friendly letter: Heading, Greeting, Body, Closing, Signature.

74

Page 12 Lesson Test

- Each lesson in the *Sourcebook* ends with the opportunity for students to reflect on their reading with the **Readers' Checklist**. This self-assessment is an informal inventory of what they learned from the reading.

- The **Lesson Test** blackline master gives a multiple-choice test on the selection and a short-essay question for a more formal assessment.

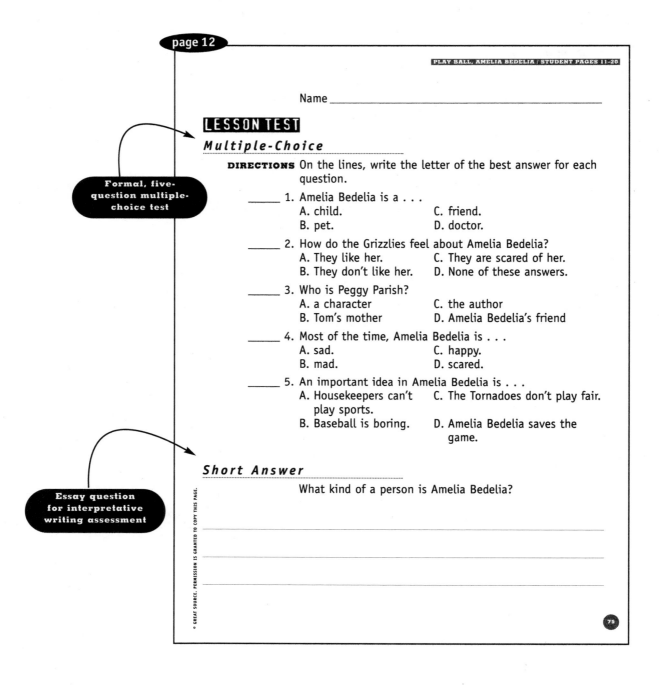

page 12

PLAY BALL, AMELIA BEDELIA / STUDENT PAGES 11–20

Name _____

LESSON TEST
Multiple-Choice

DIRECTIONS On the lines, write the letter of the best answer for each question.

_____ 1. Amelia Bedelia is a . . .
  A. child.   C. friend.
  B. pet.   D. doctor.

_____ 2. How do the Grizzlies feel about Amelia Bedelia?
  A. They like her.   C. They are scared of her.
  B. They don't like her. D. None of these answers.

_____ 3. Who is Peggy Parish?
  A. a character   C. the author
  B. Tom's mother   D. Amelia Bedelia's friend

_____ 4. Most of the time, Amelia Bedelia is . . .
  A. sad.   C. happy.
  B. mad.   D. scared.

_____ 5. An important idea in Amelia Bedelia is . . .
  A. Housekeepers can't   C. The Tornadoes don't play fair.
     play sports.
  B. Baseball is boring.   D. Amelia Bedelia saves the
                              game.

Short Answer

What kind of a person is Amelia Bedelia?

_____

_____

_____

© GREAT SOURCE. PERMISSION IS GRANTED TO COPY THIS PAGE.

75

Formal, five-question multiple-choice test

Essay question for interpretative writing assessment

Guiding Student's Reading

BY LAURA ROBB

Whenever I coach teachers, I meet with them to learn about their teaching styles and practices, their educational philosophy, and all the time I'm jotting down questions they have for me. At a school in my community, I recently met with teachers from grades three, four, and five. Their teaching experience ranged from two to ten years, and their teaching styles included a reading/writing workshop that integrated the language arts and a more structured classroom that separated topics such as reading, writing, spelling, grammar, and punctuation skills. However, among twelve teachers, three questions surfaced again and again:

1. What can I do to support *all my readers* as well as those who struggle?

2. How do I find short materials for my struggling and reluctant readers?

3. Can I apply the guided reading principals primary teachers are using to older students?

Reflective teachers constantly pose questions, for questions are the foundation of inquiry. And inquiry can lead to responsive teaching—teaching that meets the needs of each child in your classroom as well as spurs teachers to explore answers to their questions.

In this article, I will address the three questions because they are crucial to supporting teachers who understand the importance of taking each struggling or reluctant reader where he or she is and gently nudging them forward by offering chunks of independent reading time, scaffolding instruction, and by organizing and leading flexible strategic reading groups.

Independent Reading

Too often, struggling readers spend more of their time completing skill sheets than reading books they can enjoy. The skill-sheet instructional strategy comes from the traditional belief that isolated practice of such skills as finding the main idea, sequencing, word meanings, and syllabication would help students acquire the skills to read books, the newspaper, and magazines.

Contrary to tradition, research shows that one of teachers' most important tasks regarding comprehension instruction is to set aside ample time for actual text reading. Students who struggle need to read as much as or more than proficient readers—providing the texts are at their independent reading level. Such daily silent reading combined with strategy demonstrations and student practice can improve reading more than a diet of skill sheets.

Finding adequate materials for struggling readers who read one or more years below grade level is a challenge. Teachers recognize that there is a limited amount of easy-to-read material available for middle grade students—reading materials that are on topics that hold their interest from start to finish.

The **Sourcebooks**, however, are outstanding resources for teachers in need of independent reading materials. Selections are leveled from easy reading at the start of each student book to a final lesson that's near or on grade level. Since selections are excerpts from the finest literature, teachers have sixteen books per grade level that children can read independently throughout the school year. Moreover, teachers can offer other readable books by the authors students enjoy most. For those who require teacher support while reading, you can scaffold instruction by sitting side-by-side a student and guide the reading with questions, prompts, and modeling.

The Importance of Scaffolding

Scaffolding is the specific support offered to pairs, small groups, individuals, and the entire class that teachers provide before, during, and after reading. Teachers scaffold students' reading until each student demonstrates an understanding of a strategy. Gradually, the teacher withdraws support, moving students to independence.

In a typical middle grade classroom, where teachers work with a mix of reluctant and struggling, grade level, and proficient readers, scaffolding reading might start with the entire class, then move to those students who require additional help in order to understand and internalize a strategy.

Recent research shows that applying reading strategies to texts—strategies such as predicting, questioning, and making personal connections improves students' comprehension before, during, and after reading. In addition, it's also important to help students set purposes for reading before plunging them into a text, for this strategy focuses students on what's important in the selection.

Good teaching provides scaffolding for proficient and struggling readers and starts before reading, helping students activate their prior knowledge and experience so they can use what they know to connect to the authors' words and construct new understandings. During reading, scaffolding strategies build on setting purposes for reading as students actively interact with a text by using the reading purposes to underline words and phrases and write notes in the margin. After reading scaffolding improves recall and deepens comprehension as students practice such strategies as rereading and skimming to answer a question, to find details about a character or event, to locate information, or prepare for writing. Reflecting on their reading by revisiting the piece, talking to a partner, and writing about what they've read all boost comprehension and recall of key details and ideas.

Why Sourcebooks Are a Must-have Text

We have carefully structured each **Sourcebook** lesson so that it builds on the sound, current research on scaffolding instruction and the reading strategy curriculum. We've integrated the strategic parts of each lesson to heighten the impact on struggling readers of practicing and coming to understand related strategies. Here's the support your students will receive with each lesson:

Get Ready to Read: throughout the **Sourcebook**, students practice four to six research-tested activities that prepare them for reading.

Your Purpose for Reading: each lesson sets a purpose for reading that builds on the preparation activity and focuses students' reading goals.

Read and Interact with the Text: during the first reading, students become **active readers**, underlining and circling parts of the text then writing their thoughts and questions in the Notes.

Comprehension Builders: while reading students are invited to stop-and-think about the story's structure, meaning, as well as answer questions and think about relationships such as cause and effect.

Reread: asks students to go back to the text, and complete parts they haven't already completed, in order to build fluency.

Word Work: these activities help struggling readers improve their decoding strategies and learn how they can build on what they already know about words to figure out how to say new, unfamiliar words.

Getting Ready to Write: helps students prepare for their writing by creating a detailed plan of ideas.

Writing Activity: always related to the reading selection, students use their plans to write letters, poems, expository, descriptive, and narrative paragraphs.

Look Back: this reflective part of the lesson invites students to think about what they learned, why they enjoyed the piece, the meaning of the selection, or why the piece was easy or challenging to read.

Many of your students will be able to work through each lesson independently or with the support of a reading partner. However, there will be times when you will use the entire lesson or parts of a lesson with a pair or small group of students. Moreover, you'll find the *Sourcebook* lessons ideal for group instruction because short, readable selections allow you to focus on strategies and work through part of a lesson in one to two periods.

Strategic Reading Groups

"I can't read this stuff. I'll never learn how to read." These comments, made by readers who struggle, reveal how fragile these youngsters are. Unfortunately, their self-esteem is low due to all their negative experiences with reading. At school they watch classmates complete work easily and achieve success—these observations only reinforce struggling learners' negative thoughts about their ability to progress. At home, they avoid reading because they can't cope with grade-level texts. Often, teachers and parents read materials to them. However, this only improves students' listening. To improve reading, students must read books they CAN read and enjoy.

The best way to support your struggling readers is to organize groups that are flexible because they respond to the ever-changing needs of students.

Responsive Grouping

Learners improve at different rates. That's why responsive grouping, where you work with students who have common needs, is the key to moving all readers forward. Once a student understands how to apply a strategy such as predicting, posing questions, or previewing, it's time to move that child to a group that's working on another strategy.

Responsive, flexible grouping is similar to the guided reading model primary teachers use. The differences in the middle grades is that students don't change groups as frequently as emergent and beginning readers. The emphasis of instruction is on developing critical thinking strategies, interpreting the meaning of texts, and learning to find the main points an author is making. In addition, those students who need to bolster their ability to pronounce long, new words and figure out their meanings using context clues receive ongoing teacher support. The question, then, that faces all of us teachers is, "How do I monitor the progress of each child so I can respond to his/her reading needs by changing group membership?"

First teachers must systematically observe their students by doing the following:

- Jot down notes as students work independently, with a partner, or in a small group.
- Study samples of students' written work.
- Observe students during teacher-led small group strategic reading lessons.
- Hold short one-on-one conferences and listen to students answer questions about their reading process, progress, and needs.
- Use this data to adjust group membership.

The chart below, compares Responsive and Traditional Grouping. It will help you understand the benefits of responsive grouping.

Responsive Grouping	Traditional Grouping
Students grouped by assessment of a specific strategy	Students grouped by general assessments such as standardized testing.
Responds to students' needs and changes as these needs change.	Static and unchanging for long periods of time.
Strategies practiced before, during, and after reading with a variety of genres.	Selections limited to basal. Worksheets for specific skills.
Books chosen for the group at their instructional level.	Students move through a grade-level basal whether or not they read above or below grade level.
Reading is in silent, meaningful chunks.	Round-robin oral reading.
Students actively interact with the text, discuss and reflect on it, and develop critical thinking.	Students read to find out the correct answer.
Varied vocabulary with an emphasis on solving word problems while reading.	Controlled vocabulary.
Students practice and apply strategies that enable them to connect to and think deeply about their reading.	Students complete worksheets that have little to do with the story in the basal anthology.
Students learn to apply word-solving strategies to real books.	Students practice skills with worksheets. The transfer of using word-solving strategies in real books is rarely made.
Evaluation based on careful observation of students' reading in a variety of situations.	Evaluation based on skill sheets and basal reading texts.

The Sourcebooks and Responsive Grouping

The *Sourcebooks* are ideal for small group work that focuses on a specific reading or writing strategy. Selections are readable, and all the strategies are connected and/or related in each lesson. All the lessons have been structured according to the standards listed under "Responsive Grouping." Moreover, you don't have to use valuable time to search for short materials to frame a meaningful lesson that can nudge struggling readers forward.

If one child or a group of children are experiencing difficulty with a specific strategy such as previewing, taking notes, decoding, or preparing to write, the *Sourcebooks* are the perfect resource for the teacher to support and guide those students. Teachers can focus on one part of a lesson with the group or work through an entire lesson over several days. The main consideration is to offer instructional scaffolding to readers who struggle, for as you work together, you will improve their reading ability and develop their confidence and self-esteem.

Ten Suggestions for Supporting Struggling Readers

The tips that follow are from a list that I keep in my lesson plan book, so I can revisit it and make sure I am attending to the needs of every student who requires my support.

1. Be positive. Focus your energies on what students can do. Accept students where they are and use the *Sourcebook* lessons to move them forward.

2. Set reasonable and doable goals with your students. Continue to revise the goals as students improve.

3. Give students reading materials they can read independently, such as the selections in the *Sourcebook*. When students DO the reading, they will improve.

4. Get students actively involved with their learning by using strategies that ask students to interact instead of to passively listen.

5. Help students learn a strategy or information a different way if the method you've introduced isn't working.

6. Sit side-by-side and explain a point or strategy to a student who needs extra scaffolding. Closing the gap between your explanation and the student can result in improved comprehension.

7. Invite students to retell information to a partner or in small groups. Talk helps learners remember and clarify their ideas.

8. Make sure students understand directions.

9. Help struggling readers see their progress. Invite students to reflect on their progress and tell you about it. Or, tell students the progress you see.

10. Give students extra time to complete work and tests.

Closing Thoughts

Using the *Sourcebooks* with your reluctant and struggling readers can transform passive, unengaged readers into active and motivated learners. As your students complete the *Sourcebook* lessons and benefit from other parts of your reading curriculum, they will have had many opportunities to build their self-confidence, self-esteem, and develop a repertoire of helpful strategies by participating in reading, writing, and thinking experiences that are positive and continue to move them forward.

Fountas, Irene and Gay Su Pinnell. 1996. *Guided Reading: Good First Teaching for All Children*. Portsmouth, NH: Heinemann.

Gillet, Jean Wallace and Charles Temple. 1990. *Understanding Reading Problems: Assessment and Instruction*, Third edition. New York: HarperCollins.

Robb, Laura. 2000. *Teaching Reaching in Middle School*. New York: Scholastic.

BY RUTH NATHAN

During the past thirty years, many studies centering on the reading process have identified what good readers do (Pressley and Woloshyn, 1995). We know they use efficient strategies to comprehend, and that they know when and where to use them. We know, too, that good readers monitor their comprehension, and that they are appropriately reflective. That is, strong readers know when they need to read more, read again, or ask for help. Proficient readers also possess strong vocabularies and usually have vast backgrounds of experience, either real or vicarious.

In order to grow into becoming a proficient reader, studies from the fields of both psychology and education have also shown that successful instruction will most likely occur when certain needs are met (Adams, 1990). For example, it is important for readers to be reading at their instructional level when they're learning comprehension strategies and not be frustrated by text that is too difficult. Difficult text usually has more complex syntactic structures and less-frequent words. It is equally important that teachers teach a few (one or two) strategies at a time, in context, and that these strategies be repeated frequently.

Because of what we know about proficient readers *and* quality instruction, the chapters in this *Sourcebook* have embraced three keys to promote student success:

KEY ONE: Only a few comprehension strategies are taught at a time, and these comprehension strategies are taught *in* context, practiced, and repeated (Robb, 2000; Harvey and Goudvis, 2000).

KEY TWO: The literature in the *Sourcebook* is of high interest and appropriate readability. This means that the stories selected would interest readers at this age; that the syntactic complexity is low at first, becoming ever-more difficult; and that word recognition is eased by choosing books with more frequent words and fewer rare words. Only gradually do stories contain a greater number of rare words.

KEY THREE: In each chapter rare words are identified and explained. In addition, there are word recognition exercises in each chapter meant to help less-proficient readers gain in their word-recognition power. Students are shown how to use analogy to read new words; as well as how to use words parts, such as syllables and affixes, to speed word recognition.

In addition to the three keys, the authors of the *Sourcebook* have utilized many strategies *before*, *during*, and *after* reading to engage readers and to promote transfer of learning.

Each chapter begins with readers accessing their prior knowledge and suggests a reason for reading. Research has shown prior knowledge and purpose to be important factors in comprehension (Adams, 1990). During reading, students are encouraged to talk with classmates, thus articulating their beliefs while at the same time hearing other interpretations of the text (Keene and Zimmermann, 1997; Booth and Barton, 2000). In addition, during reading students are using the text pages to reflect on their understanding through invitations to both write and draw (Clagget, _____. Harvey and Goudvis, 2000). This practice goes back to the Middle Ages, but has received much support in all contemporary models of competent thinking (Pressley and Woloshyn, 1995). After reading, students are using all the language arts—reading, writing, listening, and speaking, as well as drawing, to write related entries, be it a summary, invitation, journal entry with a point of view, or creative story-ending or poem.

All in all, the *Sourcebooks* are the perfect answer to what struggling readers need to improve their comprehension and reading enjoyment. The three keys to success combined with before, during, and after reading opportunities will provide students with many meaningful and joyful experiences. Our hope is that these experiences might lead students to a life filled with unforgettable encounters with texts of all types—books, newspapers, magazines, and all texts electronic.

Four Must-Have Teacher Resources

Classrooms That Work: They Can All Read and Write, 2nd edition, by Patricia M. Cunningham and Richard L. Allington. New York: Longman, 1999.

This book covers a range of topics you will find useful: teaching reading and writing in the primary and intermediate grades, organizing your classroom, and helping struggling readers cope with difficult science and history texts. You'll visit classrooms that use Cunningham's "Four-Blocks" approach to reading and better understand how the model works in the primary grades.

Easy Mini-Lessons for Building Vocabulary by Laura Robb, New York: Scholastic, 1999.

Choose from a large menu of doable strategies that build students' vocabulary before, during, and after reading. You'll also help prepare your students for standardized tests with the "Test-Taking Tips" sprinkled throughout the book. This book offers a practical and manageable approach to teaching vocabulary.

Words Their Way: Word Study for Phonics. Vocabulary, and Spelling Instruction, 2nd edition, by Donald R. Bear, Marcia Invernizzi, Francine Johnston, and Shane Templeton, Columbus, Ohio: Merrill 2000.

This book will strengthen teachers knowledge of word study and spelling because the authors clearly explain developmental spelling and each of the stages children pass through. In addition, the book is packed with easy-to-implement word study games and lessons that can improve children's ability to read and understand multi-syllable words.

Teaching Reading in Middle School: A Strategic Approach to Teaching Reading That Improves Comprehension and Thinking, by Laura Robb, New York: Scholastic, 2000.

Readers will gain deep insights in teaching reading strategies before, during, and after reading, organizing students into teacher-led strategic reading groups, setting up a reading workshop, as well as motivating and assessing middle grade and middle school readers. A chapter on struggling readers offers suggestions for helping these students read books at their independent levels without losing self-esteem. The readable text combines literacy stories, theory, and practice, and offers a practical, research-based model.

BY LAURA ROBB

On the first day of school twenty-five to thirty third graders cross the threshold of your classroom. Each student differs in the experiences and knowledge they bring to your class. Students' reading levels vary: some will read on grade level, a group will read one to two years below grade level, and a few proficient readers will be one to two years above grade level. This snapshot raises three questions for language arts and reading teachers:

1. How do I address the needs of this wide range of reading abilities?

2. How do I find appropriate pieces for strategic group work—literature students can read.

3. What does the rest of the class do while I'm working with a group?

For two to four reading groups to be able to work independently and with their teacher, it's important to create simple, but effective reading and writing experiences that students can complete alone or with a partner. Equally as important is showing students how to use materials they'll work on while you're with a group and negotiating behavior guidelines so students don't interrupt you.

Teach Students How to Work in Pairs, Small Groups, and Independently

It can take from four to six weeks to establish routines at the start of the year. During this time students learn how to work on specific tasks without your guidance. Thoroughly explain the how-to's of each experience. For example, for independent reading, explain how you've organized your classroom library, where to log in the title and author of the book and the amount students have read, as well as behavior expectations for silent, independent reading.

While You Work with a Group Students Can . . .

Provide easy-to-manage reading and writing experiences for students making independent learning time meaningful and engaging. Such experiences can also nudge students forward and improve their reading and writing strategies and skills.

SOURCEBOOKS AND DAYBOOKS The *Reading and Writing Sourcebooks* and *Daybooks of Critical Reading and Writing* are top-notch resources for independent work and teacher-led group work. Show students how the *Sourcebooks* and *Daybooks* work by completing the first unit with them. You can order a *Daybook* at grade level and one a year above grade level to challenge students to learn at their independent reading levels.

Struggling readers can work with you in *Sourcebook* grade 3 and gain the vocabulary, skills, and strategies they need to progress. Once students understand what they must do, parts of each lesson, such as the Word Work and Write can be completed independently.

PAIRED READING partners read small sections of a book or passage and retell parts to one another.

LISTENING TO A BOOK students listen to books by *Sourcebook* authors on an audiocassette in a listening center. They can respond to this experience by drawing and/or writing about the story in a journal.

COMPLETE A JOURNAL ENTRY students can respond to their reading by identifying the main character, the problems faced and the outcomes; by describing the personality of the main character; by drawing and writing about important settings; or by showing how a character or event is similar to an experience they've had.

GROUP DRAMAS small groups select a section or chapter of a book to dramatize, using voices and gestures to reveal character.

WRITING PROJECT students can work on a piece of writing from their *Sourcebook*, *Daybook*, or writing folder.

Group Management Tips

In a forty-five minute to one hour reading block, you can meet with two reading groups (35–45 minutes total reading time—15 to 20 for each teacher-led group plus five extra minutes for transitions), and have time to go over the activities and show students where they'll work. Create a signal for immediate quiet, such as flicking the lights.

Here are some suggestions that lead to productive group work:

- Select three to four reading and writing experiences from the list on pages 6 and 7 that students will work on until everyone completes each activity.

- Post these experiences on a chart or the chalkboard.

- List the names of students under their first activity. Rotate to a new activity after 15 to 20 minutes.

- List the names of the two reading groups that will work with you that day.

- If some students finish early, they should read independently using books they can read without support.

Early in the year, take the time to establish guidelines for what students do if they have a question and you're working with reading groups. Write the four guidelines that follow on construction paper and display on a bulletin board or wall.

1. Stop and think. Try to solve your problem on your own. Think of strategies you can try that might help.

2. Ask your reading partner or a member of your group for help.

3. If your buddy or a group member can't help, ask another student.

4. If neither 1, 2, or 3 works, read your free choice reading book and wait until your teacher can help you.

Closing Thoughts

The level of success of group work depends on two things:

- Activities students can complete on their own.

- Establishing routines and behavior guidelines BEFORE inviting students to complete activities independently or with a partner.

The **Sourcebooks** and **Daybooks** are ideal resources for students because you can offer them reading and writing activities that are appropriate to their developmental needs. Moreover, as students experience success and pleasure in reading and writing, they will improve.

Here is a quick guide to the main prereading, comprehension, and reflecting strategies used in the **Sourcebooks**. Students will benefit by explicit instruction in these strategies. You can help teach these strategies by introducing them to students.

In order to help students internalize these strategies, the number and use of them was limited so that students could encounter them repeatedly throughout the book.

Overview

Prereading Strategies
  K-W-L
  Anticipation Guide
  Preview
  Think-Pair-and-Share
  Word Web

Active Reading Strategies

Comprehension Strategies
  Stop and Think
  Retell
  Double-entry Journal
  Graphic Organizer
  Story Frames

Word Work Strategies

Reflective Reading Strategies
  Understanding
  Ease
  Meaning
  Enjoyment

PREREADING STRATEGIES
K - W - L

What It Is

K-W-L is a pre- and post-reading strategy designed to facilitate students' interest in and activate their prior knowledge of a topic before reading nonfiction material. The letters *K, W,* and *L* stand for "What I Know," What I Want to Know," and "What I Learned."

Look at the example of a K-W-L chart from ***Sourcebook,*** grade 3, Lesson 6, *Cave People*.

K-W-L CHART
What I **K**now   Topic: Cave People
Lived long ago
Lived in caves
Hunted animals to survive
What I **W**ant to Know
What was their life like?
How long ago did they live?
What I **L**earned
Cave people lived during the Ice Age.
They lived by hunting reindeer with spears.

How to Introduce It

Introduce K-W-L as a whole class activity. Give students time to write 1 or 2 questions they have. Explain that they will come back to their chart after they have finished reading to write what they have learned.

Explain to students that K-W-L first pulls together what they know and then gives them questions that they can read for.

Be sure to return to the chart and list what students learned in the *L* column.

Why It Works

Brainstorming (the *K* part) activates prior knowledge. What sets K-W-L apart from other prereading strategies is that K-W-L also encourages students to ask questions (the *W* component), thereby setting meaningful purposes for their reading. Returning to the chart (the *L* component) brings closure to the activity and demonstrates the purposefulness of the task.

Comments and Cautions

Don't worry about the accuracy of what students write under the *K* column. Students can correct any errors later during the *L* part of the activity.

After students write What They Know under "K," ask them to get together in groups. This will help readers benefit from the knowledge of the whole group.

Then, as students break out of their groups to begin reading, be sure to focus them on their questions, "L, What I Want to Learn."

What It Is

An anticipation guide is a series of statements that students respond to, first individually and then as a group, before reading a selection. The intent is not to quiz students but to prompt answers and discussion. The discussion will build background and expectation and give students a reason to read.

Here is an example from the **Sourcebook,** grade 3, *Just a Few Words, Mr Lincoln:*

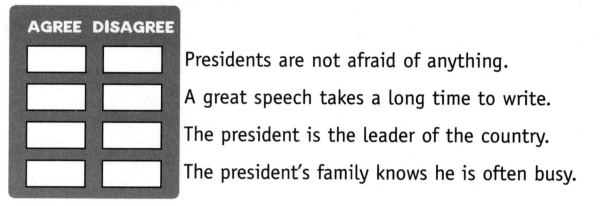

AGREE DISAGREE

Presidents are not afraid of anything.

A great speech takes a long time to write.

The president is the leader of the country.

The president's family knows he is often busy.

How to Introduce It

Have students read the statements. (When making your own guides, keep the number of statements to about 5 items. More than that makes it difficult to discuss in detail.)

Discuss the students' responses. The point of an anticipation guide is to discuss students' various answers and explore their opinions. Build the prior knowledge of each student by adding to it the prior knowledge of other students, which can be done through discussion. The discussion of Anticipation Guide statements can also be a powerful motivator, because once students have answered them they have a stake in seeing if they are "right."

Encourage students to make predictions about what the selection will be about based on the statements.

Then read the selection.

After reading the selection, have students return to their guides and re-evaluate their responses based on what they learned from the selection.

Why It Works

Anticipation guides are useful tools for eliciting predictions before reading both fiction and nonfiction. By encouraging students to think critically about a series of statements, anticipation guides raise expectations and create anticipation about the selection.

Comments and Cautions

This is a highly motivational prereading activity. Try to keep the class discussion on the subject; the teacher's role is that of a facilitator, encouraging students to examine and re-examine their responses. The more stake students have in an opinion, the more they will be motivated to read more about the issue.

The focus of the guides should be the discussion that ensues upon completion, not the correction, not the correctness of the students' responses.

You might also turn the entire anticipation guide process into a whole group activity by having students respond with either "thumbs up" or "thumbs down."

Preview or Walk-thru

What It Is

Previewing is a prereading strategy in which students read the title and skim the selection and then reflect on a few key questions. It asks the students to "sample" the selection before they begin reading and functions very much like the preview to a movie. Occasionally it is simply referred to as a walk-thru and is a less formal variation of skimming and scanning.

How to Introduce It

Previewing can be done as an individual or group activity. You might introduce it to the group and in later lessons encourage students to work on their own.

On the first time you use this activity, take time to model previewing carefully for students.

Direct them to the title. Have a student read it aloud.

Next, ask students to look at the first sentence. Have someone read it aloud.

Then give students 10–15 seconds to look over the rest of the selection. Ask them what words, names, or ideas they remember.

Finally, direct students to the last paragraph. Ask students what stands out in the last paragraph.

Then have students respond to 4–5 questions about the selection. Questions might include:

* What is the selection about?

* When does it take place?

* Who is in it?

* How does the selection end?

Read the rest of the selection.

Return to the questions and discuss the accuracy of student's predictions. Were they surprised at how the selection turned out based on their initial preview? Why or why not?

Here is an example from **Sourcebook**, grade 3, *Volcanoes*:

BEFORE YOU READ

Look over, or preview, this reading about volcanoes to get an idea of what you'll be learning about.
1. First, read the title.
2. Next, read the first and the last paragraphs.
3. Then, write 3 questions you have about volcanoes.

MY QUESTIONS

1. ....
....
....
....

Why It Works

Previews work because they provide a frame of reference in which to understand new material. Previews build context, particularly when reading about unfamiliar topics. Discussing the questions and predicting before reading helps students set purposes for reading and creates interest in the subject matter.

Comments and Cautions

Previews work best with difficult, content-intensive reading selections. Especially with nonfiction and texts with difficult vocabulary, it helps students to understand a context for a selection—what's the subject? where's the story located? who's involved?

Think-Pair-and-Share

What It Is

Think-Pair-and-Share is a prereading strategy that encourages group discussion and prediction about what students will read. Students work in pairs or groups of three or four to discuss sentences selected from the text.

How to Introduce It

Break students into groups of 3–4. Present 3–5 sentences from the selection. Ask group members to read the sentences and discuss what they mean and in what order they might appear in the text.

Encourage groups to make predictions and generate questions about the reading.

Then read the selection.

Have groups discuss the selection and the accuracy of their think-pair-and-share sentences. How many were able to correctly predict the order in which they appeared? How many could predict what the selection was about?

Here is an example from **Sourcebook,** grade 3, *Tomás and the Library Lady*:

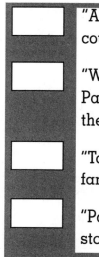

"All of a sudden something grabbed the man. He couldn't move. He was too scared to look around."

"When they got hot, they sat under a tree with Papá Grande. 'Tell us a story about the man in the forest,' said Tomás."

"Tomás was on his way to Iowa again with his family. His mother and father were farm workers."

"Papá Grande laughed. 'Tomás, you know all my stories,' he said."

Why It Works

Think-Pair-and-Share can be a powerful tool for getting students motivated to read. Small group work such as this gives students the chance to discover that they don't always have to come up with all the answers themselves. Sometimes two or three heads <u>are</u> better than one. Working in groups also provides reluctant readers with the understanding that all readers bring different ideas to the reading task. The activity also begins the critical process of "constructing meaning" of the text.

You can make the activity more tactile by cutting the sentences up into strips and passing them out to each group. Ask the groups to put the sentences in the order they think they occurred in the story.

Comments and Cautions

Have students help in building the "think-pair-and-share" activity. Have each group member write one sentence from the text on a file card. Then ask groups to exchange file cards—one group pieces together the sentences of another group.

Word Web

What It Is

A word web is a prereading activity in which students brainstorm and make connections to a key concept from the reading material. Word webs work especially well with selections about a specific idea, such as weather.

Here is an example from **Sourcebook**, grade 3, Poems About the Weather:

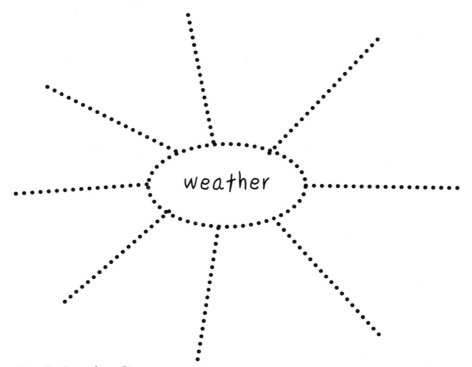

weather

How To Introduce It

Explain what a word web is. Tell students that you want to put a word in the center of the web and then think of as many other words and ideas as they can that connect to that word.

Walk students through the activity as a group. Take a general idea, such as "transportation." Ask students to give examples of transportation. Then ask them how they feel about different kinds of transportation (cars, planes, trains, spaceships, etc.).

After modeling how to complete a web, ask students to complete the one in the **Sourcebook**. Then have them share their webs with 2 or 3 other students before reading the selection.

Why It Works

Word webs are excellent tools for developing students' conceptual knowledge. They tap into students' prior knowledge and help students make connections between what they know and what they will learn.

Comments and Cautions

If students get "stuck," encourage them to write down words, phrases, examples, or images they associate with the concept. For this strategy, it is helpful to students to work together in groups. Students should experience success and create ideas about the subject before they start the selection.

ACTIVE READING STRATEGIES

The Active Reading Strategies are introduced at the beginning of the *Sourcebook* (pages 5–9). They are the heart of the interactive reading students are asked to do through the book. In **Part II** of each lesson, students are first asked to read the selection actively, marking or highlighting the text or writing comments and reactions to it. In the first reading, they read and mark. In the second reading, they are asked to write or draw their thoughts in the Response Notes beside each selection.

To maintain focus, the directions ask readers to do one thing at a time. Struggling readers do not naturally interact with a text, so these strategies are limited to only four and an example is provided in each lesson. The intent is to help them get started on the way to becoming active readers.

Examples are also provided in each lesson to model the strategy. The intent is to build the habit of reading with a pen in hand and marking up the text until it becomes a natural way for students to read.

Response Strategies

1. Make clear

2. Connect

3. Question

4. Draw

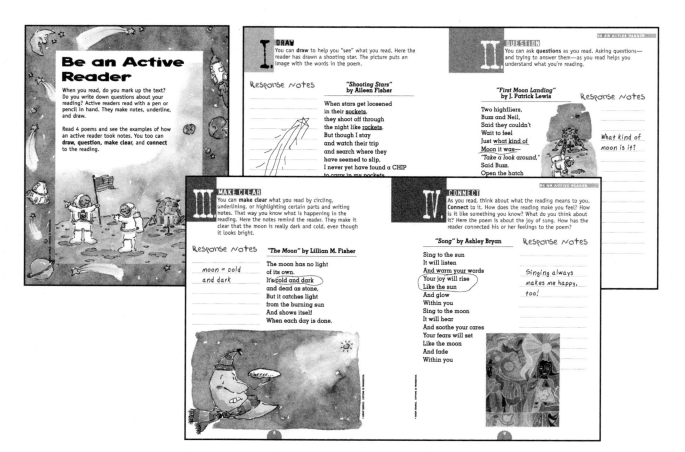

The purpose of these Response Strategies in each lesson is:

1. To help students learn how to mark up a text

2. To help students focus on specific aspects of a text and find the information they need

3. To build lifelong habits for students by repeating good reading practices

COMPREHENSION STRATEGIES
Stop and Think

What It Is

The Stop and Think strategy is a form of directed reading. It is designed to guide students' reading of a selection. Directed reading in its purest form consists of a series of steps, including readiness, directed silent reading, comprehension check and discuss, oral re-reading and follow-up activities. In the *Sourcebook*, students gain readiness in **Part I**, read silently in **Part II**, and then encounter questions that check their comprehension throughout the selection.

During the **Reread** step at the end of **Part II**, teachers are encouraged to have students reread the selection another time, and respond to the Stop and Think questions. Repeated reading of a selection tends to increase reading fluency, which in itself improves reading comprehension.

How To Introduce It

For the first selection with Stop and Think questions, point out to students the questions that are placed in the middle of the selection. Have students read the selection as directed in the instuctions in **Part II**.

Guide them through active reading of the text on the first reading and to responding to the text on a second reading. Then, after all of the students have made it through the selection, ask students to reread. On this reading, ask students to concentrate on the questions in the text. Tell students to answer each question when they come upon it.

Mention to students that the questions are the kind of questions they should be asking of themselves as they read.

Here is an example from *Sourcebook*, grade 3, *Volcanoes*:

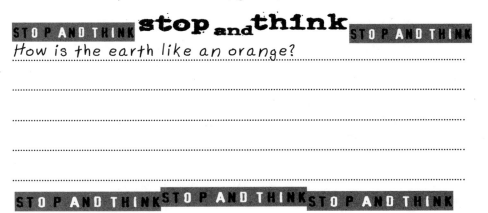

STOP AND THINK **stop** and **think** STOP AND THINK

How is the earth like an orange?

....

....

....

....

....

STOP AND THINK STOP AND THINK STOP AND THINK

Why It Works

Directed reading helps students ask the questions good readers ask of themselves. The structured format of the Stop and Think activities ensures that students will be asking the right kinds of questions.

Comments and Cautions

* Directed reading may need to be modified to fit the needs of individual students. Some students may benefit by answering these questions in groups or by working in pairs.

* Directed reading is intended to help students make meaning from the text. But, putting the questions in the text may also serve as an interruption of reading for some students. Especially for these students, be sure that students read all the way through the selection once before trying to tackle the Stop and Think questions. By increasing reading fluency, you will be increasing students' reading comprehension.

Graphic Organizer

What It Is

A graphic organizer is a visual representation of the information for a reading selection. Graphic organizers can be as simple as a web or as involved as a story chart. In either case, the purpose is to <u>show</u> information and organize it for the reader.

How To Introduce It

Start off by showing some graphic organizers. For example, show a 3-column Beginning, Middle, and End chart and a Story Frame. Tell students that they can use different kinds of graphic organizers to help them keep track of what they read.

After students understand what graphic organizers are, tell them their purpose: to organize information and make it easier to remember.

Here is an example from *Sourcebook,* grade 3, *Buffalo Bill and the Pony Express*:

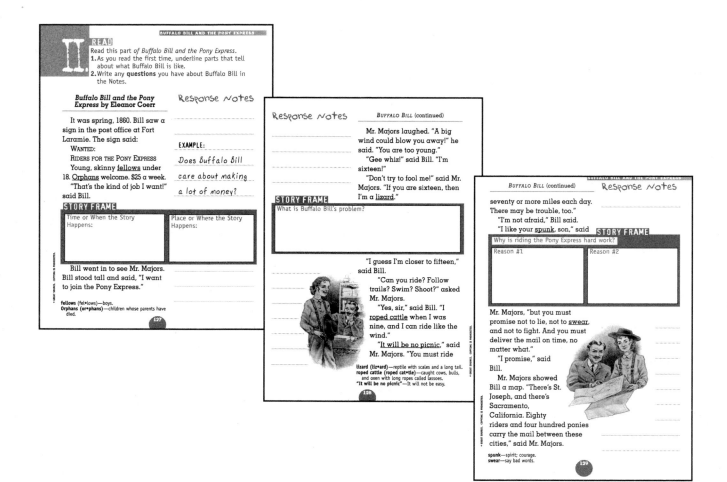

Why It Works

By making thinking visible, a graphic organizer helps students remember it. It also helps students make connections between ideas, especially in flow charts or cause-effect charts.

Comments and Cautions

You may want to introduce simple graphic organizers in your discussions of selections. A common and quite easy organizer is a Beginning, Middle, and End chart for stories.

By starting with simple organizers, students will be acquainted with graphic organizers when they encounter later in the grade 3 *Sourcebook* the Cause-Effect chart and Story Frame.

Double-Entry Journal

What It Is

A Double-entry journal is an adaptation of the more familiar response journal. Typically, the left column includes quotes from a selection, while the right column offers students the opportunity to respond to the quotation or idea. It is a very good strategy to build students' ability to comprehend and interpret a text and to make inferences.

How To Introduce It

Introduce Double-entry journals by doing one as a group with the whole class. Create a 2-column chart and put a quote from the selection in the left-hand column. Then ask students for their reactions to the quote and write them on the right-hand side. Explain to students that they have just completed a Double-entry journal and that it is a strategy to help them understand specific quotes or sentences from a text.

In time, students can choose their own quotes to comment on. In the *Sourcebook*, the quotes are always chosen for students. The benefit of selecting the quotations for students is to simplify their task of interpreting passages.

Here is an example from *Sourcebook,* grade 3, Poems About the Weather:

DOUBLE-ENTRY JOURNAL

Quote	What You Think This Means
"The world looks good enough to bite."	It sounds like something to eat—like cake.

Why It Works

Double-entry journals encourage students to become more engaged in what they are reading. With a double-entry journal, students naturally make connections between the literature and their own lives. Double-entry journals expand on students' understanding of the material because they demand that students make inferences or some kind of interpretation of the text. By beginning the interpretation of literature, students will find writing about a text easier once they focus on the quotations they select.

Comments and Cautions

Many students may not know what to write about the quotes. Encourage students to write how they feel about the quote or tell what they think a quotation means.

Find the students who need help in knowing what to write and work through several more examples with them.

What It Is

Retelling is both a comprehension strategy and assessment tool in which students tell about a selection in their own words. Retelling often works best with chronological stories and as a means of checking whether students followed the general "story" in a selection.

How To Introduce It

Introduce retelling as a whole-class activity. For example, you might read a fairy tale out loud or tell the story of the "Billy Goats Gruff" in which three Billy goats try to cross a bridge guarded by a troll. First the small goat meets the troll and persuades him to wait for his bigger brother. Then the next Billy goat meets the troll and persuades the troll to wait for his mother. Then the mother comes and kicks the troll off the bridge. Then ask a volunteer to retell the story. Then ask another volunteer. Explain that retellings will differ somewhat but have the same essential features.

Here is an example from **Sourcebook,** grade 3, *Play Ball, Amelia Bedelia*:

STOP AND RETELL stop and retell STOP AND RETELL

What do you remember about Amelia Bedelia so far?

Why It Works

Explain to students the benefit of retelling as a strategy is that they understand a story better when it is translated into their own words. Mention also that retelling helps students remember the story.

Retelling also helps students make a more personal connection to the text, which makes it more meaningful, and provides a deeper understanding of the material.

Comments and Cautions

You might have students tape record the retellings and let students listen and assess their own work.

Tell students that the goal of a retelling is not to tell a story with every detail but only to tell what is important about the story.

As much as possible, try to make students understand that one retelling is not necessarily better than another because it includes more. A retelling should be accurate and reflect the story, but longer retellings are not necessarily better than shorter ones.

Word Work: Strategies for Reading and New Words

BY RUTH NATHAN, PH.D.

There's an old saying, "If you drop gold and books, pick up the books first, then the gold" (von Hoff Johnson, 1999). Most of us who work with less-skilled readers would wish this scenario for our struggling students. But the truth is, many less-skilled readers don't enjoy reading at all. While there are many documented reasons for their feelings toward text, the most ubiquitous problem is slow, even laborious, word recognition processes. When reading words takes a great deal of attention and time, comprehension is often lost (Adams, 1990). Who would want to read if it brought no satisfaction?

The Word Work section of each lesson in the **Sourcebooks** is intended to give struggling readers strategies to read new or longer words. Once a reader reads a word a few times, rather than skipping it, word recognition time for that word decreases and soon becomes automatic. The more automatic word recognition is, the more attention is available for the important work of comprehension, reflection, and interpretation. If we want our less-skilled readers to "go for the books," not just the "gold," we have to teach them strategies to unlock the pronunciation of unknown words.

Five Useful Strategies

Recognizing complex sound/symbol combinations

Recognizing compound words

Reading new words by analogy

Syllabification

Recognizing word parts: affixes, root words

Recognizing Complex Sound/Symbol Combinations

When children first learn to read, they are taught one-to-one sound/symbol correspondences. For example, **b** says /b/ as in *ball*; **t** says /t/ as in *top*. But soon this one-to-one phenomenon is lost to the truth of the matter. Our language is a mixture of many languages, mostly Anglo-Saxon, Greek, and Latin. From Anglo-Saxon we get the *many* spellings of **long a,** as in *mate, nail, play,* and *great*. From Latin we get the "schwa" (the first sound in *about*), a sound spelled with virtually every vowel: *ahead, attitude, committee, selection,* and *selection* (Henry, 1990). And from Greek we get, the sound /f/ as in *phonograph,* not /f/ as in *fly*; or /k/ as in *chronology,* not /k/ as in *kite*. English is complex! This being the case, the **Sourcebooks** offer lessons in these complex letter/sound relationships using "word sorts," an active technique that highlights alternative spellings of the same sound (Bear, et. al., 2000).

Recognizing Compound Words

Many long English words are simply the combination of two smaller words; these are called compound words. Compounding is one of the major ways by which English words are created. *Over* combines with *pass* to become *overpass*. *Book* combines with *store* to become *bookstore*. Students benefit tremendously by knowing that one strategy for recognizing a longer word is to look for smaller words of which it might be made.

Reading New Words by Analogy

When we say readers can read a new word by using "analogy," it means that they can use a word they know to read one that looks similar from the first vowel onward. For example, if I can read *right* I can probably read *might* by removing the **r** and substituting an **m**. Both words are part of the same word family. That is to say, from the vowel onward they are identical in both spelling and sound. Reading words by analogy is a useful technique when reading sight words, words that are in "families" that don't conform to more frequent sound/symbol relationships, such as *could, would, should*.

Syllabification

Longer words usually contain many syllables. A syllable is a word or word part with one vocalic sound. For example, *front* has one syllable while *front/ier* has two. If students have a strategy for breaking longer words into syllables, then the words become easier to read. Consequently, the ***Sourcebooks*** contain word work lessons on syllabification. Fortunately the syllable patterns are generally the same in Latin based words as in those of Anglo-Saxon origin. The VCCV (*muf/fin*), VCV (*mu/sic* or *sev/en*), and VCCCV (*mon/ster* or *pump/kin*) patterns are most common (Henry, 1990). It's interesting to note, again to students' advantage, that prefixes and suffixes often consist of syllables based on these patterns (for example, *in/ter-* and *in/tro-* [VCCV], *-i/ty* [VCV]).

Recognizing Affixes: Prefixes and Suffixes

In addition to knowing the meaning of frequent prefixes (*un-, re-, dis-, in-*) and the meaning *and* uses of suffixes *(-ful, -ly, -ion)*, less-skilled readers need instruction on how the spelling of a root word might change with the addition of a suffix that begins with a vowel. For example, when the suffix *-ed* or *-ing* is added to a root word, the spelling of the word it's added to often changes. This confuses less-skilled readers. A **y** might change to an **i** as in marr*i*ed; a final consonant might double, as in run*n*ing, or a **final e** might be dropped, as in *rumbling*. Because these subtle root word changes confuse less-skilled readers, the changes must be taught explicitly. In addition, prefixes sometimes change their spelling, depending on the word they precede. For example, the prefix *in-* is spelled four ways: *in*valid, *im*portant, *ir*relevant, and *il*legal. Spelling changes in prefixes and root words challenge less-skilled readers and need to be taught explicitly. This is why all ***Sourcebook*** lessons include a word work part in them.

Taken together, the Word Work lessons in the ***Sourcebook*** reduce the chance that less-skilled readers will just skip words they think they can't read. "Go for the books" might become a reality for all children if they have strategies for recognizing new or long words. Remember, recognition of words comes first, then automaticity. Just as drivers can talk while they drive because they've automatized the driving process, readers will comprehend, reflect, and think critically about what they read if word recognition comes at no cost to reading for meaning (Stanovich, 1995).

References

Adams, Marilyn. 1990. *Beginning to Read: Thinking and Learning about Print*. Cambridge, Massachusetts: The MIT Press.

Bear, D. and Marcia Invernizzi, Shane Templeton, and Francine Johnson. 1999. *Words Their Way: Word Study for Phonics, Vocabulary, and Spelling Instruction*. Columbus, Ohio: Prentice Hall.

Booth, David and Bob Barton. 2000. *Story Works: How Teachers Can Use Shared Stories in the Curriculum*. Pembroke.

Harvey, Stephanie and Anne Goudvis. 2000. *Strategies That Work: Teaching Comprehension to Enhance Understanding*. Stenhouse.

Henry, Marcia K. 1990. *Words: Integrated Decoding and Spelling Instruction Based on Word Origin and Word Structure*. Austin, Texas: Pro-Ed.

Keene, Ellin Oliver and Susan Zimmerman. 1997. *Mosaic of Thought: Teaching Comprehension in a Reader's Workshop*. Heineman.

Pressley, Michael and Vera Woloshyn. 1995. *Cognitive Strategy Instruction That Really Improves Children's Academic Performance*. Brookline Books.

Robb, Laura. 2000. *Teaching Reading in Middle School: A Strategic Approach to Reaching Reading That Improves Comprehension and Thinking*. New York: Scholastic.

Stanovich, Keith. 1986. "Matthew effects in reading: Some consequences of individual differences in the acquisition of literacy." *Reading Research Quarterly*, 21, 360-407.

Von Hoff Johnson, Bonnie. 1999. *Wordworks: Exploring Language Play*. Golden, Colorado: Fulcrum Resources.

WORD WORK SKILLS

The notes below outline the skills included in Word Work sections of the grade 3 *Sourcebook*. The skills are listed here to help you reinforce and explicitly teach these ideas (and sometimes rules) about words. Some ideas are taught more than once and get progressively more difficult.

The purpose of the Word Work activities is to ease at-risk readers' stress over reading unknown or long words. Among the ways to help are to show students how to "see" 1) the base word of a long word that might have a prefix, suffix, or both, and that might have undergone a spelling change; 2) smaller words in compound words; 3) syllables; or 4 analogous words. Once students begin to feel comfortable with word recognition strategies, they will be able to decode more words more easily and they will be able to focus on comprehension.

1. Base Words and Adding Suffixes

One way to add a suffix to a base word is to just add it on.

miss + ed = *missed*

miss + ing = *missing*

miss + es = *misses*

A suffix is a great tool for making new words.

2. Reading Words by Analogy (Consonants and Consonant Clusters)

If you can read a word, many times you can read a word that's almost the same.

Say *king*. Now take off the "k" and put "st" in front of "ing." The new word is *sting*.

3. Compound Words

You can make a big word by joining 2 small words. The big word is called a compound word.

rain + fall = *rainfall*

out + side = *outside*

tree + top = *treetop*

4. Reading Words by Analogy (Consonants and Consonant Cluster)

You have learned that you can read a word and then read another word that's almost the same.

Say *moon*. Now take off the "m" and put "sp" in front of "oon." The new word is *spoon*.

5. Adding Suffixes

RULE #1: With words that end in silent *e*, remember to drop the *e* before adding an ending that starts with a vowel. Example: make + ing = *making*

RULE #2: With words that end in 2 consonants (*pack, yell*) or have 2 vowels that are side by side in the middle (*scoop, load*), just add the endings to the word. Example: pack + ing = *packing*; scoop + ed = *scooped*

6. Syllables

Words have beats—1, 2, 3, or more beats. Try clapping *mammoth*. You clapped 2 times because *mammoth* has 2 beats, or syllables.

Some 2-syllable words have 2 consonant letters in the middle. These letters can be the same (bo<u>tt</u>le). These letters can be different (ba<u>sk</u>et, wi<u>nd</u>ow).

7. Prefixes and Suffixes

Adding letters to the beginning and end of a word makes the word longer. It can also change the word's meaning. A prefix is a part of a word added to the beginning of a word. A suffix is a part of a word added to the end of a word.

> EXAMPLE: The smaller word is *mind*. Add the prefix "re" and the suffix "er." The new word is *reminder*.

8. Base Words

Take a prefix off the beginning of a word and a suffix off the end. The small word that's left is called a base word.

9. Dividing Words into Syllables

This selection has many 2-syllable words (words with 2 beats).

1. Look at the consonants in the middle of each word. Then write the word under the correct heading in the chart.

2. Divide each word into 2 parts by putting a line through the 2 consonants in the middle.

10. Adding *–ed* or *–ing*

Many of the words you know end in a final silent e. Here are some: *taste, bake*, and *come*.

Words that end in silent e are tricky if you are adding an ending that begins with a vowel such as *ed, ing*, and *er*. It's easy to make final silent e words longer when you follow this rule:

If a word ends in a silent *e*, drop the *e* before adding an ending that starts with a vowel.

11. Reading Words by Analogy (Consonants and Consonant Clusters)

If you can read one word, you can read a word that's like it or almost the same.

> EXAMPLE: You can read *pick*. Now take off the "p" and put "st" in front of "ick." The new word is *stick*.

12. Base Words with a Final Silent *e*

Look at the words, including the example, below.

1. Say the word.

2. Take off the ending, or suffix.

3. Write the base word.

4. Make sure you add a final silent *e* to the base word if it's needed.

13. **Compound Words**

A compound word is a long word made from 2 small words.

14. **Adding −*s* −*es* and −*ing***

Study each word in the box.

1. Put words that end in silent e in the first column.

2. Put words that end in 2 consonants in the second column.

branch	catch	move
pitch	take	drive

3. Now add -*s* or -*es* and -*ing* to each word.

15. **Finding Base Words**

This selection has many long words.

You can read them if you follow these tips:

• Take off each suffix.

• Read the small word, or base word.

• Then say the base word and the suffix.

16. **Adding Suffixes**

You can make a small word longer by adding prefixes to the beginning and suffixes at the end.

1. Look at the prefixes and suffixes in the box.

2. Use them to make the small words in the chart into bigger words.

Prefixes:	Suffixes:
sur-, re-, un-	*-ing, -ed, -ful, -er*

REFLECTIVE READING STRATEGIES

The Reflective Reading strategies occur in **Part V** of each lesson. They help students take away more from what they read. All too often students are asked, "Did you get it?" Reading seems like a code they have been asked to decipher but cannot. Struggling readers especially need to understand that there is more to reading than "Did you get it?"

How can we turn around struggling readers if the only payoff for reading is "getting it"? Good readers read for a variety of reasons: to entertain themselves, to expand their understanding of a subject, or simply because they have to read. Yet good readers naturally take away more from what they read. For example:

- We read sports pages because they are **enjoyable**.

- We read about as skiing because it has personal **meaning** to us.

- We read cartoons and magazines because they are **quick and easy** to browse.

- We read directions about setting up a stereo because we gain an understanding of how it works.

As teachers, we need to help struggling readers see beyond "getting it" on a multiple-choice test. So, **Part V** of each lesson in the *Sourcebook* is a "reflective" assessment, a looking-back, so students can see what they <u>gained</u> from the lesson.

Continue your paragraph below.

WRITERS' CHECKLIST

Capitalization

☐ **Did you begin all of your sentences with a capital letter?**

EXAMPLE: *Frog babies are called tadpoles.*

V. LOOK BACK

What details about frogs can you remember? Write the details below.

Think about Your Reading

READERS' CHECKLIST

Meaning

☐ **Did you learn something from the reading?**
☐ **Did you have a strong feeling about the reading?**

40

© GREAT SOURCE. COPYING IS PROHIBITED.

The other important goal of **Part V** is to ask students to think about their reading. The metacognitive part of reading—what was hard, what was easy, what strategy was used—comes once students reflect and collect their thoughts.

Students need to "think about their reading." Allow time at the end of each lesson for students to write their thoughts. These holistic assessments will offer valuable insight about what students did and did not understand and will prove to be very useful as diagnostic tools. Students will also benefit by learning to monitor their comprehension on their own.

The purpose of the Reflective Assessment in each lesson is:

1. To model for students the questions good readers ask of themselves after reading

2. To expand the reasons why students want to read

3. To build lifelong habits for students by repeating best reading practices

Reflective Assessment

1. Understanding

Did you understand the reading?

Can you tell a friend what the reading is about?

2. Ease

Was the reading easy to read?

Were you able to read it smoothly?

3. Meaning

Did you learn something from the reading?

Did you have a strong feeling about the reading?

4. Enjoyment

Did you like the reading?

Would you recommend the reading to a friend?

Play Ball, Amelia Bedelia

Background

Peggy Parish's Amelia Bedelia stories are among the most beloved of all children's books. In *Play Ball, Amelia Bedelia,* Amelia Bedelia manages to wreak havoc at the Grizzlies' big game against the Tornados, thanks to her habit of taking all instructions literally.

When a player calls in sick the day of the big game, the Grizzlies beg the funny maid to take the boy's place. In her usual inimitable style, Amelia Bedelia proceeds to whack a base when she's told to make a "base hit," worries about clothing tags instead of tagging a player out, and grabs first, second, and third base when her players tell her it's OK to "steal." Even with these mishaps, however, Amelia Bedelia still manages to save the day.

BIBLIOGRAPHY Students might enjoy reading another Amelia Bedelia story by Peggy Parish, or one told by Parish's nephew, Herman Parish. Have students choose from among the following: *Amelia Bedelia Helps Out; Good Work, Amelia Bedelia; Merry Christmas, Amelia Bedelia;* and *Good Driving, Amelia Bedelia.* All of these books are within the same Lexile range as *Play Ball, Amelia Bedelia.*

How to Introduce the Reading

Read aloud the introductions to *Play Ball, Amelia Bedelia* with students. Help create in students a sense of expectation about the selection. Arouse their curiosity by asking the question, "Would you want to play in a game that was new to you?" Help students make a prereading connection between the text and their own lives.

By creating a sense of expectation, you set the stage for reading. This is an all-important first step in getting ready to read.

Other Reading

Read aloud other Amelia Bedelia books or other stories written at this same reading level. Among the titles at the same reading level (Lexile 200–220) are:

(Lexile 220)   (Lexile 210)   (Lexile 220)

65

Play Ball, Amelia Bedelia

STUDENT PAGES 00-00

Skills and Strategies Overview

PREREADING	predicting
READING LEVEL	Lexile 220
VOCABULARY	◆loaded ◆worried ◆stealing ◆scooped ◆puzzled
RESPONSE	question
COMPREHENSION	retell
WORD WORK	suffixes
PREWRITING	brainstorm
WRITING	letter/commas
ASSESSMENT	enjoyment

OTHER RESOURCES

The first **four** pages of this teacher's lesson describe Parts I–V of the lesson in the student book. Also included are the following **six** blackline masters to reinforce the lesson.

Vocabulary

Prereading

Comprehension

Word Work

Prewriting

Assessment

1. BEFORE YOU READ

Read through the introduction (pages 64–65) with students. These opening paragraphs are meant to pique students' interest in the reading to come. Help students make some initial connections between the story topic and their own lives. Then assign the prereading activity, making **predictions**. (Refer to the Strategy Handbook on page 48 for more help.)

Motivation Strategy

MOTIVATING STUDENTS Borrow a copy of *Play Ball, Amelia Bedelia* from the library and do a read-aloud of the first several pages of the book, up to the point at which Amelia Bedelia bats for the first time. This short activity will give students some context for the excerpt in the ***Sourcebook*** and also will serve as an excellent introduction to Parish's tone and writing style.

CONNECTING WITH STUDENTS Ask students to tell about a time something funny happened when they were playing a team sport. Have them say what happened and why it was funny. Help students forge a connection between the topic of the story and their own experiences.

Words to Know

CONTEXT CLUES Use the **Words to Know** blackline master on page 70 as a way to troubleshoot vocabulary problems. After working through the page, you might decide to teach a short vocabulary lesson on using **context clues.**

To begin, show students the key vocabulary words in *Play Ball, Amelia Bedelia*: *loaded, worried, stealing, scooped,* and *puzzled.* Explain that these (and other) words are defined at the bottom of the page, but that you'd like them to try to predict the meaning of the words first, before checking the footnoted definition. Tell the class: "Sometimes the author will leave clues in nearby sentences about the meaning of a difficult word. For example, I see the word *worried* on page 00. I don't know what this word means, so I'll look for some clues. In the sentences before the 'worried' sentence, I see that the team is nervous because it is the last inning, bases are loaded, and the Grizzlies need to score four runs to win. I'd feel nervous if I were one of the Grizzlies. Could *worried* mean 'nervous'? Now that I've made a prediction, I can check the definition at the bottom of the page to see if I am right."

Prereading Strategies

PREDICTIONS As a prereading activity, students are asked to make **predictions** about the story. Making predictions about a text can help pique student interest while at the same time give them a purpose for reading. They read in order to find out if their predictions actually come true.

PICTURE WALK For another prereading activity, take a **picture walk** of *Play Ball, Amelia Bedelia*. Explain to the class that during a picture walk, the reader looks at the art or photographs on each page, without reading any of the text. As you know, the art that accompanies a selection can provide valuable clues about the topic, tone, and sometimes even the author's main idea or message. Students should use the information they've gleaned from their picture walks to make predictions about the story.

To extend the activity, use the **Before you Read** blackline master on page 71.

MY PURPOSE Always establish a reading purpose for students before they begin an assignment. Move beyond the overly-general "read to find out what happens" and create a purpose that gives students something to look for or think about as they read.

II. READ

Response Strategy

FIRST READING Before students begin their first reading, explain the response strategy of asking during-reading questions. Point out the example in the Response Notes on page 13. Explain that this is a **question** one reader has about the story. Students will have other questions that they want to ask. Each time a question occurs to them, they should make a note of it in the margin.

Comprehension Strategy

SECOND READING Be sure students understand that, as they are reading Parish's story, they will need to stop occasionally in order to retell the events described. **Retelling** a story or an article can help readers make connections between events and ideas. Retelling can also help readers clarify in their own minds exactly what has occurred.

For more comprehension practice, use the **Comprehension** blackline master on page 72.

Discussion Questions

COMPREHENSION 1. What do you know about Amelia Bedelia? (*Encourage students to tell about Amelia Bedelia's appearance, personality, playing skills, and so on.*)

2. What mistakes does she make during the game? (*She "steals" the bases and runs all the way home when the team tells her to "run home."*)

CRITICAL THINKING 3. What's funny about this story? (*Have students support their opinions by pointing to specific words and sentences in the story.*)

4. Does *Play Ball, Amelia Bedelia* have a happy or a sad ending? (*Again, be sure students support their answers with evidence from the text. Easy inferential questions like this one will help sharpen students' ability to make strong and well-supported inferences about a text.*)

5. How does the team feel about Amelia Bedelia? (*Possible: At first they are a little worried. Later, they are thrilled when she makes a run.*)

Reread

THIRD READING The directions on page 16 ask students to reread the story, keeping a close eye out for the funny things Amelia Bedelia says and does. If you find students had trouble answering one or more of the Discussion Questions, you may want to do a whole-class rereading of the text. Stop at the bottom of each page and ask a volunteer to retell what has happened up to that point. When we reread, word recognition is faster, which leaves more time to make inferences or figure out the main idea of the work.

Word Work

SUFFIXES The Word Work lesson on page 17 affords you an excellent opportunity to introduce the idea of **suffixes** to students. Point out to students –ed, -ing, and –es suffixes. Before they begin the exercise, you might have students return to a page in the Amelia Bedelia story and circle words they can find that contain any of these three suffixes. First write the suffixes on the board. Then have students work to find as many as they can.

For additional practice with suffixes, see the **Word Work** blackline master on page 73.

III. GET READY TO WRITE

Prewriting Strategies

BRAINSTORM Students will **Brainstorm** a list of the funny things that Amelia Bedelia does so that they can write a letter to a friend. Work together as a class on this activity or have students work in small groups. You may choose to have students write full sentences for their lists or simply make a few notes. Explain that they will turn these notes into sentences later when they write their letters.

Have students use the **Get Ready to Write** blackline master on page 74.

IV. WRITE

Read aloud the directions on page 19 to help students understand the assignment. Remind them that their **letters** should be about Amelia Bedelia and the funny things she does in the story. Point out the sample letter on page 18. Then teach the five parts of a friendly letter: heading (which includes the date and return address), greeting, body, closing, and signature. Point out that a comma separates the day from the year. In addition, commas are used after the greeting and closing. Also show students that although each word of the greeting is capitalized, only the first word of the closing takes a capital letter.

After students have written a first draft, have them stop and think carefully about what they've written. They should ask themselves: Have I offered plenty of details about the story? Do I stay focused on the funny things that Amelia Bedelia says and does?

WRITING RUBRIC Use this rubric to help with a quick assessment of students' writing.

Do students' letters

- include a description of Amelia Bedelia?

- contain details about the funny parts of the story?

- follow the proper form for a friendly letter?

Grammar, Usage, and Mechanics

When students are ready to edit their work, refer them to the **Writers' Checklist.** Read aloud the question on the checklist regarding proper use of commas and explain that students should ask this question of themselves. If they find themselves answering no to any part of the question, they'll need to do some revising. You might have to support some students by helping them get started with revisions.

V. LOOK BACK

Reflect with students on their **enjoyment** of *Play Ball, Amelia Bedelia*. Point out the **Readers' Checklist** and have the class discuss their answers to the questions. Explain that these are two of the questions that good readers ask themselves at the end of every story.

To test students' comprehension, use the **Lesson Test** blackline master on page 75.

Name _____

WORDS TO KNOW

Before Reading

DIRECTIONS Read each sentence.

Then say what you think the underlined words mean.

If you don't know, make a guess. Use the rest of the sentence to help you.

1. The trunk was so <u>loaded</u> with boxes that there was no space left.

I think loaded means _____

2. I am <u>worried</u> that I'll trip and fall down the stairs.

I think worried means _____

3. She <u>scooped</u> up the ball and threw it to third base.

I think scooped means _____

4. I'm so <u>puzzled</u> by this math problem that I can't figure it out.

I think puzzled means _____

Practice

Now use the word *worried* in a sentence. Your sentence should help the reader understand what *worried* means.

_____

_____

Name _____

BEFORE YOU READ

Picture Walk

DIRECTIONS Take a picture walk through *Play Ball, Amelia Bedelia*.

Look at every picture.

Then answer these questions.

My Picture Walk of *Play Ball, Amelia Bedelia*

1. Which picture do you like the best? Say why.

_____

_____

2. What do you learn about Amelia Bedelia from the pictures?

_____

_____

3. What pictures are funny? What makes them funny?

_____

_____

4. What do you predict the story will be about?

_____

_____

Name _____

COMPREHENSION

Web

DIRECTIONS Use this web to show what you know about Amelia Bedelia. Write one word on every line.

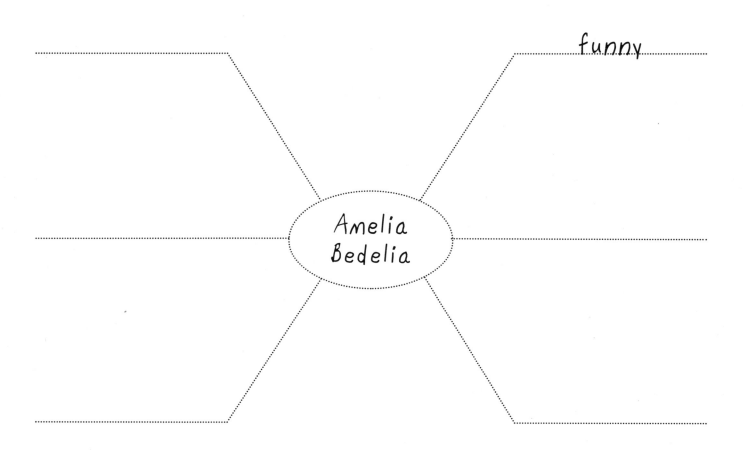

funny

Amelia Bedelia

Name _____

WORD WORK

After Reading

DIRECTIONS Add suffixes to these words to make new words. Write the new words on the lines.

1. go + ing = _____

2. fix + es = _____

3. reach + es = _____

4. load + ed = _____

5. miss + ed = _____

6. steal + ing = _____

Practice

DIRECTIONS Find the words with suffixes in these sentences. Circle the suffixes.

Example: He miss(ed) his turn at bat.

7. We loaded onto the bus.

8. The coach shouted at the team.

9. Stella mixes the lemonade for the fans.

10. We are starting the game in an hour.

Name _____

GET READY TO WRITE

Writing a Letter

DIRECTIONS Follow these steps to write your letter.

STEP 1 Choose the person you will write to.

I will write to:
_____

STEP 2 Decide what you will write about. Circle your topic.

I will write about . . .

Why *Play Ball, Amelia Bedelia* is a funny book.

Why you should read *Play Ball, Amelia Bedelia*.

Why Amelia Bedelia would be a great housekeeper.

STEP 3 Find two details from the story that you want to put in your letter. Write them here.

detail #1
_____

_____

detail #2
_____

_____

STEP 4 Next write a good first sentence for your letter.

My first sentence:
_____

STEP 5 Make sure you use these 5 parts of the friendly letter: Heading, Greeting, Body, Closing, Signature.

Name _____

LESSON TEST

Multiple-Choice

DIRECTIONS On the lines, write the letter of the best answer for each question.

_____ 1. Amelia Bedelia is a . . .
A. child.   C. friend.
B. pet.   D. doctor.

_____ 2. How do the Grizzlies feel about Amelia Bedelia?
A. They like her.   C. They are scared of her.
B. They don't like her.   D. None of these answers.

_____ 3. Who is Peggy Parish?
A. a character   C. the author
B. Tom's mother   D. Amelia Bedelia's friend

_____ 4. Most of the time, Amelia Bedelia is . . .
A. sad.   C. happy.
B. mad.   D. scared.

_____ 5. An important idea in Amelia Bedelia is . . .
A. Housekeepers can't   C. The Tornadoes don't play fair.
   play sports.
B. Baseball is boring.   D. Amelia Bedelia saves the
                                game.

Short Answer

What kind of a person is Amelia Bedelia?

_____

_____

_____

Poems About the Weather

BACKGROUND

For the book *Weather,* noted poet and anthologist Lee Bennett Hopkins gathered together works by Ogden Nash, Langston Hughes, Lilian Moore, and others to produce an anthology of poetry that is a fun and memorable tribute to the elements. Reprinted in the **Sourcebook** are three well known poems: "Winter Morning," "Go Wind," and "Mister Sun."

For years, Lee Bennett Hopkins has been a passionate champion of poetry for children. He says, however, that poetry was for him a learned rather than an inborn passion: "As a young child growing up in the projects in New Jersey," he explains, "poverty—not poetry—surrounded me. I discovered the power of poetry when I became a classroom teacher and saw quickly how magically the genre worked with my students. I wove poetry throughout every area of the curriculum from mathematics to physical education."

BIBLIOGRAPHY Students might enjoy reading another of Hopkins's anthologies of poetry. Encourage them to choose one of the following:

How to Introduce the Reading

Ask a volunteer to read aloud the introduction to the lesson on page 21. Then have several students offer answers to the questions listed: "How do you feel on a rainy day?" "How do you feel on a sunny day?" "Do you enjoy snow, wind, and fog?" Encourage students to explain their answers and offer examples from their own lives. A short discussion on the topic of weather will serve as an excellent warm-up for the poems students are about to read. In addition, it may help set at ease any students who feel intimidated by the genre of poetry.

Other Reading

Most children are fascinated with weather. You can make a valuable connection to your science curriculum by suggesting students read one of the following:

SNOW IS FALLING by Franklyn M. Branley

HOW'S THE WEATHER?: A LOOK AT WEATHER AND HOW IT CHANGES by Melvin and Gilda Berger

PINK SNOW AND OTHER WEIRD WEATHER by Jennifer Dussling

(Lexile 320)   (Lexile 300)   (no Lexile rating)

"Winter Morning," "Go Wind," and "Mister Sun"

STUDENT PAGES 21–30

Skills and Strategies Overview

PREREADING	word web
READING LEVEL	Lexile NP*
RESPONSE	draw
VOCABULARY	◇spreading ◇slushy ◇fling ◇trading
COMPREHENSION	Double-entry journal
WORD WORK	consonants and consonant clusters
PREWRITING	brainstorm
WRITING	poem / spelling
ASSESSMENT	ease

*NP = Not Prose and cannot be Lexiled

OTHER RESOURCES

The first **four** pages of this teacher's lesson describe Parts I–V of the lesson. Also included are these **six** blackline masters. Use them to reinforce key elements of the lesson.

Vocabulary

Prereading

Comprehension

Word Work

Prewriting

Assessment

BEFORE YOU READ

Explain to students that they're about to read three different poems that all have to do with the same topic: weather. Have students tell about funny, scary, or interesting weather experiences of their own. Then ask them to turn to the prereading activity, a **word web**. (Refer to the Strategy Handbook on page 51 for more help.)

Motivation Strategy

MOTIVATING STUDENTS Borrow a copy of *Weather* from the library and do a read-aloud of several of the poems not reprinted in the *Sourcebook*. Show students that reading poetry is fun, not scary or hard. Use your voice to impart a sense of enthusiasm about the topic and genre.

Words to Know

CONTEXT CLUES Use the **Words to Know** blackline master on page 82 as a way to troubleshoot vocabulary problems. After working through the page, you might decide to teach a short vocabulary lesson on using **context clues.**

Post the key vocabulary words for this lesson on the board: *spreading, slushy, fling,* and *trading.* Then teach a brief lesson on how to use context clues to find the meaning of an unfamiliar word. Tell students to look for the clues about the word's meaning in the sentences surrounding the unfamiliar word. For example, if a student doesn't know the meaning of the word *spreading,* he or she can check the surrounding lines of verse. Nash compares a coating of snow to the frosting on a cake. This may give students a clue that *spreading* means the kind of smoothing they do when they help someone put icing on a cake.

Prereading Strategies

WORD WEB As a prereading activity, students are asked to make a **word web** for the word *weather.* A web like the one on page 22 will help activate students' prior knowledge about the topic while at the same time allow them to make some initial connections between the literature and their own lives. Students can share their webs with a reading partner or the whole class. Leave a couple of the most interesting webs on the board for the duration of the lesson. Students can refer to them as they read and as they complete the writing assignment in **Part IV.**

GRAPHIC ORGANIZER As a further prereading activity, ask students to brainstorm a list of sensory words that they associate with the word *weather.* This quick activity will give students the chance to play with language in much the same way that a poet plays with language. Create a chart that asks for "sight, "sound," and "touch" words describing a particular weather phenomenon such as storms or fog.

Or, if you prefer, use the graphic organizer printed on the **Before You Read** blackline master on page 83.

MY PURPOSE Read aloud the purpose statement on page 22 and be sure students understand that you'd like them to look for weather words as they are reading. Students may want to "borrow" some of these words when they write weather poems of their own.

READ

Response Strategy

FIRST READING Before students begin their first readings, explain the response strategy, **draw.** Refer to the explanation on page 23 of the student book, or explain in your own words that drawing helps you make pictures in your mind as you read. Most students will welcome the opportunity to draw and doodle as they are reading.

Comprehension Strategy

SECOND READING During their reading of the poems in the *Sourcebook*, students will need to stop three separate times and record their thoughts in a **Double-entry journal.** Using a double-entry journal encourages active response to text. Explain to students that their responses should be personal reactions to a word, line, or idea in the poem. Their goal is to *react,* not summarize. To help students get started, work together on the first journal entry on page 23. Read the quotation aloud and ask various students how they might respond.

For more help with **Comprehension,** assign the blackline master on page 84.

Discussion Questions

COMPREHENSION 1. According to "Go Wind," what kinds of things does the wind do? *(push, shake, take, make things fly, and so on)*

2. With whom does Mister Sun trade places? *(the moon)*

CRITICAL THINKING 3. How does Ogden Nash feel about snow? *(Answers will vary. Students might want to quote the last two lines of the poem in response to this question.)*

4. What's funny about the last two lines of Lilian Moore's poem? *(Possible: The speaker has been telling the wind to push, but when it pushes, she tells it to back off.)*

5. Which of the poems did you like best? Why? *(Ask students to fully explain their opinions.)*

Reread

THIRD READING The directions on page 26 ask students to reread the three poems and pay close attention to the weather words they circled on their first reading. The purpose of this activity is twofold: first, it will show students that doing an additional reading can enhance their understanding and enjoyment of a work. Second, it will reinforce students' understanding of the language of the poems, which is an important first step in thinking about a poet's style.

Word Work

CONSONANTS AND CONSONANT CLUSTERS The Word Work lesson on page 27 can help you introduce or review **consonants** and **consonant clusters** with students. To get things started, put a list of the consonants and clusters on the board. Model for students how to make words from them: "I'm thinking of the word *wish*. If I take off the *w* and put a *d* in its place, I have a new word: *dish*."

For additional practice with consonants, see the **Word Work** blackline master on page 85.

GET READY TO WRITE

Prewriting Strategies

BRAINSTORM The directions on page 28 ask students to get ready to write a poem of their own. To begin, they'll **brainstorm** a list of weather words and the sounds they make. Ask a volunteer to read aloud the examples at the top of the chart. Show students how these sound words can add excitement to their writing. Sensory words like these give readers the "you are there" feeling that is such an important part of enjoying what you read.

Have students use the **Get Ready to Write** blackline master on page 86.

IV. WRITE

Students are asked to write a **poem** about weather that incorporates some of the sound words they noted at the prewriting stage. (Explain again that these types of words can make their writing more interesting to read.) Remind the class that not all poems rhyme, although your more advanced students might like to try writing a four-line poem using end-rhyme. If students have trouble getting started, have them model their writing on one of the poems in the *Sourcebook*.

WRITING RUBRIC Use this rubric to help with a quick assessment of students' writing.

Do students' poems

• have a specific weather element (such as snow, wind, or sunshine) as a subject?

• contain two or more sensory words that describe the weather element?

• include an illustration that relates to the subject matter (or mood) of the poem?

Grammar, Usage, and Mechanics

When students are ready to proofread their work, refer them to the **Writers' Checklist** at the top of page 30. Ask them to read each word in the poem, checking carefully for spelling errors. To help, assign proofreading partners and have them lightly circle in pencil any spelling errors. The writer should then correct the word by checking a dictionary or a class word list. Here are some commonly misspelled words that relate to the topic of weather:

afraid	dance	different	early	fall	listen	loud	noise	quiet	spring

V. LOOK BACK

Take a moment at the end of the lesson for students to reflect on the relative **ease** or **difficulty** with which they read the three poems. Point out the **Readers' Checklist** and have the class discuss their answers to the questions. If students say that the poems were hard, find out why. Make notes about strategies you might use for future lessons on poetry.

To test students' comprehension, use the **Lesson Test** blackline master on page 87.

Name _____

WORDS TO KNOW

Before Reading

DIRECTIONS Read each sentence.

Then tell what you think the underlined words mean.

If you don't know, make a guess. Use the rest of the sentence to help you.

1. She was <u>spreading</u> grass seed on the dirt, so the grass would grow.

I think spreading means _____

2. When the snow began to melt, the sidewalks became <u>slushy</u>.

I think slushy means _____

3. Don't <u>fling</u> that snowball at my face!

I think fling means _____

4. I was <u>trading</u> baseball cards with Sean when it began to rain.

I think trading means _____

Practice

Now use the word *fling* in a sentence. Your sentence should help the reader understand what *fling* means.

_____

_____

_____

Name _____

BEFORE YOU READ

Graphic Organizer

DIRECTIONS Think about a storm you watched. What did you see and hear?

Then think of words that describe the storm.

Write some sight words in the first column. Write some sound words in the second column.

A Storm

Sight words	Sound words
lightning flashing	Boom! Crash!

Name _____

COMPREHENSION

Summarize
....

DIRECTIONS On the lines below, tell what the three poems are about. Use full sentences.

"Winter Morning" by Ogden Nash is about
_____

_____

_____

_____

"Go Wind" by Lilian Moore is about
_____

_____

_____

_____

"Mister Sun" by J. Patrick Lewis is about
_____

_____

_____

_____

Name _____

WORD WORK

After Reading

DIRECTIONS Use the consonants and consonant clusters in the box to build new words. Write the new words on the lines. (One example has been done for you.)

fr   w   f   cl   spr   sn   gl   fl   n

1. row   flow

2. stay

3. bee

4. trip

Practice

DIRECTIONS Read these words. Circle the consonant blends. Then write a sentence using one of the words.

5. from   6. climb

7. glimmer   8. stop

My sentence: _____

_____

_____

_____

_____

Name _____

GET READY TO WRITE

Writing a Poem

DIRECTIONS Follow these steps to write your poem.

STEP 1 Decide what you will write about. Circle your topic.

I will write about . . .
_____

a big storm   a sunny day

hail   fog

STEP 2 Say how this weather makes you feel.

It makes me feel
_____

_____

STEP 3 Write words that describe how this weather looks and sounds.

How it looks

How it sounds

STEP 4 Write your poem in your *Sourcebook*.

Name _____

LESSON TEST

Multiple-Choice

DIRECTIONS On the lines, write the letter of the best answer for each question.

_____ 1. In the poem "Winter Morning," snow on the lake looks like . . .

A. sugar. C. salt.

B. powder. D. ice cream.

_____ 2. In the first two poems, what word does **not** describe the weather?

A. frosty C. stumps

B. slushy D. swoosh

_____ 3. In the third poem, what shakes things and makes them fly?

A. the snow C. the sun

B. the wind D. the rain

_____ 4. In the poem "Mr.Sun," What do the words "shades of night" mean?

A darkness C. wind

B. clouds in the sky D. sunlight

_____ 5. In all three poems, the weather acts like . . .

A. a clock. C. an animal.

B. a television. D. a person.

Short Answer

What words or phrases from the poems help you see the weather? Pick 3 and explain your answer.

_____

_____

_____

Frogs

BACKGROUND

In *Frogs,* Laura Driscoll invites readers on a five-senses journey into the world of these amazing amphibians. Driscoll shows a poet's love of language when she describes the sounds and sights of a frog's world.

Driscoll's book about frogs is the type that even the most reluctant readers can really enjoy. Students who normally feel intimidated will be able to read Driscoll's book without having to worry. If there's time, find a copy of Driscoll's whole book in your local library. The cut paper frogs she uses to illustrate her book are as lively and fun as the words themselves.

BIBLIOGRAPHY Students might enjoy reading another Laura Driscoll book. For example, *The Bravest Cat! The True Story of Scarlett* is the heart-warming true story of a stray cat who rescued her five kittens from a burning building in 1996.

(Lexile 310)

(Lexile 310)

(no Lexile rating)

How to Introduce the Reading

Read the introduction to *Frogs* and ask students about their experiences (or siblings' and friends' experiences) with frogs. Arouse their curiosity by asking: "What can you learn about frogs?" and "What would you *like* to learn about frogs?" Finish your introduction by having students imitate the sound a frog makes. Their funny noises will help set a light-hearted mood for the lesson.

Other Reading

Encourage students to enjoy poetry. Work now to develop a love for the sounds and style of a good poem. To help, read aloud from one of these modern classics:

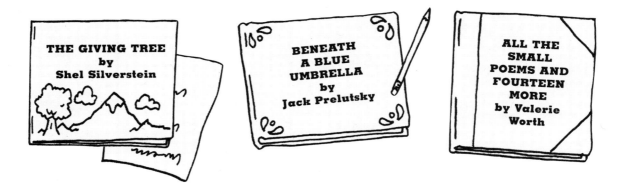

Frogs

Skills and Strategies Overview

PREREADING anticipation guide

READING LEVEL Lexile NA*

RESPONSE make things clear

VOCABULARY ◇webbed ◇hatch ◇breathe ◇shrink ◇disappear

COMPREHENSION stop and think

WORD WORK compound words

PREWRITING narrowing a topic

WRITING expository paragraph / capitalization

ASSESSMENT meaning

*NA = Lexile not available

OTHER RESOURCES

The first **four** pages of this teacher's lesson describe Parts I–V of the lesson. Also included are these **six** blackline masters. Use them to reinforce key elements of the lesson.

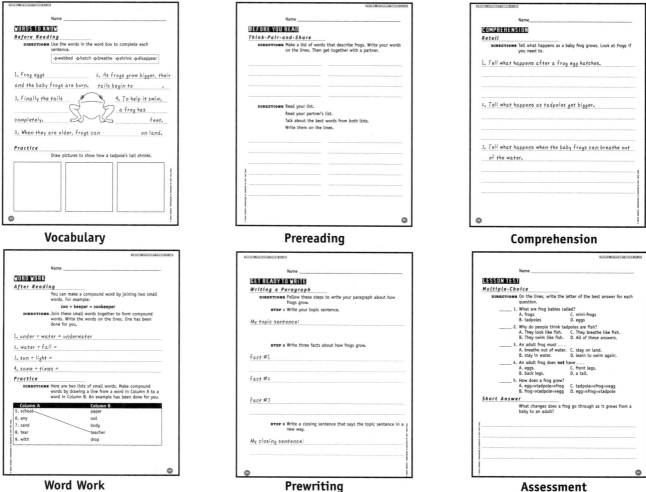

Vocabulary

Prereading

Comprehension

Word Work

Prewriting

Assessment

BEFORE YOU READ

Think about any students in your class who struggled with the poems in Lesson 2. Consider establishing a slower pace now, or offering additional reading support. When you feel the class is ready, ask the class to complete the prereading activity for this lesson, an **anticipation guide**. (Refer to the Strategy Handbook on page 48 for more help.)

Motivation Strategy

MOVTIVATING STUDENTS As a warm-up to *Frogs*, have students read aloud the poems they wrote for Lesson 2. Encourage them to read with as much expression as they can, so that the whole class can truly enjoy the "sound" of the poets' work. Use this short activity to once again reinforce the notion that reading can be an enjoyable experience.

Words to Know

CONTEXT CLUES Use the **Words to Know** blackline master on page 94 as a way of troubleshooting vocabulary problems. After working through the page, you might decide to teach a short vocabulary lesson on using **context clues.**

To begin, show students the key vocabulary words in *Frogs: webbed, hatch, breathe, shrink,* and *disappear.* Explain that four of the five words are defined at the bottom of the page. (*Breathe,* which appears on page 34, is not defined.) Tell the class that you'd like them to circle the words as they come across them in the text. When they stop to circle, they should think quickly about what the word means. If they're not sure, they can make a note in the Response Notes and then ask for help when they've finished reading.

Prereading Strategies

ANTICIPATION GUIDE **Anticipation guides** are easy to create and interesting for students to do. They work especially well with lower-level readers because they give students a "head start" on topic and theme work. Have the class work independently on the guide, marking √ for answers with which they agree, and X for answers with which they disagree. Then pair students off and ask them to compare answers. Have students explain their answers to each other, using personal experiences as support for their answers.

THINK-PAIR-AND-SHARE As an additional prereading activity, have students work together on a **think-pair-and-share** that explores their knowledge of frogs. Have them begin by listing words (five or more) that describe frogs. They can compare their lists and form a shared list of descriptive words.

To extend the activity, photocopy the **Before You Read** blackline master on page 95 and have students use it for their notes.

MY PURPOSE Point out the reading purpose on the bottom of page 32. Be sure students understand that their purpose will be to find out about baby frogs and how they grow. If you plan to do a read-aloud of the selection, remind students of this purpose at several different points during the oral reading.

II. READ

Response Strategy

FIRST READING When students are ready to do their first readings, explain the response strategy of **make things clear.** Tell the class that good readers think carefully about the words they are reading and *what they mean*. The response strategy of making things clear shows students how important it is to keep track of these silent clarification comments that they make unconsciously as they're reading. Later, when they begin the prewriting activity, have students return to their Response Notes and read what they've written.

Comprehension Strategy

SECOND READING At two separate points during their reading of *Frogs*, students will need to pause to answer **stop and think** questions that are meant to help them reflect on the facts of the reading. The stop and think questions in the *Sourcebook* serve several purposes. First, they help slow the speed with which students read. A slower reader is quite often a more careful reader. Second, they allow students to self-assess their own comprehension of the selection. If the student can't answer the question, he or she knows to reread in the area of the question. This is helpful for low-level readers who have a hard time skimming an entire text in search of one detail.

For more help with **Comprehension**, assign the blackline master on page 96.

Discussion Questions

COMPREHENSION 1. What are some characteristics of frogs? (*Possible: They live in ponds, have webbed feet, begin life as tiny eggs, and so on.*)

CRITICAL THINKING 2. What sound word did you hear in Driscoll's *Frogs*? (*Ker-plunk!*)

3. What fact from *Frogs* surprised you? (*Encourage students to explain their reactions.*)

4. In what ways are frogs different from fish? (*Have students use the facts of the poem to help them make their comparisons.*)

Reread

THIRD READING Your students will benefit from an additional reading of *Frogs*. Try reading it aloud. Have students follow along in their books and listen for details about how frogs grow. Each time they hear a new detail, they can make a star in their books. Later, when they need to write about frog development, students can simply return to the starred parts of *Frogs*.

Word Work

COMPOUND WORDS You've probably noticed that most young learners enjoy working with **compound words.** They enjoy putting together smaller words to create compounds, and feel proud that they're able to read and understand so many "big" words. Make the most of students' interest by teaching a short lesson on compounds. Then have them complete the exercise in the middle of page 36.

For additional practice with compounds, see the **Word Work** blackline master on page 97.

III. GET READY TO WRITE

Prewriting Strategies

NARROWING A TOPIC As an initial prewriting activity, students will retell how a frog grows from an egg to an adult. Write a sequence organizer on the board and then ask volunteers to name each step in the process. Encourage students to return to the text to find important facts. They'll use these facts as support for their **topic sentences** when they write their paragraphs. Although they're given the option of using a sentence that has been written for them, you might take the time now to practice writing topic sentences. Remind the class that a topic sentence does two things: 1) It names the subject and 2) It tells what part of the subject the writer will be talking about.

Have students use the **Get Ready to Write** blackline master on page 98.

IV. WRITE

Read aloud the directions on page 39 so that you're sure students understand that their assignment is to write an **expository paragraph** about the changes a frog undergoes after it is hatched from an egg. Help students get into the habit of using a standard paragraph structure, by first writing a topic sentence, then two to three supporting details, followed by a closing sentence that restates the topic sentence.

After students have written a first draft, have them exchange papers with an editing partner. Ask: "Has the writer offered at least three details from the text that show the development of a frog?"

WRITING RUBRIC Use this rubric to help with a quick assessment of students' writing.

Does the student's paragraph

• open with a topic sentence that states the subject and focus of the paragraph?

• contain three or more accurate details about the development of frogs?

• end with an appropriate closing sentence?

Grammar, Usage, and Mechanics

When students are ready to proofread their work, refer them to the **Writers' Checklist** and teach a short lesson on **capitalization.** Ask student editors to lightly circle capitalization errors and allow time for writers to make corrections.

V. LOOK BACK

Reflect with students on the **meaning** of *Frogs*. Point out the **Readers' Checklist** on page 40. Help students discuss what the piece meant to them personally.

To test students' comprehension, use the **Lesson Test** blackline master on page 99.

Name _____

WORDS TO KNOW

Before Reading

DIRECTIONS Use the words in the word box to complete each sentence.

◇webbed ◇hatch ◇breathe ◇shrink ◇disappear

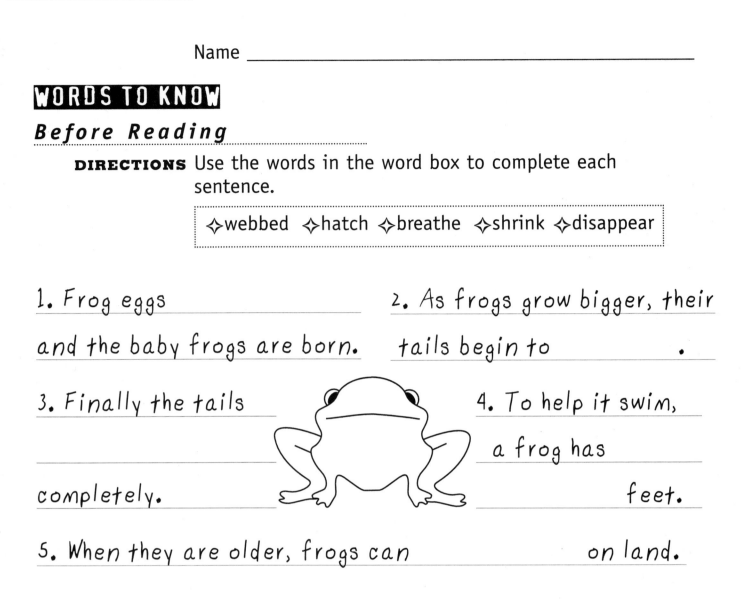

1. Frog eggs _____ and the baby frogs are born.

2. As frogs grow bigger, their tails begin to _____ .

3. Finally the tails _____ completely.

4. To help it swim, a frog has _____ feet.

5. When they are older, frogs can _____ on land.

Practice

Draw pictures to show how a tadpole's tail *shrinks*.

Name _____

BEFORE YOU READ

Think-Pair-and-Share

DIRECTIONS Make a list of words that describe frogs. Write your words on the lines. Then get together with a partner.

_____   _____

_____   _____

_____   _____

DIRECTIONS Read your list.

Read your partner's list.

Talk about the best words from both lists.

Write them on the lines.

_____   _____

_____   _____

_____   _____

Name_____

COMPREHENSION

Retell

DIRECTIONS Tell what happens as a baby frog grows. Look at *Frogs* if you need to.

1. Tell what happens after a frog egg hatches.

_____

_____

2. Tell what happens as tadpoles get bigger.

_____

_____

3. Tell what happens when the baby frogs can breathe out of the water.

_____

_____

Name _____

WORD WORK

After Reading

You can make a compound word by joining two small words. For example:

zoo + keeper = zookeeper

DIRECTIONS Join these small words together to form compound words. Write the words on the lines. One has been done for you.

1. under + water = underwater

2. water + fall =

3. sun + light =

4. some + times =

Practice

DIRECTIONS Here are two lists of small words. Make compound words by drawing a line from a word in Column A to a word in Column B. An example has been done for you.

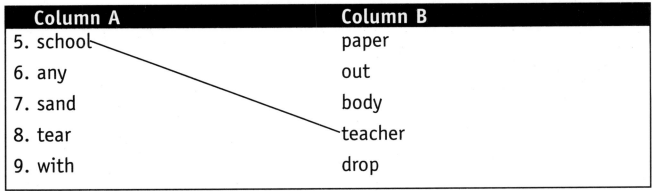

Column A	Column B
5. school	paper
6. any	out
7. sand	body
8. tear	teacher
9. with	drop

Name _____

GET READY TO WRITE

Writing a Paragraph

DIRECTIONS Follow these steps to write your paragraph about how frogs grow.

STEP 1 Write your topic sentence.

My topic sentence: _____

_____

STEP 2 Write three facts about how frogs grow.

fact #1 _____

fact #2 _____

fact #3 _____

STEP 3 Write a closing sentence that says the topic sentence in a new way.

My closing sentence: _____

_____

Name _____

LESSON TEST

Multiple-Choice

DIRECTIONS On the lines, write the letter of the best answer for each question.

_____ 1. What are frog babies called?
A. frogs   C. mini-frogs
B. tadpoles   D. eggs

_____ 2. Why do people think tadpoles are fish?
A. They look like fish.   C. They breathe like fish.
B. They swim like fish.   D. All of these answers

_____ 3. An adult frog must . . .
A. breathe out of water.   C. stay on land.
B. stay in water.   D. learn to swim again.

_____ 4. An adult frog does **not** have . . .
A. eggs.   C. front legs.
B. back legs.   D. a tail.

_____ 5. How does a frog grow?
A. egg⇒tadpole⇒frog   C. tadpole⇒frog⇒egg
B. frog⇒tadpole⇒egg   D. egg⇒frog⇒tadpole

Short Answer

What changes does a frog go through as it grows from a baby to an adult?

_____

_____

_____

_____

I'll Catch the Moon

BACKGROUND

Nina Crews's *I'll Catch the Moon* is the story of a resourceful seven-year-old girl who would very much like to build a ladder from her New York City apartment to the moon. Crews's story is a delightful combination of reality and fantasy that is sure to capture your students' imagination. The rhythmic cadence of the writing lends a dreamlike quality to the prose, while the frank, first-person point of view keeps the story grounded in the reality of the "honk, blink, stop, go" of a New York City street.

Nina Crews is the daughter of Donald Crews *(Freight Train)* and Ann Jonas *(Round Trip),* both of whom have had enormous success in the field of children's literature. Trained as an artist and photographer, Nina started her career as a commercial animation producer. Her first picture book, *One Hot Summer Day,* was published in 1995. It was followed by *I'll Catch the Moon* and *Snowball.*

BIBLIOGRAPHY Students might enjoy reading another book by Nina Crews. Have them choose from among the following, all of which are at a similar reading level to *I'll Catch the Moon* (Lexile 300):

ONE HOT SUMMER DAY

SNOWBALL

YOU ARE HERE

How to Introduce the Reading

Ask students to turn to the opening of Lesson 4 on page 41. Read aloud the introductory paragraph, which is meant to pique students' interest in the subject of the unit. Then ask for volunteers to respond to the three questions about "moon travel." If you have time, ask students to create a list of "must-haves" for their trip to the moon. Have them illustrate their lists at home or during class free time.

Other Reading

As a warm-up to *I'll Catch the Moon,* read aloud one of these engaging and visually stimulating books for young learners:

(Lexile 330)   (no Lexile rating)   (Lexile 330)

I'll Catch the Moon

Skills and Strategies Overview

PREREADING word web

READING LEVEL Lexile 300

VOCABULARY ◇floats ◇outer space ◇helicopters ◇comet ◇passing

RESPONSE draw

COMPREHENSION stop and think

WORD WORK consonants and consonant clusters

PREWRITING web / topic sentence

WRITING descriptive paragraph / commas in a series

ASSESSMENT ease

OTHER RESOURCES

The first **four** pages of this teacher's lesson describe Parts I–V of the lesson. Also included are these **six** blackline masters. Use them to reinforce key elements of the lesson.

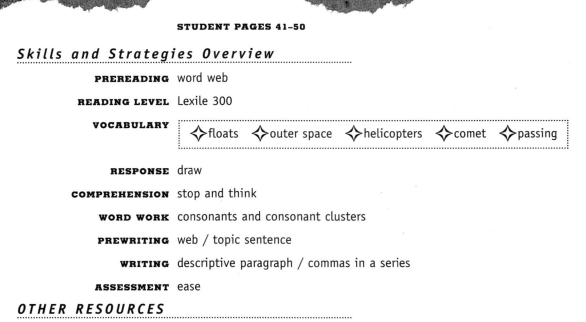

Vocabulary

Prereading

Comprehension

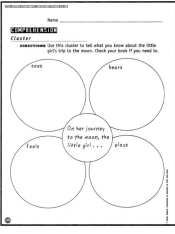

Word Work

Prewriting

Assessment

1. BEFORE YOU READ

Read aloud the directions at the top of page 42. Ask students to close their eyes and picture the moon. What words, images, and ideas come to mind? Then ask them to complete the prereading activity, a **word web.** (Refer to the Strategy Handbook on page 51 for more help.)

Motivation Strategy

MOTIVATING STUDENTS Open the lesson by explaining that *I'll Catch the Moon* is a story about a girl who builds a ladder from her city apartment to the moon. Ask the class: "How would you get to the moon if a rocket were not available?" Encourage students to use their imaginations and brainstorm a list of possible methods of travel. A short brainstorming session on this topic will help you set an appropriate "dreamlike" mood for students' reading of Crews's story.

Words to Know

CONTEXT CLUES Use the **Words to Know** blackline master on page 106 to troubleshoot vocabulary problems. After working through the page, you might decide to teach a short vocabulary lesson on using **context clues.**

To begin, show students the key vocabulary words in *I'll Catch the Moon: floats, outer space, helicopters, comet,* and *passing*. Explain that these (and other) words are defined at the bottom of the page, but that you'd like students to predict what they think the words mean before checking the dictionary definition. Quite often, you can figure out what a word means in a particular context by thinking about a time you've heard the word before. Tell the class: "I see that the moon *floats,* and I'm not sure what *floats* means. I know that sometimes I *float* in the water. Could 'floats' have something to do with hanging in a liquid like water? Now that I've made a prediction, I can check the definition at the bottom of the page to see if I am right."

Prereading Strategies

WORD WEB As a prereading activity, students are asked to make a **web** for the word *moon*. Encourage students to move beyond words that describe the moon in a literal way ("round") and think of sensory words that could help a reader really *picture* what the moon is like. Ask: "What do you think the moon feels like? What would you smell if you were standing on the moon? What would you hear and taste?"

PICTURE WALK As a further prereading activity, have students take a **picture walk** of *I'll Catch the Moon*. Ask students to say how the pictures make them feel and what they remind them of. Which picture best captures their imagination? What makes the picture interesting or unique? Help students see the playful quality of the art. The playfulness of the pictures matches the playfulness of Crews's text.

To support this activity, use the **Before You Read** blackline master on page 107.

MY PURPOSE The reading purpose on page 42 asks students to pay attention to the motivation behind the little girl's trip to the moon. Why does she want to take a pretend trip to the moon? Have students keep this question in mind as they're reading. When they've finished their second reading, lead a short discussion about the text using this question as a starter.

II. READ

Response Strategy

FIRST READING As they read Crews's story, students should try to **draw** the action Crews describes. Each time they "see" something new, they should make a sketch in the Response Notes. Visualizing while reading keeps the reader actively involved in the text. It's a way of keeping focused and on track.

Comprehension Strategy

SECOND READING As they read *I'll Catch the Moon,* students will stop at several different points and think about the action of the story. **Directed Reading** of a story or article can help readers make connections between events and ideas. It can also help readers clarify in their own minds what exactly has occurred. This is a particularly good strategy to use with selections that are challenging or involve a topic that is remote from students' personal experiences. It's important that they don't interrupt their reading for much longer than a minute or so.

For more help with **Comprehension,** assign the blackline master on page 108.

Discussion Questions

COMPREHENSION 1. Where does the little girl in the story live? *(in a city)*

2. What does she want to do once she reaches the moon? *(catch it)*

CRITICAL THINKING 3. What words would you use to describe the little girl? *(Possible: smart, imaginative, determined)*

4. How do you think the little girl feels about the moon? *(Possible: She loves it and thinks it would make a good playmate.)*

5. Why do you think the little girl wants to take a pretend trip to the moon? *(Answers will vary. Ask students to discuss possible motivations and then say how they think her "trip" turned out.)*

Reread

THIRD READING On their third reading of the selection, students should watch carefully for details of the little girl's trip. What does she see, hear, and feel? Have students make notes in the Response Notes and draw any additional pictures that come to mind.

Word Work

CONSONANTS AND CONSONANT CLUSTERS The Word Work lesson on page 47 offers further practice on reading words by analogy. Point out to students how easy it is to create (and spell) new words once they become familiar with a few shorter words. By seeing how many words are similar, except for a few **consonants** or **consonant clusters**, students will be able to add the words they can decode.

For additional practice with consonants, see the **Word Work** blackline master on page 109.

GET READY TO WRITE

Prewriting Strategies

WEB The directions on page 48 ask students to build a **web** of ideas involving their own trips to the moon. Specifically, students will need to list words and phrases that describe what they see and do on their journeys. Invite the class to be as creative as possible. Encourage students to come up with fantastic sights and activities. After they finish their webs, students will write a topic sentence for their paragraphs. Have them read the model at the bottom of the page and then create a sentence that is similar.

Have students use the **Get Ready to Write** blackline master on page 110.

WRITE

Students' assignment in this lesson is to write a **paragraph** that describes their trip to the moon. Explain to the class that you want them to write what they see, hear, and feel on their journeys. They should try to use words that help their own readers visualize what they are describing. Have them open with the topic sentence they wrote on page 48. In the body of the paragraph, they'll incorporate ideas from their webs. They should end with a closing sentence that is a restatement of the topic sentence.

After students have written a draft, have them stop and think carefully about what they've written. They should ask themselves: *Have I offered lots of interesting descriptive details in my writing? Do I stay focused on my imaginary journey?*

WRITING RUBRIC Use this rubric to help with a quick assessment of students' writing.

Do students' descriptive paragraphs

• tell where they're going and how they feel about the trip?

• contain details about what they *see* and *hear?*

• end with a sentence that ties things together and acts as a restatement of the topic sentence?

Grammar, Usage, and Mechanics

When students are ready to proofread their work, refer them to the **Writers' Checklist** and explain the rule for using commas in a series. For practice, write some word series on the board and have students insert commas where they're needed.

LOOK BACK

Reflect with students on their responses to *I'll Catch the Moon*. Were they able to read it with **ease**? Why or why not? Point out the **Readers' Checklist** and have the class discuss their answers to the questions.

To test students' comprehension, use the **Lesson Test** blackline master on page 111.

Name _____

WORDS TO KNOW

Before Reading

DIRECTIONS Read this paragraph. It has 5 underlined words from the story. Write the meaning of each underlined word. Use the other words in the paragraph to help you.

> Space shuttles can fly around the stars in <u>outer space</u>. Airplanes and <u>helicopters</u> cannot. If you go to outer space, you will see that a planet's moon looks like it <u>floats</u> over the planet. You might see <u>comets</u> made of frozen gases <u>passing</u> by the planet Earth.

1. *I think* outer space *means* _____

2. *I think* helicopters *means* _____

3. *I think* floats *means* _____

4. *I think* comets *means* _____

5. *I think* passing *means* _____

Practice

Now write a sentence about a comet. Your sentence should show you know what *comet* means.

_____

_____

_____

Name _____

BEFORE YOU READ

Picture Walk

DIRECTIONS Take a picture walk through *I'll Catch the Moon*.

Look at every picture.

Then answer these questions.

My Picture Walk of *I'll Catch the Moon*

1. Which picture do you like best? Say why.	2. How do the pictures make you feel?
3. What do you learn about the girl from the pictures?	4. Do you predict you will like this story? Say why.

Name _____

COMPREHENSION

Cluster

DIRECTIONS Use this cluster to tell what you know about the little girl's trip to the moon. Check your book if you need to.

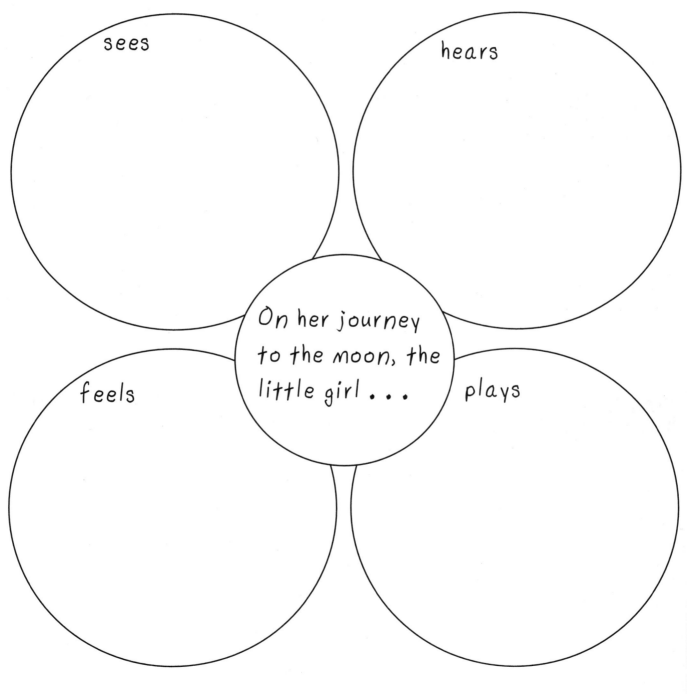

sees

hears

On her journey to the moon, the little girl . . .

feels

plays

Name _____

WORD WORK

After Reading

DIRECTIONS Use the consonants and consonant clusters in the box to build new words.

Write the new words on the lines. (An example has been done for you.)

st	gr	c	sl	r	p	scr	m	t	l	b	s	f

Old word   **New word**

1. catch   scratch

2. jump

3. ladder

4. star

5. floats

Practice

DIRECTIONS Use the consonant clusters in the box to make words of your own.

sm	fr	gr

6. owl

7. own

8. art

Name _____

GET READY TO WRITE

Writing a Descriptive Paragraph

DIRECTIONS Follow these steps to write your descriptive paragraph.

STEP 1 Write a topic sentence. Use this sentence starter:

On my trip to the moon, I
_____

_____

STEP 2 Write three details that tell about your trip.

detail #1 What I saw: _____

_____

_____

detail #2 What I heard: _____

_____

_____

detail #3 How I felt: _____

_____

_____

STEP 3 Write your paragraph in your *Sourcebook*.

Name_____

LESSON TEST

Multiple-Choice

DIRECTIONS On the lines, write the letter of the best answer for each question.

_____ 1. Where does the girl in the story live?
A. in the country   C. in the city
B. on a farm   D. in the suburbs

_____ 2. How will the girl get to the moon?
A. She will fly.   C. She will go in a rocket.
B. She'll climb a ladder. D. She will ride the cow.

_____ 3. What will she do when she gets to the moon?
A. play games   C. run and jump
B. travel   D. All of these answers

_____ 4. The girl thinks of the moon as . . .
A. her pet.   C. a friend.
B. a family member.   D. a place she will never go.

_____ 5. In the girl's imagination, what do the stars have?
A. a nose   C. ears
B. a mouth   D. eyes

Short Answer

Why do you think the girl imagines a trip to the moon?

_____

_____

_____

_____

Volcanoes

BACKGROUND

Nicholas Nirgiotis's *Volcanoes: Mountains That Blow Their Tops* is an easy-to-read introduction to one of nature's most spectacular phenomena: erupting volcanoes. Nirgiotis provides information about how volcanoes are formed, what causes them, and the effect an eruption can have on a planet. Nirgiotis's style of combining scientific facts with true stories about volcanic eruptions is sure to capture the interest of your young scientists.

The excerpt reprinted in the *Sourcebook* focuses on the how and why of volcanoes. Nirgiotis helps readers visualize the make-up of a volcano by comparing it to an orange. When the layers of the peel (or volcanic crust) are peeled away, the interior (mantle) is revealed. He also details the physics behind magma in easy-to-understand language. Your lower-level readers will have no trouble following his descriptions.

BIBLIOGRAPHY Students might enjoy reading other nonfiction books about scientific subjects. Have them do a search in the school library or ask them to choose one of the following books, all of which have Lexile ratings that are close to the rating assigned to *Volcanoes: Mountains That Blow Their Tops* (Lexile 310).

(Lexile 320)   (Lexile 350)   (Lexile 330)

How to Introduce the Reading

Read the introduction to *Volcanoes* aloud and ask students to answer the questions on the page: *What do you know about volcanoes? What are they? What do they look like? What makes them explode?* To further pique students' interest, put together a classroom library of volcano books that students can thumb through. Since students will mostly be looking at the photos, feel free to choose books that are a bit above their reading level. Some interesting titles include*: Volcanoes and Other Natural Disasters* by Harriet Griffey; *Volcanoes* by Seymour Simon; *The Mount St. Helens Volcano* by William Bankier; and *Why Do Volcanoes Blow Their Tops? Questions and Answers About Volcanoes and Earthquakes* by Gilda and Melvin Berger.

Other Reading

Read aloud other science books written at this same reading level. There are many good books available, including these three:

(Lexile 330)　　　　　　(Lexile 350)　　　　　　(Lexile 330)

Volcanoes

Skills and Strategies Overview

PREREADING	preview
READING LEVEL	Lexile 310
VOCABULARY	✦volcano ✦stirred ✦layers ✦plates ✦ash
RESPONSE	make things clear
COMPREHENSION	stop and think
WORD WORK	word endings
PREWRITING	main idea/details chart
WRITING	expository paragraph / capitalization
ASSESSMENT	enjoyment

OTHER RESOURCES

The first **four** pages of this teacher's lesson describe Parts I–V of the lesson. Also included are these **six** blackline masters, which you can use to reinforce key elements of the lesson.

Vocabulary

Prereading

Comprehension

Word Work

Prewriting

Assessment

BEFORE YOU READ

Read aloud the directions at the top of page 52. Explain that students are about to read a nonfiction article about volcanoes. Ask students to think of volcano facts they'd like to have confirmed by the reading. Write a list of the facts on the board. Help students see that one reason for reading is to find out information or answers to important questions. Then have the class complete the prereading activity, a **preview**. (Refer to the Strategy Handbook on page 49 for more help.)

Motivation Strategy

MOTIVATING STUDENTS Before class begins, check your library for an interesting film or video on volcanic eruptions. Show the film to the class as a warm-up for the reading. This activity will help students who are mainly visual learners, or students who sometimes have a difficult time gleaning information from reading. If the film is particularly good, it may also serve to pique interest in the reading.

Words to Know

CONTEXT CLUES Use the **Words to Know** blackline masters on page 118 as a way to troubleshoot vocabulary problems. After working through the page, you might decide to teach a short vocabulary lesson on using **context clues**.

As students read, point out key vocabulary words such as *volcano, stirred, layers, plates*, and *ash*. Ask for volunteers to pronounce the words and offer definitions without checking the footnoted definition. Then ask for sample sentences that use the words. Help students become accustomed to hearing the words in many different contexts.

Prereading Strategies

PREVIEW Before they read, students will do a **preview** of *Volcanoes*. A preview is a helpful prereading strategy because it gives readers a glimpse of what's to come. Thumbing through the pages they are about to read can help students learn about the subject and anticipate any comprehension problems they might have. To that end, you might have students note any glossed words that are unfamiliar. Also have them glance at the questions that interrupt the text. Their quick previews of these items will show them what's expected when it comes time to read. Students should finish their previews by writing three questions they have about volcanoes.

K-W-L As a further prereading activity, have students complete a **K-W-L** for *Volcanoes*. Ask them to note what they know or have heard about volcanoes (including the names of famous volcanoes) in the K column. Their questions belong in the W column. After they've finished reading, have students fill out the L column in anticipation of the writing assignment.

To extend the activity, use the **Before You Read** blackline master on page 119.

MY PURPOSE Always establish a reading purpose for students before they begin an assignment. Move beyond the overly-general "Read to find out what happens" and create a purpose that gives students something specific to look for or think about as they read.

II. READ

Response Strategy

FIRST READING When students are ready to begin their first readings, take a moment to remind them of the purpose of the **make things clear** response strategy. Give students an example of the kind of clarification comment they might make in the Response Notes. (For example, they might write "A part of a volcano is underground, where you can't see it" next to the last lines of the first paragraph on page 53.)

Comprehension Strategy

SECOND READING As they read, students will need to discover the facts about volcanoes. The **Stop and Think** questions that interrupt the text will help them reflect on the facts they've learned and then draw conclusions about what those facts might mean. If you like, have students read through the article once, without stopping. On their second reading, they can pause at each **Stop and Think**.

For more help with **Comprehension,** assign the blackline master on page 120.

Discussion Questions

COMPREHENSION 1. What are "plates"? *(the top layers of the earth)*

2. What happens when magma finds a crack between the plates? *(It spurts out. This is the start of a volcano.)*

CRITICAL THINKING 3. What is the difference between magma and lava? *(Refer students to the explanation of these two terms on pages 54 and 55 and then have them answer the question.)*

4. What are some of the things you'd see if you were watching a volcano erupt? *(Have students piece together what they've learned and then visualize an eruption before answering.)*

5. What is the main idea of Nirgiotis's article? *(Possible: Hot magma in the earth makes the volcano blow its top.)*

Reread

THIRD READING The directions on page 56 ask students to reread *Volcanoes* for a second or third time. On this reading, they should pay particular attention to their original purpose: find out how and why a volcano erupts. When they've finished this reading, have them spend a few moments completing the L column on the **Before You Read** blackline master on page 119.

Word Work

WORD ENDINGS Words with **silent *e* endings** are a puzzle for young readers, low-level readers, and students who speak English as a second language. Carefully review the rule for adding an *-ing* or *-ed* ending to a word that ends in silent *e*. Then ask students to complete the exercise on page 57. Reinforce your silent *e* teaching throughout the year. Every other week or so, put a few silent *e* words up on the board and ask students to add *–ing* and *–ed* endings to the words.

For additional practice with suffixes, see the **Word Work** blackline master on page 121.

III. GET READY TO WRITE

Prewriting Strategies

MAIN IDEA/SUPPORTING DETAILS Before they begin the chart on page 58, you might review with students some tips on how to find the **main idea** in an article.

step 1 Check the title. The most important idea is sometimes in the title.

step 2 Look at the first and last sentences of every paragraph.

step 3 Watch for key words in italics or boldface. These words often point the way to the main idea.

Once students have read the main idea at the top of the volcano, they can begin gathering details. Remind the class that each detail they list should relate to the main idea.

Have students use the **Get Ready to Write** blackline master on page 122.

IV. WRITE

Students' assignment for this lesson is to write an **expository paragraph** about volcanoes. They'll open their paragraphs with the topic sentence on page 59. Then they'll choose the three strongest details from the organizer and add these to the body of the paragraph. They'll end with a closing sentence that wraps things up and leaves readers with something to think about.

WRITING RUBRIC Use this rubric to help with a quick assessment of students' writing.

Do students' paragraphs

• show they understand the process involved in volcanic eruption?

• include three strong details from the text in support of the topic sentence?

• end with a closing sentence that is interesting and creative?

Grammar, Usage, and Mechanics

When students are ready to proofread their work, refer them to the **Writers' Checklist** at the top of page 60. Read the two items aloud and ask the class to make sure that they can answer "yes" to both questions. Then have them proofread their paragraphs for spelling errors. If students get stuck, have them work with an editing partner, or do a small-group edit of a single paragraph to model the process of finding and correcting capitalization errors.

V. LOOK BACK

Reflect with students on their **enjoyment** of *Volcanoes*. Point out the **Readers' Checklist** and have the class discuss their answers. Explain that these are the questions that good readers ask themselves after they finish a reading assignment.

To test students' comprehension, use the **Lesson Test** blackline master on page 123.

Name _____

WORDS TO KNOW

DIRECTIONS Read the sentences in Column A.

In Column B, look for the meaning of the underlined words.

Draw a line between the sentence in A and the correct word definition in B.

Column A	Column B
1. When a <u>volcano</u> blows up, you don't want to be standing nearby.	a. different parts
2. I <u>stirred</u> the salt and milk into the bowl.	b. mountain with a hole that can shoot out lava, ash, and gases
3. The earth is made of many <u>layers</u> of rock.	c. top layers of earth
4. Magma pushes up on the earth's <u>plates.</u>	d. powder left behind when something burns
5. When a volcano erupts, <u>ash</u> fills the sky.	e. mixed

Practice

Write a sentence that tells what happens when a *volcano* erupts.

_____

_____

_____

_____

Name _____

BEFORE YOU READ

K-W-L

DIRECTIONS Think of what you've heard about volcanoes.

Write what you know in the K column.

Write your questions about the topic in the W column.

Save the L column for later.

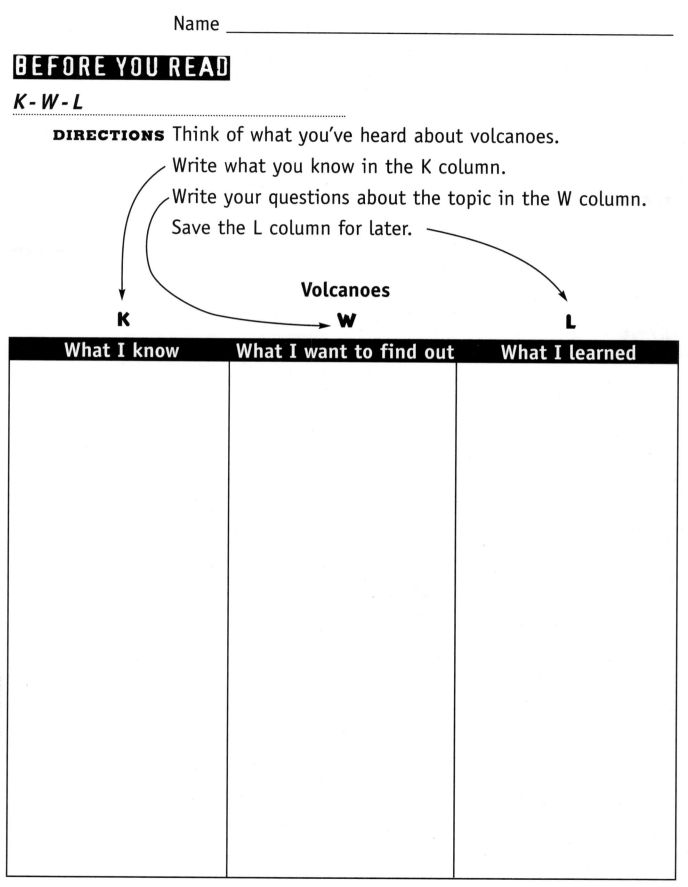

Volcanoes

K   **W**   **L**

What I know	What I want to find out	What I learned

Name _____

COMPREHENSION

Graphic Organizer

DIRECTIONS Use this organizer to show what happens when a volcano blows its top. Check your book if you need to.

First,
magma pushes on the plates and moves up through a crack.

↓

Next,

↓

Then,

↓

After that,

↓

Finally,

Name _____

WORD WORK

After Reading

DIRECTIONS Add suffixes to these words to make new words. Write the new words on the lines.

1. bake + ing = _____

2. scoop + ed = _____

3. compute + ing = _____

4. save + ed = _____

5. state + ment = _____

6. care + ful = _____

Practice

DIRECTIONS Add the suffix to the word to complete these sentences. Then write the word. One has been done for you.

7. The hot ash (fill + -ed) the sky.   *filled*

8. It (seem + -ed) like night. _____

9. We were (hide + -ing) in the house. _____

10. When it was over, we (smile + -ed). _____

11. That was a (taste + -less) piece of pie. _____

12. Mother was (grate + -ful) for the party. _____

Name _____

GET READY TO WRITE

Sketch

Sometimes drawing before you write can make the definitions of words come more easily.

DIRECTIONS Draw a picture of a volcano blowing its top.

Then label these parts of your drawing: *plates, magma, crater,* and *lava.*

Name _____

LESSON TEST

Multiple-Choice

DIRECTIONS On the lines, write the letter of the best answer for each question.

_____ 1. A long time ago, people thought a volcanic eruption came from . . .
A. the weather.   C. eating oranges.
B. the god of fire.   D. None of these answers

_____ 2. What is the top layer of the earth called?
A. the mantle   C. the crust
B. the skin   D. the magma

_____ 3. The mantle is so hot that it causes . . .
A. ash in the sky.   C. volcanoes to blow up.
B. the weather to change.   D. rock to melt.

_____ 4. For a volcano to erupt, you must have . . .
A. a god of fire.   C. plates moving.
B. a hard crust.   D. magma pushing through a crack in the plates.

_____ 5. After a volcano erupts, why is it dark?
A. Ash blocks the sun.   C. Volcanoes only erupt at night.

B. Lava covers the sun. D. The volcano makes it rain.

Short Answer

What do you think is the main idea of *Volcanoes*?

_____

_____

_____

Cave People

BACKGROUND

In the book *Cave People,* Linda Hayward invites young readers to travel back in time to the Ice Age. On their journey, readers will meet the Neanderthals and learn what they looked like, where they lived, and how they survived the dangers that faced them every day of their lives.

The Neanderthal were a primitive people who lived approximately fifty thousand years ago. They were an early group of *Homo sapiens* that inhabited much of Europe and the Mediterranean lands during the late Pleistocene Epoch, about 100,000 to 30,000 years ago. Neanderthal remains have also been found in the Middle East, North Africa, and western Central Asia.

The Neanderthals were short, stout, and powerfully built. Skull remains show that their faces had heavy brows, large teeth, and small cheekbones. These ancient peoples were cave dwellers, although they occasionally built camps in the open air. They wore clothing, used fire, hunted small and medium-sized animals (e.g., small deer), and scavenged from the kills of large carnivores such as the mammoth. Their weapons were made of stone and wood.

Recent evidence has shown that the Neanderthals coexisted for several thousand years with the modern humans, the *Cro-Magnon.* No one is sure why the Neanderthal population died out, although it's possible that their demise stemmed from competition with the *Cro-Magnon.*

BIBLIOGRAPHY Students might enjoy reading the books shown below. All three range in Lexile levels from 290 to 390. *Cave People,* the subject of this lesson in the ***Sourcebook,*** has a Lexile level of 330.

OH, THE THINGS YOU CAN SAY FROM A-Z	WET FOOT, DRY FOOT, LOW FOOT, HIGH FOOT	ALL STUCK UP
(Lexile 290)	(Lexile 310)	(Lexile 390)

How to Introduce the Reading

Read the introduction to *Cave People*. Offer background on the Neanderthals as needed. Then ask students to answer the question posed on page 61 of their books. How do they think their lives would be different if they were living among cave people? To extend the discussion, create a Venn diagram that compares life 50,000 years ago to life today. Have students add to the Venn before and after they read.

Other Reading

These three books can help you make additional links to your social studies curriculum:

(Lexile 360)   (no Lexile rating)   (Lexile 330)

Cave People

Skills and Strategies Overview

PREREADING K-W-L

READING LEVEL Lexile 330

VOCABULARY ◇mammoth ◇spotted ◇reindeer ◇spears ◇ridges

RESPONSE make things clear

COMPREHENSION stop and think

WORD WORK syllables

PREWRITING 5Ws chart

WRITING news story / end punctuation

ASSESSMENT understanding

OTHER RESOURCES

The first **four** pages of this teacher's lesson describe Parts I–V of the lesson. Also included are the following **six** blackline masters to reinforce key elements of the lesson.

Vocabulary

Prereading

Comprehension

Word Work

Prewriting

Assessment

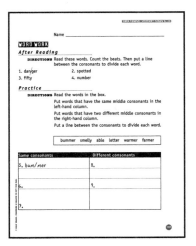

BEFORE YOU READ

Before students begin the lesson, ask what they know about the Ice Age. When did it take place and what was it like? (Students may know that it took place a long time ago, and that it was quite cold, and that the land was relatively barren.) Ask them to keep this knowledge in mind as they complete the prereading activity, a **K-W-L.** (Refer to the Strategy Handbook on page 47 for more help.)

Motivation Strategy

MOTIVATING STUDENTS To help motivate students and familiarize them with the subject, find one or two books from your library about the Ice Age. (For example, the *Eyewitness Visual Dictionary: Prehistoric Life* offers an excellent visual introduction to the subject.) Encourage students to discuss what they see in the illustrations and compare it to what they know from other sources, such as books, TV shows, movies, and so on.

Words to Know

CONTEXT CLUES Use the **Words to Know** blackline master on page 130 as a way of troubleshooting vocabulary problems. After working through the page, you might decide to teach a short vocabulary lesson on using **context clues.**

Discuss with students the key vocabulary words for this selection: *mammoth, spotted, reindeer, spears,* and *ridges.* Have them make a note when they come across these words in the reading, and then encourage them to define the words in context before checking the footnoted definition. Students will benefit from the additional work with using context clues.

Prereading Strategies

K-W-L As a prereading activity, students are asked to complete a **K-W-L.** A K-W-L can be helpful to those students who have trouble settling down to read and write. In addition to assisting with organization, a K-W-L gives students the chance to activate prior knowledge about a subject. After recording what they already know, they can think carefully about "gaps" in their knowledge. This way, *they* (as opposed to *you)* decide what they need to learn about the Neanderthal.

QUICKWRITE As an alternate prereading strategy, ask students to do a **quickwrite** that relates to the topic of the lesson. If you like, assign a topic from the list below and ask students to write for one minute about this topic without stopping. Later, they may want to use some of their ideas in their news stories (see **Part IV** on page 67). Possible topics for a quickwrite include:

- How I'd feel if I Lived in a Cave
- Growing Up During the Ice Age
- What It's Like to Hunt a Woolly Mammoth

To extend the activity, use the **Before You Read** blackline master on page 131.

MY PURPOSE Students' purpose for reading Hayward's article will be to find out what the lives of the Neanderthal were like—specifically, how they lived, what they hunted, and what challenges they faced in their struggle to survive.

II. READ

Response Strategy

FIRST READING As they read, students will once again make notes that show they understand what they are reading. The **make things clear** response strategy encourages students to think carefully about the facts and details they read, and then draw conclusions about what those facts and details mean. Before they begin, point out the example in the Response Notes on page 63. Explain that this is one conclusion they might draw from the facts on the page. Students might come up with completely different ideas, all of which they should mark in the Response Notes.

Comprehension Strategy

SECOND READING As they are reading Hayward's article, students will need to stop occasionally and answer **Stop and Think** questions designed to test their factual recall of the text. For some of the questions (e.g. "How are Neanderthals like people today?"), students will need to make connections between the text and their own lives. Encourage them to be brief in their responses. It's important that they don't leave the reading itself for an extended period of time. They should be able to answer each **Stop and Think** question in a minute or less.

For help with **comprehension**, assign the blackline master on page 132

Discussion Questions

COMPREHENSION 1. What do you know about the Neanderthal? *(Possible: They lived in caves, had a unique facial structure, and had to face all kinds of dangers every day.)*

2. What is one animal that the Neanderthal hunted? *(reindeer)*

CRITICAL THINKING 3. What was dangerous about life during the Ice Age? *(Possible: There was very little protection from the elements and the wildlife, including mammoth and wild lions.)*

4. What do you think it was like to be a child in a Neanderthal family? *(Encourage students to use what they know from outside sources in addition to what they know from Hayward's article to answer this question. If students are stumped, discuss it as a class.)*

Reread

THIRD READING Before they begin writing, students should take the time to reread Hayward's article. This is an important habit to cultivate in students, especially when the assignment is somewhat challenging. As they reread, have students keep in mind their own reading purpose. They should also take a moment to review the notes they made in the margins of the text. Which of their notes help them meet their reading purpose?

Word Work

SYLLABLES The Word Work lesson on page 65 may be a review for some students and fresh material for others. Explain how to clap the syllables of words and then practice doing so with several **two-syllable words.** Have students clap along with you until you are sure they can really "hear" the syllable breaks.

For additional practice with syllables, see the **Word Work** blackline master on page 133.

III. GET READY TO WRITE

Prewriting Strategies

5Ws CHART If students are not familiar with the **5Ws**, carefully explain the importance of understanding the who, what, where, when, why (and sometimes how) of a topic. Be sure they know that this type of organizer can help them see the main idea and supporting details of a piece of writing. Help students get into the habit of completing a quick 5-W's organizer each time they read nonfiction. If your students are unfamiliar with this strategy, try completing the chart on page 66 in class. Duplicate the chart on the board or on an overhead. Ask volunteers to suggest details for each section. Then have students work individually on their closing sentences.

Have students use the **Get Ready to Write** blackline master on page 134.

IV. WRITE

Read aloud the directions on page 67. Students are to write a **news story** about cave people on a big hunt. Explain that all good news stories tell who, what, where, when, and why. Remind the class to use their organizers to help them with the body of the paragraph.

After students have written a first draft, have them exchange papers with an editing partner. Editors should read the news story and ask: "Does the story give three or more interesting details about the big hunt?" If the answer is no, the editor should suggest a detail or two that might improve the writing.

WRITING RUBRIC Use this rubric to help with a quick assessment of students' writing.

Do students' news stories

• open with a topic sentence that names the topic and what's important or interesting about it?

• contain three or more details about the big hunt?

• end with a closing sentence that ties things together?

Grammar, Usage, and Mechanics

When students are ready to proofread their work, refer them to the **Writers' Checklist.** Read aloud the question on the checklist and review the rules for **end punctuation**. For practice, ask students to punctuate some sample sentences.

V. LOOK BACK

Reflect with students on their **understanding** of *Cave People*. Point out the **Readers' Checklist** and have the class discuss their answers to the questions. Were there parts of the article that confused them? If so, what could they have done to clear up their confusion? (They might have reread, asked a question, or visualized what is described.)

To test students' comprehension, use the **Lesson Test** blackline master on page 135.

Name _____

WORDS TO KNOW

Before Reading

DIRECTIONS Read each sentence.

Then say what you think the underlined words mean.

Use the rest of the sentence to help you.

1. The huge <u>mammoth</u> reminds me of an elephant.

I think mammoth *means* _____

2. I looked around and <u>spotted</u> a deer before it ran into the woods.

I think spotted *means* _____

3. In Alaska, herds of <u>reindeer</u> give food and milk to people.

I think reindeer *are* _____

4. The Neanderthals used <u>spears</u> to kill their food.

I think spears *means* _____

5. I felt <u>ridges</u> on the rock when I ran my fingers along its side.

I think ridges *means* _____

Practice

Now use the word *spotted* in a sentence. Your sentence should help the reader understand what *spotted* means.

_____

_____

Name _____

BEFORE YOU READ

Quickwrite

DIRECTIONS Choose a topic from the list below.

Then write for 1 minute about your topic.

Write everything you can think of.

My topic (circle one):

How I'd Feel if I Lived in a Cave   Growing Up During the Ice Age

What It's Like to Hunt a Woolly Mammoth

My Quickwrite

_____

_____

_____

_____

_____

_____

_____

_____

_____

Name _____

COMPREHENSION

Shared Reading

DIRECTIONS Work with a reading partner to answer these questions. Write your answers in your book. Use complete sentences.

1. Who were the *Neanderthals*?

_____

_____

2. What did they eat?

_____

_____

3. Where did they live?

_____

_____

4. Why were their lives difficult?

_____

_____

5. Would you have liked to live during the *Ice Age*? Explain.

_____

_____

Name _____

WORD WORK

After Reading

DIRECTIONS Read these words. Count the beats. Then put a line between the consonants to divide each word.

1. dan/ger

2. spotted

3. fifty

4. number

Practice

DIRECTIONS Read the words in the box.

Put words that have the same middle consonants in the left-hand column.

Put words that have two different middle consonants in the right-hand column.

Put a line between the consonants to divide each word.

bummer smelly able letter warmer farmer

Same consonants	Different consonants
5. bum/mer	8.
6.	9.
7.	10.

Name _____

GET READY TO WRITE

Writing a News Story

DIRECTIONS Use this organizer to plan your news story.

A **topic sentence** tells the subject of the paragraph and the part of the subject you will talk about.

My topic sentence:

Detail #1	Detail #2	Detail #3

The **details** explain or describe the subject.

Name _____

LESSON TEST

Multiple-Choice

DIRECTIONS On the lines, write the letter of the best answer for each question.

_____ 1. Why didn't the Neanderthals kill mammoths?
    A. Mammoths were too big.
    B. Mammoths were dead.
    C. The Neanderthals didn't have weapons.
    D. None of these answers

_____ 2. To get food, a Neanderthal . . .
    A. went to a store.
    B. hunted animals.
    C. picked corn.
    D. worked on a farm.

_____ 3. For the Neanderthal, the weather was . . .
    A. very hot.
    B. windy.
    C. very cold.
    D. rainy.

_____ 4. Which of these sentences describes a Neanderthal?
    A. They had small teeth.
    B. They had a bony ridge on their head.
    C. They were tall.
    D. They had no hair.

_____ 5. Life was hard for the Neanderthals because . . .
    A. they had to protect themselves.
    B. they had to stay warm.
    C. they had to hunt for food.
    D. All of these answers

Short Answer

What did you learn about the Neanderthals?

_____

_____

_____

Look at Your Eyes

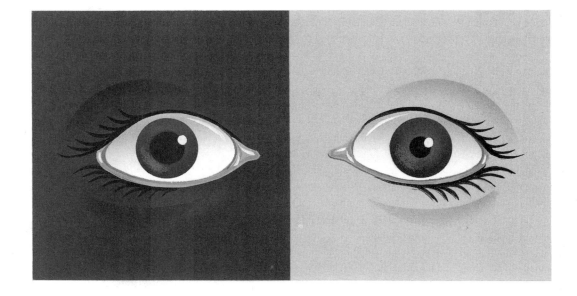

BACKGROUND

Paul Showers's nonfiction book *Look at Your Eyes* is a lighthearted, though factual, study of the human eye. Originally published in 1962, Showers's book is narrated by a young boy who stares deep into his own eyes while standing in front of the bathroom mirror. The young narrator examines the different parts of his eye—pupils, lashes, lids, and brow—and explains the function of each and how they work together.

Showers's book is one that students may want to read near a mirror so that they can imitate the actions of the narrator. After students finish reading the excerpt in the ***Sourcebook***, read aloud other sections of the book. Students can become eye "doctors" if you have several mirrors handy for them to use to examine the different parts of their own eyes.

BIBLIOGRAPHY Students might enjoy reading another book that tells about the five senses and why they're important. Have them choose one of these three:

HOW MANY TEETH? by Paul Showers (Lexile 370)

YOUR FIVE SENSES by Bobbi Katz (Lexile 370)

YOU CAN'T SMELL A FLOWER WITH YOUR EAR: ALL ABOUT YOUR FIVE SENSES by Joanna Cole (Lexile 400)

How to Introduce the Reading

Ask students to say what would happen to their eyes if they were to go from a dark room into the light. Would they squint or keep their eyes wide open? Explain that moving from dark to light affects the size of their pupils. Have students tell the location of the pupil and say what they know about its function. A short discussion on this topic will serve as an excellent warm-up to the subject of Showers's book excerpt. It will also offer some prereading reinforcement of the reading purpose in the lesson.

Other Reading

Read aloud these high-interest nonfiction books. Use them as valuable cross-curricular links to social studies or science.

THE DRINKING GOURD by F. N. Monjo

MY PUPPY IS BORN by Joanna Cole

STORM CHASERS: TRACKING TWISTERS by Gail Herman

(Lexile 370)   (Lexile 380)   (Lexile 380)

Look at Your Eyes

STUDENT PAGES 69–76

Skills and Strategies Overview

PREREADING	preview
READING LEVEL	Lexile 370
VOCABULARY	✧pupil ✧smaller ✧bigger ✧window ✧light
RESPONSE	question
COMPREHENSION	cause and effect
WORD WORK	prefixes and suffixes
PREWRITING	narrowing a topic
WRITING	expository paragraph / commas in compound sentences
ASSESSMENT	meaning

OTHER RESOURCES

The first **four** pages of this teacher's lesson describe Parts I–V of the lesson. Also included are the following **six** blackline masters. Use them to reinforce key elements of the lesson.

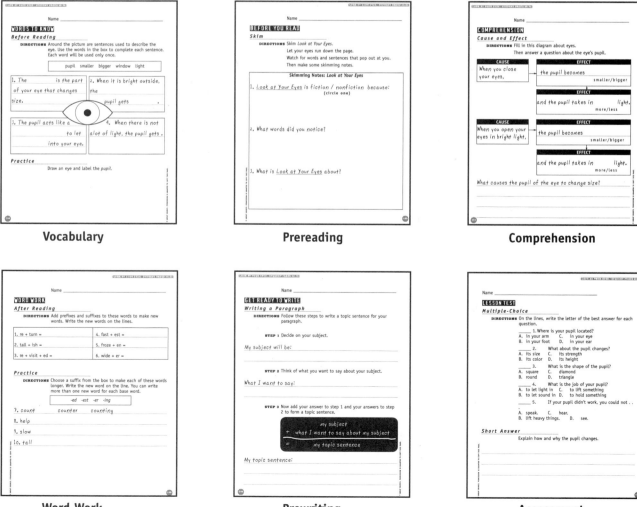

Vocabulary

Prereading

Comprehension

Word Work

Prewriting

Assessment

BEFORE YOU READ

Read aloud the directions for the prereading activity, a **preview.** For variety, ask reading partners to work together on their previews. Pair students with lower and higher reading abilities. Encourage partners to point out what they notice and why it seems important. Each student can then make his or her own previewing notes in the book. (Refer to the Strategy Handbook on page 49 for more help.)

Motivation Strategy

MOTIVATING STUDENTS For a fun opening activity, divide students into pairs and ask each to describe his or her partner's eyes: their color, size, and so on. Also have them describe their partner's brows and lashes. What do they notice? When they've finished, ask students to report what they saw. Point out to the rest of the class any observations that seem particularly insightful or unique.

Ask students to make a list of family members and give each person's eye color. What patterns do they notice? (Parents with blue eyes have blue-eyed children, and so on.) Have students ever seen anyone with two different colored eyes?

Words to Know

CONTEXT CLUES Use the **Words to Know** blackline master on page 142 as a way to troubleshoot vocabulary problems. After working through the page, you might decide to teach a short lesson on using **context clues.**

To begin, show students the key vocabulary words for the lesson: *pupil, smaller, window, light,* and *bigger.* Ask volunteers to pronounce and define each word. Then have them practice using the words in sentences. Encourage students to use these words often over the course of the lesson. Do this in hopes that the words become a permanent part of students' vocabularies.

Prereading Strategies

PREVIEW During a **preview**, the reader looks carefully at the first and last paragraphs of the selection, and then glances through the rest of the text, paying particular attention to headlines, questions, vocabulary words, art, and captions. A preview can familiarize the reader with the topic of the selection and will often provide valuable clues about the author's main idea. Encourage students to make notes after they finish their previews. The diagram on page 70 is an example of how they might record their notes.

SKIM As an additional prereading activity, have students do a **skim** of the selection. During a skim, readers glance through the selection quickly, looking for words and phrases that reveal information about the topic. Skimming gives readers an idea of what they can expect during their close readings, and can alert them to words, phrases, or ideas that might cause difficulty during their careful readings. As you know, this may be particularly helpful to those students who feel intimidated by nonfiction.

To extend the activity, use the **Before You Read** blackline master on page 143.

MY PURPOSE Point out the reading purpose at the bottom of page 70. Ask a volunteer to read it aloud. To be sure students understand their purpose, rephrase it slightly as "Find an answer to this question: *Why does the pupil of your eye change size?*" Clear up any confusion about the purpose before making the reading assignment.

II. READ

Response Strategy

FIRST READING Discuss the response strategy of **questioning**. Point out the example given on page 71 and explain that this is just an example of a question that might occur to students as they are reading. Other readers might have completely different questions. Request that students write at least one question per page of text. Help them get into the habit of noting questions automatically as they read.

Comprehension Strategy

SECOND READING Before students begin their first readings, point out the **cause-effect** interrupter, which appears on page 71. Be sure students understand what cause and effect means. If necessary, model the relationship between the two by showing the effect of a "cause" you demonstrate, such as closing the door (effect: outside noise is muted).

For more help with **Comprehension** assign the blackline master on page 144.

Discussion Questions

COMPREHENSION 1. Why does the pupil grow smaller when you open your eyes after having them closed for a bit? *(It needs less light, so it contracts. In the dark, the pupil gets larger to take in as much light as possible.)*

CRITICAL THINKING 2. How is a pupil like a window? *(Possible: It lets light into your eye like a window lets light into a room.)*

3. Do you think it's possible to see without a pupil? *(Possible: No, the eye needs light in order to process visual images.)*

4. What would you say is the main idea of Paul Showers's article? *(Possible: The pupil changes size when the light changes.)*

Reread

THIRD READING As you know, reading a selection for a second (or third) time can greatly increase comprehension. Tell students that when they reread, they should watch carefully for information about how and why the pupil changes. What brings on the change? What would happen if the pupil could not change in size? Encourage students to make additional notes in the margins of the text.

Word Work

PREFIXES AND SUFFIXES The Word Work lesson on page 73 offers students a review of forming new words by adding **prefixes** and **suffixes** to base words. Consider posting a prefix and suffix chart on a bulletin board. List common prefixes (including *re-, un-,* and *dis-*) and suffixes (*-ing, -ed,* and *-s* or *-es*) and their definitions. Students can refer to the chart as they consider how the meaning of the base word changes when a prefix or suffix is added.

For additional practice with prefixes and suffixes, see the **Word Work** blackline master on page 145.

III. GET READY TO WRITE

Prewriting Strategies

NARROWING A TOPIC Be sure to offer plenty of time for students to complete the prewriting page. Students will begin by writing a **topic sentence** for their paragraphs. To help, show them this simple formula:

subject + what I want to say about the subject = a good topic sentence.

Eyes change + when the light changes = Your eyes change every time the light changes.

Have students use the **Get Ready to Write** blackline master on page 146.

IV. WRITE

Read aloud the directions on page 75. Be sure students understand that their assignment is to write an **expository paragraph** about how and why their eyes change. The notes they made on the cause-effect interrupters should be very helpful. Remind the class to read these notes and the notes they made on the prewriting chart before they begin drafting their paragraphs.

After students have written a first draft, have them stop and think carefully about what they've written. They should ask themselves: *Have I explained why eyes change?* If not, they need to return to their paragraphs and do some rewriting.

WRITING RUBRIC Use this rubric to help with a quick assessment of students' writing.

Do students' expository paragraphs

• open with a topic sentence about why the eyes change?

• include three or more details that explain how and why they change?

• end with a closing sentence that states their feelings about the topic? (See the bottom of page 74.)

Grammar, Usage, and Mechanics

Commas probably cause more trouble than any other punctuation mark. For this reason, you may want to use the **Writers' Checklist** as a starting point for a brief lesson in comma usage. Be sure that students know that a comma must be used to separate the two parts of a compound sentence. Explain that a joining word *(and, but, so,)* is simply not "strong enough" to hold up the two parts of a sentence by itself. A comma also must be used.

V. LOOK BACK

Point out the **Readers' Checklist** and reflect with students on the **meaning** of the selection. What did Showers's article mean to them personally?

To test students' comprehension, use the **Lesson Test** blackline master on page 147.

Name _____

WORDS TO KNOW

Before Reading

DIRECTIONS Around the picture are sentences used to describe the eye. Use the words in the box to complete each sentence. Each word will be used only once.

pupil smaller bigger window light

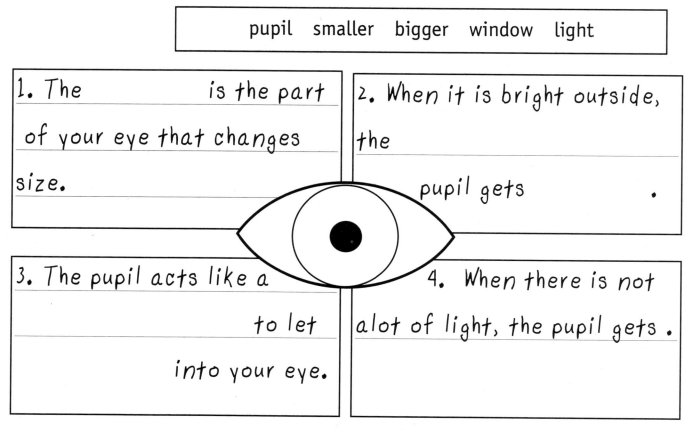

1. The _____ is the part of your eye that changes size.

2. When it is bright outside, the _____ pupil gets _____ .

3. The pupil acts like a _____ to let _____ into your eye.

4. When there is not alot of light, the pupil gets _____ .

Practice

Draw an eye and label the *pupil*.

Name _____

BEFORE YOU READ

Skim

DIRECTIONS Skim *Look at Your Eyes*.

Let your eyes run down the page.

Watch for words and sentences that pop out at you.

Then make some skimming notes.

Skimming Notes: *Look at Your Eyes*

1. Look at Your Eyes is fiction / nonfiction because:
                        (circle one)

_____

_____

_____

2. What words did you notice?

_____

_____

_____

3. What is Look at Your Eyes about?

_____

_____

_____

Name _____

COMPREHENSION

Cause and Effect

DIRECTIONS Fill in this diagram about eyes.

Then answer a question about the eye's pupil.

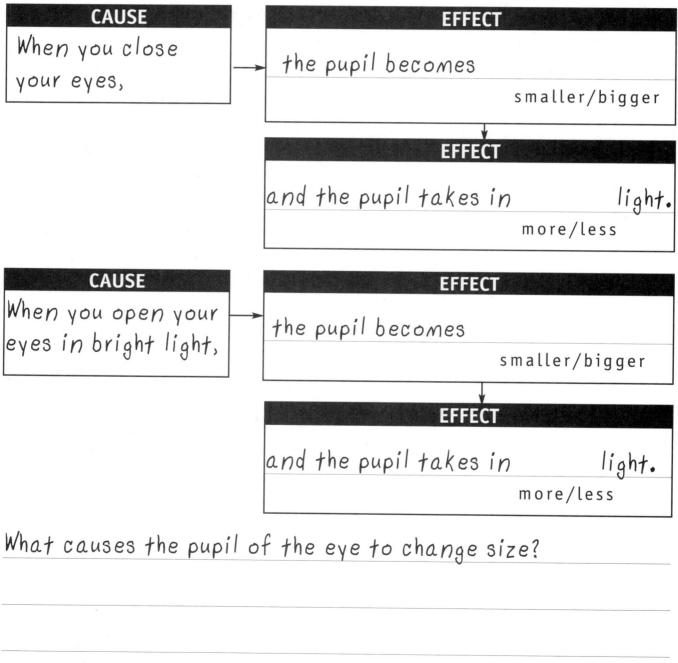

CAUSE
When you close your eyes,

EFFECT
the pupil becomes
smaller/bigger

EFFECT
and the pupil takes in   light.
more/less

CAUSE
When you open your eyes in bright light,

EFFECT
the pupil becomes
smaller/bigger

EFFECT
and the pupil takes in   light.
more/less

What causes the pupil of the eye to change size?

_____

_____

Name _____

WORD WORK

After Reading

DIRECTIONS Add prefixes and suffixes to these words to make new words. Write the new words on the lines.

1. re + turn =	4. fast + est =
2. tall + ish =	5. froze + en =
3. re + visit + ed =	6. wide + er =

Practice

DIRECTIONS Choose a suffix from the box to make each of these words longer. Write the new word on the line. You can write more than one new word for each base word.

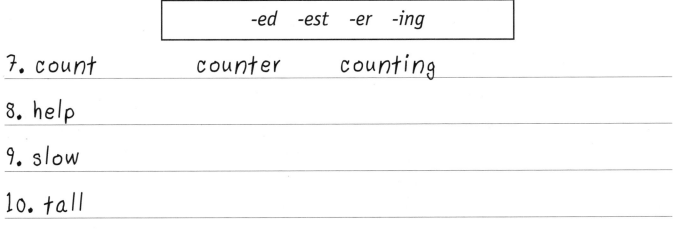

-ed   -est   -er   -ing

7. count   counter   counting _____

8. help _____

9. slow _____

10. tall _____

Name _____

GET READY TO WRITE

Writing a Paragraph

DIRECTIONS Follow these steps to write a topic sentence for your paragraph.

STEP 1 Decide on your subject.

My subject will be:

_____

_____

STEP 2 Think of what you want to say about your subject.

What I want to say:

_____

_____

STEP 3 Now add your answer to step 1 and your answers to step 2 to form a topic sentence.

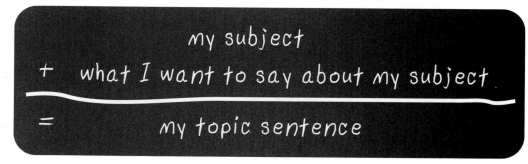

my subject
+ what I want to say about my subject
―――――――――――――――――――――――
= my topic sentence

My topic sentence:

_____

_____

Name _____

LESSON TEST

Multiple-Choice

DIRECTIONS On the lines, write the letter of the best answer for each question.

_____ 1. Where is your pupil located?
   A. in your arm   C. in your eye
   B. in your foot   D. in your ear

_____ 2. What about the pupil changes?
   A. its size   C. its strength
   B. its color   D. its height

_____ 3. What is the shape of the pupil?
   A. square   C. diamond
   B. round   D. triangle

_____ 4. What is the job of your pupil?
   A. to let light in C. to lift something
   B. to let sound in D. to hold something

_____ 5. If your pupil didn't work, you could not . . .
   A. speak.   C. hear.
   B. lift heavy things. D. see.

Short Answer

Explain how and why the pupil changes.

_____

_____

_____

BACKGROUND

Just a Few Words, Mr. Lincoln is Jean Fritz's fascinating account of the events surrounding Abraham Lincoln's famous 1863 speech at Gettysburg, Pennsylvania. Since most third-graders have not studied American history in any great detail yet, your class may benefit from some background information on Lincoln, the Civil War, and the Battle of Gettysburg.

Abraham Lincoln was the 16th president of the United States (1861–65). He preserved the Union during the Civil War and brought about the emancipation of the slaves. When Lincoln was elected in 1860, a group of eleven Southern states voted to secede from the Union. They were furious that Lincoln (a Republican) wanted to keep the Union together and end the spread of slavery to new states. These Southern states formed their own government, called the Confederacy. In 1861, the Civil War began when the Confederacy fired upon Fort Sumter.

The Battle of Gettysburg took place on July 1–3, 1863. Although Union forces won the battle, it was a terrible bloodbath for both the North and the South. In November of the same year, Lincoln traveled to Gettysburg to dedicate a cemetery on the battlefield. Interestingly, Lincoln's speech, now recognized as an example of superb oration, caused only a small stir when it was first delivered. Lincoln, in fact, called the speech "a flat failure" and was said to have been a little embarrassed by it.

BIBLIOGRAPHY Students might enjoy reading another book about a famous American. You might suggest they try one of these titles, all of which have a Lexile rating similar to that of *Just a Few Words, Mr. Lincoln* (Lexile 390).

GEORGE WASHINGTON CARVER: THE PEANUT SCIENTIST by Patricia C. and Frederick McKissack

(Lexile 400)

SACAGAWEA by Jan and Kathleen Thompson Gleiter

(Lexile 410)

THE STORY OF THOMAS ALVA EDISON, INVENTOR by Margaret Davidson

(Lexile 410)

How to Introduce the Reading

Ask a volunteer to read aloud the introduction to the selection on page 77. Then have the class tell what they know about Abraham Lincoln. What kind of president was he? Why do people still study him today? Offer background information to the class as you see fit, or create a "fact" chart on the board about Lincoln and Gettysburg that students can refer to as they read. This may help students who feel intimidated at the thought of reading about "real" historical events.

Other Reading

You may want to suggest other critically acclaimed stories written at this same reading level. Here are three possibilities:

(Lexile 390)

(Lexile 400)

(Lexile 400)

Just a Few Words, Mr. Lincoln

Skills and Strategies Overview

PREREADING think-pair-and-share

READING LEVEL Lexile 390

VOCABULARY ◇honor ◇foolish ◇crowded ◇visitors ◇telegram

RESPONSE connect

COMPREHENSION stop and think

WORD WORK base words

PREWRITING brainstorm

WRITING journal entry / commas

ASSESSMENT understanding

OTHER RESOURCES

The first **four** pages of this teacher's lesson describe Parts I–V of the lesson. Also included are the following **six** blackline masters. Use them to reinforce key elements of the lesson.

Vocabulary

Prereading

Comprehension

Word Work

Prewriting

Assessment

BEFORE YOU READ

Explain that Fritz's novel is historical fiction. This means that it has as its setting a period in history and that the action revolves around true historical events. Some of the characters are fictional, and others are true historical figures. When you feel students are ready to begin, assign the prereading activity, a **think-pair-and-share**. (Refer to the Strategy Handbook on page 50 for more help.)

Motivation Strategy

MOTIVATING STUDENTS Read a story aloud or borrow a copy of the audiotape version of *Just a Few Words, Mr. Lincoln*. Read or play the first part for the class (stop when you get to the part reprinted in the *Sourcebook*). Give students the chance to "hear" the characters in the story before they read about them.

CONNECTING WITH STUDENTS Ask students to tell about a time they were so worried about someone or something that they couldn't get their work done. What happened? Why was the worry such a distraction? How did things turn out in the end? A short discussion on this topic will help students make an initial connection to Fritz's story.

Words to Know

CONTEXT CLUES Use the **Words to Know** blackline master on page 154 as a way of troubleshooting vocabulary problems. After working through the page, you might decide to teach a short vocabulary lesson on using these and other words from the story.

To begin, show students the key vocabulary words for this lesson: *honor, foolish, crowded,* and *telegram*. Ask students where they've heard these words before and what they think they mean. (Be sure students know how to pronounce each.) Then have pairs of students write "temporary" definitions for each word on the board. As they're reading, students should look for context clues that offer more complete definitions for each word. As a last step, have students check the dictionary definitions of the words that appear on the bottom of each page.

Prereading Strategies

THINK-PAIR-AND-SHARE Students are asked to complete a **think-pair-and-share** activity as a warm-up to Fritz's story. In a think-pair-and-share, students work together to solve sentence "puzzles" related to the selection. In this case, they'll read a series of four statements about the presidency and then say whether they agree or disagree with the statements. Of course, it's not important that students know the right answer at this point. The purpose of this activity is to help them do some initial thinking about the topic of the reading.

CLUSTERING As an additional prereading activity, ask students to make an Abraham Lincoln cluster to show what they know about this famous man. Clustering can help students recall information in an organized way, as if they were following a train of thought. This activity will also serve as an excellent warm-up to the prewriting cluster students will complete in **Part III**.

To extend the activity, use the **Before You Read** blackline master on page 155.

MY PURPOSE Always establish a reading purpose for students before they begin an assignment. Move beyond the overly-general "Read to find out what happens" and create a purpose that gives students something to look for or think about as they read. Point out the reading purpose at the bottom of page 78. Have a volunteer read it aloud and another volunteer rephrase it. Be sure all students know exactly what their reading purpose is.

II. READ

Response Strategy

FIRST READING Walk students through the process of making personal **connections** to a piece of literature. Model the technique by saying: "I read this sentence about Tad being sick, and I remember a time that I was really sick. I'll make a note about that time in the margin of my book. Something about my experience may help me understand Tad's experience in the story."

Comprehension Strategy

SECOND READING **Stop and Think** questions give students the chance to pause for a moment and gather their thoughts about the reading up to that point. This is a big help to students who have a hard time processing a great deal of information in one sitting. Explain to students that as they read the story about Lincoln, they'll need to stop four different times to answer questions. If you decide to do a whole-class read-aloud of the selection, be sure to offer ample time for every student to write his or her own answers to the questions. Hold off discussing answers until after you've finished reading the selection.

For more help with **Comprehension** assign the blackline master on page 156.

Discussion Questions

COMPREHENSION 1. Why are Mr. and Mrs. Lincoln so worried? *(Tad is very sick.)*

2. What is the purpose of Lincoln's trip to Gettysburg? *(He will make a speech to dedicate a cemetery.)*

CRITICAL THINKING 3. What does this story tell you about the relationship between Lincoln and his son, Tad? *(Possible: It shows that Lincoln was a loving, involved father.)*

4. In what ways are you like Abraham Lincoln? Support your answer. *(Answers will vary. Have students support what they say with evidence from the selection.)*

5. Based on what you know, how do you think Lincoln felt about his trip to Gettysburg? *(Have students think about the reactions of Lincoln, Tad, and Mary Lincoln.)*

Reread

THIRD READING Instead of rereading all of *Just a Few Words, Mr. Lincoln,* students should focus on reviewing the notes they made in the margins of the text. What connections were they able to make to Fritz's story? In what ways does Lincoln remind them of themselves? If students had trouble making connections, walk them through the story one page at a time. Stop at the bottom of each page and ask for comments. Have students say what seems familiar about the action described or the feelings expressed.

Word Work

BASE WORDS The Word Work lesson on page 85 of the lesson presents an opportunity for you to teach a lesson on **base words.** Explain the definition of a base word and then have students fill in items a–h on the chart. For further practice, students can complete the **Word Work** blackline master on page 157.

III. GET READY TO WRITE

Prewriting Strategies

BRAINSTORM As a prewriting activity, students will **brainstorm** ideas about a time they did not want to leave home. Before they begin, explain how this topic relates to the selection. Then have the class fill out the chart on page 86. Request that they include as many details as they can think of. Also encourage students to write whatever comes to mind. Full sentences are not needed here and can sometimes slow a student's thinking.

Have students use the **Get Ready to Write** blackline master on page 158.

IV. WRITE

Remind students that a **journal entry** is a piece of personal writing. They'll be writing about themselves, their friends, or their families, rather than their response to the text. However, students will want to read over their Response Notes comments before they begin. Their during-reading notes may remind them of situations or events they'd like to tell about in their journal entries.

After students have written a first draft, have them read over their work and decide if they've given enough details describing the event. Tell the class that a good rule of thumb is three interesting details per paragraph.

WRITING RUBRIC Use this rubric to help with a quick assessment of students' writing.

Do students' journal entries

• open with a topic sentence that names the event to be described and how the writer felt?

• contain details about an event in an order that makes sense, such as chronological order?

• end with a closing sentence that ties things together and says how the writer felt when the experience was over?

Grammar, Usage, and Mechanics

When students are ready to proofread their work, refer them to the **Writers' Checklist.** Read aloud the question on the checklist and ask students to apply it to their own writing. Since they'll be writing a journal entry, you might also take a moment to explain that a **comma** belongs between the day and the date at the top of the page.

V. LOOK BACK

Point out the **Readers' Checklist** and reflect with students on their **understanding** of *Just a Few Words, Mr. Lincoln.* Find out if the length of the selection intimidated students. If so, think about strategies that might help students break up longer readings. See the Strategy Handbook (pages 46–56) for suggestions.

To test students' comprehension, use the **Lesson Test** blackline master on page 159.

Name _____

WORDS TO KNOW

Before Reading

DIRECTIONS Read the paragraph below.

Tell what you think the underlined words mean. Use the rest of the sentence to help you.

> Gettysburg was <u>crowded</u> with many people who wanted to <u>honor</u> President Lincoln. There were many <u>visitors</u>. Mr. Lincoln didn't want to say anything silly or <u>foolish</u>, so he was quiet at first. He was waiting for a <u>telegram</u> from home, telling him that his son Tad was getting better.

1. I think crowded means _____

2. I think honor means _____

3. I think visitors means _____

4. I think foolish means _____

5. I think telegram means _____

Practice

Write a sentence about a time you had *visitors* to your house.

_____

_____

_____

Name _____

BEFORE YOU READ

Cluster

DIRECTIONS Work with a partner.

Say what you know about President Lincoln.

Fill in the cluster circles with facts and details.

His work

His home

Abraham Lincoln

Springfield, Illinois

His beliefs

Name _____

COMPREHENSION

Story Map

DIRECTIONS Fill out this story map about *Just a Few Words, Mr. Lincoln*.

Give as many details as you can.

Setting
Where the story takes place:

When it takes place:

Character names plus one word describing each one

Problem

How the problem is solved

Name _____

WORD WORK

After Reading

DIRECTIONS Read this list of words. Each word has a prefix (*re-* or *un-*) or a suffix (*-ed* or *-ing*).

Cross out the prefixes and suffixes.

Write the base word on the line. One has been done for you.

1. cry~~ing~~   cry

2. unmade

3. retry

4. walked

5. undo

6. remarkable

Practice

DIRECTIONS Circle the base in each of these words. An example has been done for you.

7. un(tie)

8. falling

9. unwinding

10. reread

Name _____

GET READY TO WRITE

Writing a Journal Entry

DIRECTIONS Think about the event you want to describe in your journal entry. What happened first? What happened next? Plan what you will say on this organizer.

It all started when

I felt

So I

Then I

The whole thing ended when

After it was over, I felt

Name _____

LESSON TEST

Multiple-Choice

DIRECTIONS On the lines, write the letter of the best answer for each question.

_____ 1. Who is sick in this story?
   A. President Lincoln   C. Mrs. Lincoln
   B. Tad   D. Mr. Everett

_____ 2. Why does President Lincoln have to go to Gettysburg?
   A. to stop a war   C. to make a speech
   B. to vote on a bill   D. to clean up a battlefield

_____ 3. Why didn't President Lincoln speak when the singers asked him to?
   A. He had nothing   C. He thought he might say
      to say.   something foolish.
   B. He was tired.   D. A. and C.

_____ 4. How did President Lincoln feel when he received the telegram?
   A. angry   C. relieved
   B. silly   D. tired

_____ 5. In this story, what seems very important to President Lincoln?
   A. meeting people   C. being President
   B. traveling   D. his family

Short Answer

In what ways does this story about President Lincoln remind you of something that happened to you?

_____

_____

Why I Sneeze, Shiver, Hiccup, and Yawn

BACKGROUND

In *Why I Sneeze, Shiver, Hiccup, and Yawn*, Melvin Berger explains some common automatic reflexes and why they are important. In this book and in others, Berger uses a clear, succinct, and engaging writing style that even lower-level readers find hard to resist. As an added bonus, Berger offers a set of easy reflex-related experiments that you can use in the classroom or ask students to perform at home.

Melvin Berger is the author of more than 200 children's books. Many of these are "Let's Read and Find Out Science" titles, including *Germs Make Me Sick*, *Chirping Crickets*, and *Switch On, Switch Off*.

BIBLIOGRAPHY Students might enjoy reading another book by Melvin Berger. These three are all of high interest to students in the third grade:

(Lexile 460)   (Lexile 460)   (Lexile 430)

How to Introduce the Reading

Spark students' interest in Berger's text by asking them to tell funny sneeze, shiver, hiccup, or yawn stories to the class. Model a story of your own (for example, about a time a student couldn't stop hiccuping). Then ask what the stories all have in common. Students might notice that sneezing, shivering, hiccuping, and yawning are impulses (reflexes) that are pretty much automatic.

Then tell students that the article they're about to read explains what these and other reflexes are, and why we have so much trouble controlling them.

Other Reading

Use these titles to make a cross-curricular link to science or social studies. Read them aloud or make them a part of your classroom library:

(Lexile 490)   (Lexile 460)   (Lexile 460)

Why I Sneeze, Shiver, Hiccup, and Yawn

STUDENT PAGES 89–100

Skills and Strategies Overview

PREREADING K-W-L

READING LEVEL Lexile 390

RESPONSE make things clear

VOCABULARY ◆bundle ◆sense ◆jerks ◆completely ◆automatically

COMPREHENSION stop and think

WORD WORK two-syllable words

PREWRITING main idea and supporting details

WRITING expository paragraph / capitalization

ASSESSMENT enjoyment

OTHER RESOURCES

The first **four** pages of this teacher's lesson describe Parts I–V of the lesson. Also included are these **six** blackline masters. Use them to reinforce key elements of the lesson.

Vocabulary

Prereading

Comprehension

Word Work

Prewriting

Assessment

1. BEFORE YOU READ

Read aloud the introduction to the lesson on page 89. Ask students to answer the three questions on the page: *Have you ever just started to hiccup? Have you ever tried to stop sneezing? Why do most people make these funny noises?* See what kind of prior knowledge students have about the topic of reflexes. Then assign the prereading activity, a **K-W-L**. (Refer to the Strategy Handbook on page 47 for more help.)

Motivation Strategy

CONNECTING WITH STUDENTS Ask students to suggest "cures" for these reflexes: hiccuping or repeated sneezing. Have them say why the cures do or don't work, and what their experiences have been. Students' anecdotes will generate class interest in the scientific explanation of the two reflexes.

Words to Know

CONTEXT CLUES Use the **Words to Know** blackline master on page 166 to troubleshoot vocabulary problems. After working through the page, you might decide to teach a short vocabulary lesson on using **context clues.**

To begin, show students the key vocabulary words in *Why I Sneeze, Shiver, Hiccup, and Yawn:* *bundle, sense, jerks, completely*, and *automatically*. One of the words, *bundle* is not defined at the bottom of the page. Students will need to use context clues to define this and other unfamiliar words. Model this process by saying, "I don't know the meaning of the word *bundle*. I see, however, that it is used to describe nerves in the spinal cord. I know from the reading that the spinal cord has more than one nerve, so I predict that *bundle* means "bunch." I'll check a dictionary later, if I want to be absolutely sure."

Prereading Strategies

K-W-L The purpose of a **K-W-L** is to activate prior knowledge. It can also show students how to take responsibility for their own knowledge "gaps." In the K column, students will make notes about sneezing, shivering, hiccuping, and yawning. In the **W** column, students will write things they want to know about the subject. After they finish reading, students should return to the K-W-L and write what they learned in the L column. A K-W-L can show students that ultimately they (and not you) are responsible for their own learning.

ANTICIPATION GUIDE As a further prereading activity, have students complete an **anticipation guide** that tests their prior knowledge of the topic discussed in Berger's article. Write a series of statements that relate to the reading. Then have students check whether they agree or disagree with each statement. When students have finished reading, ask them to return to the statements and review them again. This quick activity can show students that they really can learn new information from a reading.

To extend the activity, use the **Before You Read** blackline master on page 167

MY PURPOSE Point out the reading purpose on page 90. It's particularly important that you give students a reading purpose when the assignment is to read nonfiction. Many students need something specific to look for so as to avoid getting lost in facts and details. Be sure students understand their purpose for reading Berger's article. If necessary, rephrase the purpose statement by saying, "Find out why people sneeze, shiver, yawn, and hiccup."

II. READ

Response Strategy

FIRST READING As they read, students will mark to **make clear** important facts or details, especially those that relate to their reading purpose. Invite them to use a highlighter to mark specific words and sentences that they think are interesting or puzzling. Then, in the Response Notes, students should write what they think the word or sentence means and how it relates to the topic of reflexes.

Comprehension Strategy

SECOND READING The **Stop and Think** questions scattered throughout Berger's article invite students to pause and retell what they've learned so far. This strategy is a helpful one to use with nonfiction, as it forces students to reflect on important information as they go, rather than wait until the end to gather facts and details. Have students use their interrupter notes to help them write their paragraphs for **Part IV**.

For more help with **Comprehension,** assign the blackline master on page 168.

Discussion Questions

COMPREHENSION 1. What are the two parts of the nervous system? *(the nerves, the brain and spinal cord)*

CRITICAL THINKING 2. How are nerves like telephone wires? *(They transmit messages back and forth.)*

3. Can you control your reflexes? *(Possible: Some reflexes are involuntary and some are semi-voluntary.)*

4. What do sneezes, shivers, hiccups, and yawns all have in common? *(They are reflexes. It is hard to stop them, and all are done automatically.)*

5. What other reflexes do you have? *(Answers will vary. Students might suggest blinking, coughing, gagging, and vomiting.)*

Reread

THIRD READING As they reread, students should watch for additional details about why they sneeze, shiver, hiccup, and yawn. Before they begin, have them read again the purpose statement on page 90. Their purpose for this rereading is to find even more details related to this statement. On this reading, students might make a second set of notes in a different color pen. When they finish, they can review what they wrote. This second set of notes will show them how valuable a third reading can be. Not even the best readers will take *everything* in on a first reading.

Word Work

TWO-SYLLABLE WORDS The Word Work lesson on page 96 is another lesson on syllables and dividing words that have two consonants in the middle. Remind the class that **two-syllable words** with two consonants in the middle are divided between the two consonants, no matter if the consonants are the same or different: *let/tuce; mus/cle.*

For additional practice with this rule, see the **Word Work** blackline master on page 169.

III. GET READY TO WRITE

Prewriting Strategies

MAIN IDEA AND SUPPORTING DETAILS

As a prewriting activity, students will complete a **main idea and supporting details** chart. To begin, discuss with students the definition of a main idea: *A main idea is what the reading is all about. It is the author's central, or most important, idea.* In the body of the paragraph, the author supports the main idea with a series of details—facts, descriptions, quotations, and so on. Most of the time, the author won't make a direct statement about the main idea. Instead, he or she expects readers to make inferences (reasonable guesses) about the central idea of the piece.

Have students use the **Get Ready to Write** blackline master on page 170.

IV. WRITE

In their **expository paragraphs**, students should define and then describe each of these reflexes: sneezing, shivering, hiccupping, and coughing. In addition, they'll explain why these reflexes occur. As always, they should open their paragraphs with a topic sentence that identifies the subject of the paragraph and what they plan to say about the subject. They'll need to offer three or more details for support in the body of the paragraph.

After students have written a first draft, have them stop and carefully reread what they've written. Ask them: "Did you define and describe each of the reflexes? Did you say what causes them? " If they must answer no to either question, they need to go back and do some rewriting.

WRITING RUBRIC Use this rubric to help with a quick assessment of students' writing.

Do students' paragraphs

- open with a topic sentence that explains why a person sneezes, shivers, hiccups, and yawns?

- discuss the reflexes in the body of the paragraph, using details from the reading and a dictionary?

- close with a sentence that says what they think about the reflexes?

Grammar, Usage, and Mechanics

When students are ready to proofread their work, have them look at the **Writers' Checklist** at the top of page 100. Review the rules for **capitalization:** The first word of every sentence is capitalized, as are important words in the title and the pronoun *I.* Offer additional practice by posting this sentence on the board. Ask a volunteer to find the capitalization errors:

my mother and i had a sneezing fit after we stacked the hay.

V. LOOK BACK

Reflect with students on their **enjoyment** of Berger's article. Point out the **Readers' Checklist** and have the class discuss their answers to the questions.

To test students' comprehension, use the **Lesson Test** blackline master on page 171.

Name _____

WORDS TO KNOW

Before Reading

DIRECTIONS Read these sentences. Look at each underlined word.

Then choose the correct meaning of the word.

If you're not sure, make a guess.

1. Mario sees a <u>bundle</u> of flowers and picks one up.
   (baby, bunch)

2. He can <u>sense</u> something is about to happen.
   (feel, hear)

3. He sniffs the flower and sneezes <u>automatically</u>.
   (with a lot of thought, without a lot of thought)

4. Mario <u>jerks</u> his head away from the flower, but it is too late.
(slowly moves, quickly moves)

5. To stop sneezing, Mario crumples the flower <u>completely</u>.
   (all the way, only a little)

Practice

Blinking is something you do *automatically*. Think of another thing you do *automatically*. Write about it here and use the word *automatically* to tell about it.

I _____ *automatically.*

_____

_____

_____

Name _____

BEFORE YOU READ

Anticipation Guide

DIRECTIONS Read these statements.

If you agree with the statement, circle *agree*.

If you disagree, circle *disagree*.

Save the **After Reading** part for later.

Before Reading		After Reading
agree disagree	1. Hiccups are funny.	agree disagree
agree disagree	2. You can always stop a sneeze.	agree disagree
agree disagree	3. Jumping up and down is a reflex.	agree disagree
agree disagree	4. There is one spinal cord in your body.	agree disagree
agree disagree	5. Nerves carry messages to your brain.	agree disagree

Name _____

COMPREHENSION

Directed Reading

DIRECTIONS Work with a reading partner. Answer these questions. You may have to skim parts of *Why I Sneeze, Shiver, Hiccup, and Yawn* to do so.

1. What is a reflex?

_____

_____

2. What examples of reflexes can you think of?

_____

_____

3. What is the job of the nerves in your body?

_____

_____

4. What happens when you touch something hot?

_____

_____

Name _____

WORD WORK

After Reading

DIRECTIONS Read the words in the box.

Count the beats in each word.

Divide each word into 2 parts by putting a line through the 2 consonants in the middle.

fiction jumping trouble helmet
million nervous cotton

1. fic/tion

2. _____

3. _____

4. _____

5. _____

6. _____

7. _____

Practice

DIRECTIONS Think of a 2-syllable word with 2 consonants in the middle. Write it on the line. Draw a line between the 2 syllables.

My 2-syllable word: _____

Name _____

GET READY TO WRITE

Writing a Paragraph

Get ready to write your paragraph about why you sneeze, shiver, hiccup, and yawn. In it, you will need to <u>define</u> and <u>describe</u> these reflexes. Use a dictionary to help you define them.

DIRECTIONS Write the dictionary definitions in the left column.

Write how the reflex sounds in the right column.

What the dictionary says	How it sounds
sneeze:	sneeze:
shiver:	shiver:
hiccup: *A quick catching of the breath in the throat.*	hiccup: *HIC!*
yawn:	yawn:

Name _____

LESSON TEST

Multiple-Choice

DIRECTIONS On the lines, write the letter of the best answer for each question.

_____ 1. What part of your body carries messages back and forth?

A. nerves   C. feet
B. brain   D. nose

_____ 2. When your hand touches a hot object, the message sent to your brain is . . .

A. Touch it again!   C. Move your hand!
B. Run!   D. Sneeze!

_____ 3. Which one of the following do you **not** do automatically?

A. sneeze   C. put your seat belt on
B. yawn   D. hiccup

_____ 4. Which is **not** part of the nervous system?

A. nerves   C. spinal cord
B. stomach   D. brain

_____ 5. What do sneezes, shivers, hiccups, and yawns all have in common?

A. They make you happy. C. They are reflexes.
B. They all hurt.   D. They get you in trouble.

Short Answer

What did you learn from this reading?

_____

_____

_____

_____

Marvin Redpost: Alone in His Teacher's House

BACKGROUND

Marvin Redpost: Alone in His Teacher's House is the fourth in a series of Marvin Redpost books written by the award-winning children's author, Louis Sachar. In this book and others, Sachar uses his uncanny insight into the thoughts and feelings of children to help him tell a hilarious and poignant story of a boy who badly needs to do something right for a change.

When Marvin's teacher asks Marvin if he'll care for her aging dog, Waldo, while she's away for the week, Marvin is thrilled. He tries his best to take good care of the dog so that he can prove to others (and perhaps himself) that he is mature and responsible. Shortly after he takes on the job, however, Waldo dies, and Marvin is overwhelmed by feelings of guilt, sadness, and anger at his friends for the way they tease him about the dog's death.

This excerpt from Sachar's story comes from the first part of the novel. Marvin's teacher has left town after giving specific instructions on how to care for Waldo. Marvin finds, however, that some of the instructions are pretty hard to follow. His biggest problem, he decides, is to figure out how to get Waldo to eat.

BIBLIOGRAPHY Students might enjoy reading another of Louis Sachar's books. There are many that are appropriate for this reading level, including his Wayside School series: *Wayside School Gets a Little Stranger, Sideways Stories from Wayside School,* and *Wayside School Is Falling Down.* In addition, you might recommend the following:

MARVIN REDPOST: CLASS PRESIDENT

(Lexile 440)

JOHNNY'S IN THE BASEMENT

(Lexile 450)

MARVIN REDPOST: A FLYING BIRTHDAY CAKE?

(Lexile 460)

How to Introduce the Reading

Read aloud the introduction to *Marvin Redpost: Alone in His Teacher's House* with students. Ask students to think of a time they were asked to take care of a pet or to help someone else with the job. What happened? Did anything go wrong? Did everything go right? Encourage students to tell funny stories about past events. Allow students' own experiences to set the mood for the reading.

Other Reading

You may want to recommend or read aloud other stories written at this same reading level. Choose from among these high-interest books:

(Lexile 420)   (Lexile 430)   (Lexile 430)

Marvin Redpost: Alone in His Teacher's House

Skills and Strategies Overview

PREREADING think-pair-and-share

READING LEVEL Lexile 410

VOCABULARY ✦gritty ✦enthusiastic ✦impress ✦offered

RESPONSE connect

COMPREHENSION double-entry journal

WORD WORK endings for words with a silent *e*

PREWRITING character map

WRITING journal entry / apostrophes in contractions

ASSESSMENT understanding

OTHER RESOURCES

The first **four** pages of this teacher's lesson describe Parts I–V of the lesson. Also included are these **six** blackline masters. Use them to reinforce key elements of the lesson.

Vocabulary

Prereading

Comprehension

Word Work

Prewriting

Assessment

BEFORE YOU READ

To set the mood and give students some story context, borrow a copy of *Marvin Redpost: Alone in His Teacher's House* and read the first few pages aloud to students. Students might enjoy hearing Marvin's exchange with his teacher when she asks him to take care of Waldo. Then have them complete the prereading activity, a **think-pair-and-share**. (Refer to the Strategy Handbook on page 50 for more help.)

Motivation Strategy

MOTIVATING STUDENTS
To motivate students, ask them to predict possible problems Marvin Redpost might encounter while pet-sitting Waldo. (You may already have heard about some possible "disasters" when the class told about pet-sitting problems of their own.) Make a prediction chart on the board. See if any students are able to predict Marvin's exact problem (and solution).

Words to Know

CONTEXT CLUES
Use the **Words to Know** blackline master on page 178 as a way to troubleshoot vocabulary problems. After working through the page, you might decide to teach a short vocabulary lesson on using **context clues.**

To begin, show students the key vocabulary words in Sachar's story: *gritty, enthusiastic, impress*, and *offered*. Explain that these (and other) words are defined at the bottom of the page, but that you'd like them to try to guess at the meaning of the words first, before checking the footnoted definition. Tell the class: "Sometimes the author will leave clues in nearby sentences about the meaning of a difficult word. For example, I see the word *worried* and I'm not sure what it means. I'll look for clues in surrounding sentences, and find that Marvin is very concerned that the dog won't eat. Does *worried* mean "concerned"?

Prereading Strategies

THINK-PAIR-AND-SHARE
As a prereading activity, students will complete a **think-pair-and-share** that relates to the central conflict in Sachar's story. Encourage students to listen carefully to each other's ideas. If they disagree with a possible solution, have them say why. Ask each pair to report to the class on their answers to question #2. Listen for answers that seem particularly unique or interesting. You might use some of these ideas as story-starters when you feel students are ready to write their own short stories.

WEB
As an additional prereading activity, ask students to complete a **web** that describes a pet they know well. This quick activity will help you forge a strong link between the story and students' own lives. It can also prepare students for the connect comments you'd like them to make as they're reading. Have students make their own web, listing five or more characteristics of the pet. If there's time, allow them to exchange webs to see what pet stories their classmates can tell.

For a ready-made web, use the **Before You Read** blackline master on page 179.

MY PURPOSE
As they read Sachar's story, students will need to watch for details that reveal something about Marvin's character. Explain that Sachar doesn't make a direct statement about Marvin's personality. Instead, he expects readers to make inferences about Marvin using the evidence provided.

READ

Response Strategy

FIRST READING The response strategy of **connecting** will help students fulfill their reading purpose. The directions at the top of page 103 instruct students to mark parts of the story that show what Marvin is like. In particular, they should watch for clues about his personality. They should ask themselves, "Does Marvin seem like a responsible boy or is he scatterbrained? Is he a trouble-maker or well-behaved?" Many of the clues they find on this first reading will come in handy when it's time to do some writing about the main character of Sachar's story.

Comprehension Strategy

SECOND READING As they are reading, students should think about how Marvin's experiences compare to their own, or how Marvin himself reminds them of themselves. The **Double-entry journal** boxes will help. Scattered throughout the story are two separate journal boxes. Ask students to read the quotation on the left side of each box and then respond to the quote on the right side with what they think the quote means. This leads students to make inferences about Marvin. If you think students will benefit, do the first journal box as a whole class. Model a response and explain why you made the inference you did.

For more help with **Comprehension** assign the blackline master on page 180.

Discussion Questions

COMPREHENSION 1. What is Marvin's major problem? *(He can't get Waldo to eat.)*

2. Why does Marvin buy the liver? *(to tempt the dog)*

CRITICAL THINKING 3. What's funny about this story? *(Possible: Marvin eats the dog food; he thinks the dog will hate the liver because he hates liver.)*

4. How does Marvin feel about his pet-sitting job? *(Answers will vary. Remind students to support what they say with evidence from the story.)*

5. What kind of a person is Marvin? Support your answer. *(Possible: He is smart and hardworking. His ideas on how to get Waldo to eat show that he is creative as well.)*

Reread

THIRD READING The directions on page 110 ask students to reread the story. Once again, they'll need to keep a close eye on Marvin's character and parts of the story with which they can make a personal connection. As they reread, students should also review the notes they made on their first readings. They may want to add to their initial observations in the double-entry journal.

Word Work

SILENT E The Word Work lesson on page 111 offers students some additional practice on words with **silent *e*** endings. Review the rule for adding an ending to this type of word and then assign the exercise at the bottom of the page. Notice that many of the words in the exercise come from *Marvin Redpost: Alone in His Teacher's House.*

For additional practice with silent e, see the **Word Work** blackline master on page 181.

III. GET READY TO WRITE

Prewriting Strategies

CHARACTER MAP For a prewriting activity, students will create a **character map** that explores four of Marvin's character traits. Explain to the class that you'd like them to think of one or more words that describe Marvin (four words are supplied on the page). Then they'll need to think of proof for their inferences. The proof they write on the map must come directly from the text. Help readers see that their personal inferences about Marvin are valid so long as they are supportable with evidence from the selection.

Have students use the **Get Ready to Write** blackline master on page 182.

IV. WRITE

Students should understand that their assignment is to write a **journal entry** about Marvin. They'll name three character traits and then support their inferences with proof from the story. Have them use the map they created on page 112 for help.

After students have written a first draft, have them ask themselves: *Did I tell three things about Marvin and his personality? Did I support my ideas with evidence from the selection?* If they must answer no to one of these questions, they should do some rewriting.

WRITING RUBRIC Use this rubric to help with a quick assessment of students' writing.

Do students' journal entries

- open with a topic sentence that names three of Marvin's character traits ?

- contain three or more details supporting the inferences about his character?

- end with a closing sentence that says how the writer feels about Marvin?

Grammar, Usage, and Mechanics

When students are ready to proofread their work, refer them to the **Writers' Checklist** and teach a brief review lesson on **apostrophes in contractions**. Be sure students know that an apostrophe takes the place of the missing letters when they form contractions in their own writing. Encourage students to use contractions in informal writing, such as friendly letters and journal writing. Review these common contractions:

she is ⇒ she's   he will ⇒ he'll   they are ⇒ they're

V. LOOK BACK

Point out the **Readers' Checklist** and discuss with students their **understanding** of the Marvin Redpost story. Were there parts that were hard for them to understand? Did the length cause difficulty for some? Have students suggest strategies they could use in the future to aid in comprehension.

To test students' comprehension, use the **Lesson Test** blackline master on page 183.

Name _____

WORDS TO KNOW

Before Reading

DIRECTIONS Read the conversation below. Write what you think the underlined words mean. Use the rest of the sentence to help you.

> **Mom:** "I can't believe you ate dog food. Was it good?"
>
> **Marvin:** "It wasn't bad. It was really <u>gritty</u>, like getting a mouthful of sand."
>
> **Mom:** "Your teacher was very <u>enthusiastic</u> and excited about her trip."
>
> **Marvin:** "I'm glad. I want to <u>impress</u> her by doing a good job."
>
> **Mom:** "I'm proud of you! When I <u>offered</u> to cook, you did it yourself."

1. I think gritty means _____

2. I think enthusiastic means _____

3. I think impress means _____

4. I think offered means _____

Practice

Use *gritty* in a sentence that shows what it means.

_____

_____

_____

Name _____

BEFORE YOU READ

Web

DIRECTIONS Think of a pet you know well.

Write words and sentences on the web that describe the pet.

Add more lines to the web if you need to.

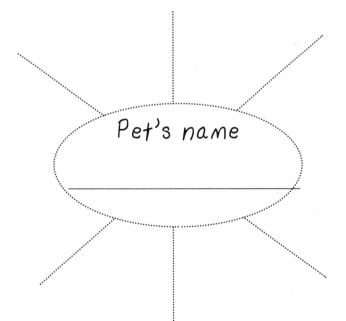

Name _____

COMPREHENSION

Character Map

DIRECTIONS Tell about Marvin Redpost on this character map.
Write as many details as you can think of.

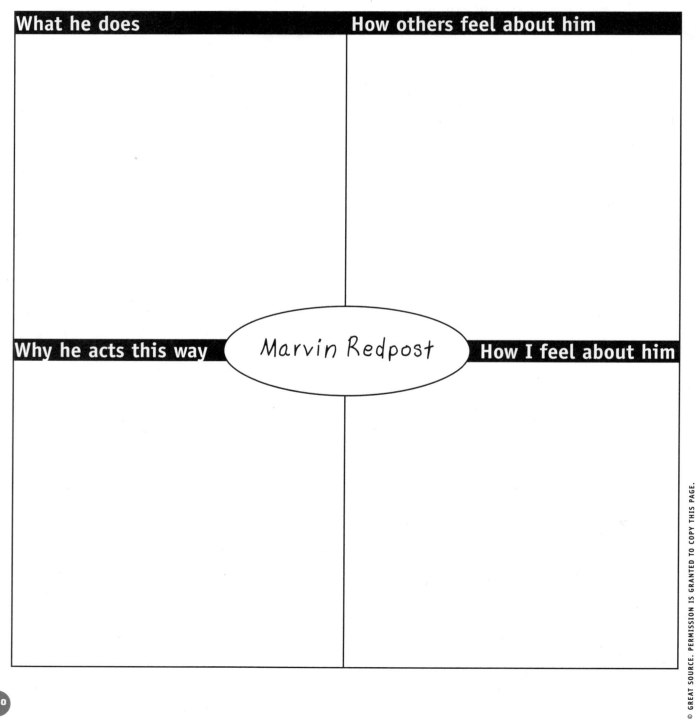

| What he does | How others feel about him |

| Why he acts this way | Marvin Redpost | How I feel about him |

Name _____

WORD WORK

After Reading

DIRECTIONS Some words drop a final *e* when adding a suffix that begins with a vowel. Add *-ed* and *-ing* to the words below. Write the new words on the lines. One has been done for you.

1. fine + ed =   fined

2. shape + ing =

3. baste + ed =

4. take + ing =

5. guide + ed =

Practice

DIRECTIONS Take the *-ed* or *-ing* ending off these words. Write the new word on the line. One has been done for you.

6. smiled   smile

7. liked

8. having

9. writing

10. stayed

Name _____

GET READY TO WRITE

Writing a Journal Entry

DIRECTIONS Follow these steps to write your journal entry.

STEP 1 Write three words that describe Marvin.

Marvin is . . .

_____   _____

_____

STEP 2 Write a topic sentence that uses the three words.

Marvin Redpost is _____ ,

_____ , and _____ .

STEP 3 Find examples from the story that support your topic
sentence. Find one example for each word.

example #1 _____

_____

example #2 _____

_____

example #3 _____

_____

Name _____

LESSON TEST

Multiple-Choice

DIRECTIONS On the lines, write the letter of the best answer for each question.

_____ 1. Marvin is taking care of a dog for . . .
   A. his grandmother.   C. his neighbor.
   B. his friend.   D. his teacher.

_____ 2. What problem does Marvin have?
   A. Waldo won't eat.   C. Marvin ran out of food.
   B. Waldo is lost.   D. Marvin lost the key to the house.

_____ 3. What does Marvin buy with his own money for Waldo?
   A. liver   C. a toy
   B. dog bones   D. canned dog food

_____ 4. How does Marvin feel when his family comes with him to see Waldo?
   A. sad   C. happy
   B. mad   D. scared

_____ 5. An important idea in this story is . . .
   A. Dog food tastes gross.   C. Dogs are smart.
   B. Don't give up!   D. Dogs like cooked food.

Short Answer

What kind of a person is Marvin? Use the events in the story to explain your opinion.

_____

_____

_____

BACKGROUND

In *Hungry, Hungry Sharks,* Joanna Cole provides a feast of details for children who are hungry for information about sharks. Cole describes the many kinds of sharks inhabiting the earth's waters today. In addition, she offers plenty of facts about size, habits, and habitats of the most "popular" of the species.

Cole was born in Newark, New Jersey, in 1944 and spent many years working as an elementary school librarian. As a librarian, she rediscovered her interest in children's literature and recalled her childhood fascination with the scientific world.

Cole's numerous science books reflect her love of all aspects of the natural world, from dinosaurs, to cockroaches, to tiny plants on a forest floor. Reviewers consistently cite her ability to instill a sense of awe in children and many have credited her with breathing new life into the genre of children's nonfiction.

BIBLIOGRAPHY Students might enjoy reading another science book by Joanna Cole. Suggest that they choose from among the following popular books:

(Lexile 410)   (Lexile 420)   (Lexile 390)

How to Introduce the Reading

Read the introduction to *Hungry, Hungry Sharks* aloud. Activate students' prior knowledge about the topic by asking them to say what they know about sharks. Have them discuss shark facts, shark stories, and any movies they've seen. Ask: *What's interesting about sharks? Is there anything scary about them?* Allow students to tell what they know before they begin reading the selection.

Other Reading

There are many nonfiction children's books that are written with the intent of capturing children's interest in the natural world. Have students try reading one of these books, all of which have Lexile scores close to that of *Hungry, Hungry Sharks*.

(Lexile 410)   (Lexile 410)   (Lexile 420)

Hungry, Hungry Sharks

Skills and Strategies Overview

PREREADING	preview
READING LEVEL	Lexile 410
RESPONSE	make things clear
VOCABULARY	✧shoot ✧torpedoess ✧chunks ✧packs ✧ship
COMPREHENSION	stop and think
WORD WORK	consonants and consonant clusters
PREWRITING	web
WRITING	descriptive paragraph / spelling
ASSESSMENT	meaning

OTHER RESOURCES

The first **four** pages of this teacher's lesson describe Parts I–V of the lesson. Also included are these **six** blackline masters. Use them to reinforce key elements of the lesson.

Vocabulary

Prereading

Comprehension

Word Work

Prewriting

Assessment

I. BEFORE YOU READ

Show some shark pictures that you have printed from a website or chosen from a library book. See which sharks students can identify. If possible, find pictures of blue sharks, which are the focus of this excerpt from Cole's book. (Good resources include *The Best Way to See a Shark* by Alan Fowler; *Eyewitness Activity Files: Sharks* by Deni Brown; and *Eyewitness Shark*, a VHS video). When you feel students are ready, assign the prereading activity, a **preview**. (Refer to the Strategy Handbook on page 49 for more help.)

Motivation Strategy

CONNECTING WITH STUDENTS Ask students to tell ocean stories of their own: beach visits, books they've read, aquarium trips, and so on. Have them bring in ocean memorabilia if possible and build a "visitor's booth" for students who are interested in taking a trip to the beach.

Words to Know

SYNONYMS Use the **Words to Know** blackline master on page 190 as a way to troubleshoot vocabulary problems. After working through the page, you might decide to teach a short vocabulary lesson on **synonyms.**

To begin, show students the key vocabulary words for this lesson: *shoot, torpedoes, chunks, packs,* and *ship*. Explain that these and other words are defined at the bottom of the page, but that you'd like students to think about synonyms for the words *before they begin reading*. Put a synonym chart on the board and see what students can come up with. Consult a thesaurus beforehand if you need some help. (An excellent online thesaurus can be found at www.merriam-webster.com.)

Vocabulary word	Synonym
chunks	parts

Prereading Strategies

PREVIEW As a prereading activity, students will do a **preview** of the selection and then fill out a web that explores their knowledge of sharks. Remind students that on a preview, they don't read every word. Instead, they let their eyes roam down each page of the reading. They pay attention only to repeated or boldface words and names that pop out at them. If necessary, assign a set time for the preview—a minute or two—to avoid the problem of students getting lost on the first or second page.

QUICKWRITE As an additional prereading activity, have students do a 1-minute **quickwrite** about sharks. Ask them to write for a minute about the topic without pausing. Tell them you won't be grading for sentence structure, grammar, and so on. What's important here is to get them thinking about what they already know about the topic of sharks.

To extend the activity, use the **Before You Read** blackline master on page 191.

MY PURPOSE Students' purpose for reading Cole's article will be to find three details about sharks. Encourage them to number the details in the Response Notes columns. (They'll likely find more than three.) Students will use these notes to help them with the writing assignment in **Part IV**.

II. READ

Response Strategy

FIRST READING Before students begin their first readings, explain the response strategy of **make things clear.** Students will mark important facts and details by underlining or highlighting, and then clarify what the facts and details mean in the Response Notes. Point out the sample response on page 117 and help students understand that this is an example of a comment one reader made to clarify what the author is saying.

Comprehension Strategy

SECOND READING Use the questions below to assess students' comprehension of what they've read. Can they name the **main idea** of the article? Can they identify **supporting details?** If not, refer them back to the text. Show them how to skim for an answer to a question or to clear up confusion about a fact or detail. Use your finger to trace down the middle of the page until you find the fact you're looking for. Help students develop the habit of using this rereading strategy on their own.

For more help with **Comprehension,** assign the blackline master on page 192.

Discussion Questions

COMPREHENSION 1. Why do blue sharks follow ships? *(They are attracted to the noise and chase the garbage that is thrown in the water.)*

CRITICAL THINKING 2. What tells you that this is a nonfiction article? *(Help students see the difference between fiction and nonfiction. Nonfiction provides information. Fiction is quite often written to entertain, intrigue, and so on.)*

3. Are blue sharks your enemies? Explain. *(Help students understand that, although these fish are not necessarily friendly to humans, they're not enemies either.)*

4. What have you learned about blue sharks? *(Ask students to read facts from their Response Notes. Clear up any confusion or misconceptions.)*

Reread

THIRD READING When they reread Cole's article, students should search for additional details that help meet their reading purpose. Ask them to mark the three most important details as #1, #2, and #3. If you have a small group of students who are struggling with the article, take them aside and do an oral reading of the piece. Point out important facts that they should note in the Response Notes.

Word Work

CONSONANTS AND CONSONANT CLUSTERS Use the Word Work lesson on page 121 to reinforce students' understanding of **consonants** and **consonant clusters.** Review problematic clusters such as *ick, br, sh,* and *th.* Offer students the opportunity to practice forming more words than required on the page.

For additional practice, see the **Word Work** blackline master on page 193.

III. GET READY TO WRITE

Prewriting Strategies

WEB To begin, students will complete a **web** that explores their knowledge of blue sharks. Encourage them to return to the text as necessary to fill in any knowledge gaps. In some cases, the notes they've made in the Response Notes can be used to complete the ovals on the web. If you have time, pull the whole class together for a group brainstorming session on blue sharks. Duplicate the web on the board and ask for volunteers to write facts or details that apply. Students can refer to this class web as they write their descriptive paragraphs.

Have students use the **Get Ready to Write** blackline master on page 194.

IV. WRITE

Be sure students understand that their assignment is to write a **descriptive paragraph** about blue sharks. Students should offer physical descriptions as well as information about habits and habitat. Stress the importance of creating a cohesive paragraph, with a beginning, a middle, and an end. Their topic sentence belongs in the opening. Specific facts and details are discussed in the body. In the closing, students should say how they feel about blue sharks and/or what they learned from Cole's article.

When students have finished drafting, review with them the structure of their paragraphs. Be sure they've included three or more details about blue sharks in the body of the paragraph. Point out that rewriting is an important step in the writing process. Even the best writers do some rewriting before they turn over a final copy.

WRITING RUBRIC Use this rubric to help with a quick assessment of students' writing.

Do students' descriptive paragraphs

• open with a topic sentence that states the subject and focus of the paragraph?

• include three or more descriptive details about blue sharks?

• close with a sentence that tells how the writer feels about blue sharks and/or the reading?

Grammar, Usage, and Mechanics

When students are ready to proofread their work, refer them to the **Writers' Checklist.** Remind the class that a spell-check program on a computer will not catch every spelling error. Good writers use a spell-check and read hard copy as well.

V. LOOK BACK

Point out the **Readers' Checklist** discuss Cole's article and its **meaning.** Were students able to glean valuable information from the writing? If not, why? Is there a more effective strategy that they could use when reading nonfiction?

To test students' comprehension, use the **Lesson Test** blackline master on page 195.

Name _____

WORDS TO KNOW

Before Reading

DIRECTIONS Look at the picture of the shark.

Use words from the box to complete each sentence.

If you don't know a word, make a guess.

◇torpedoes ◇packs ◇shoot ◇ships ◇chunks

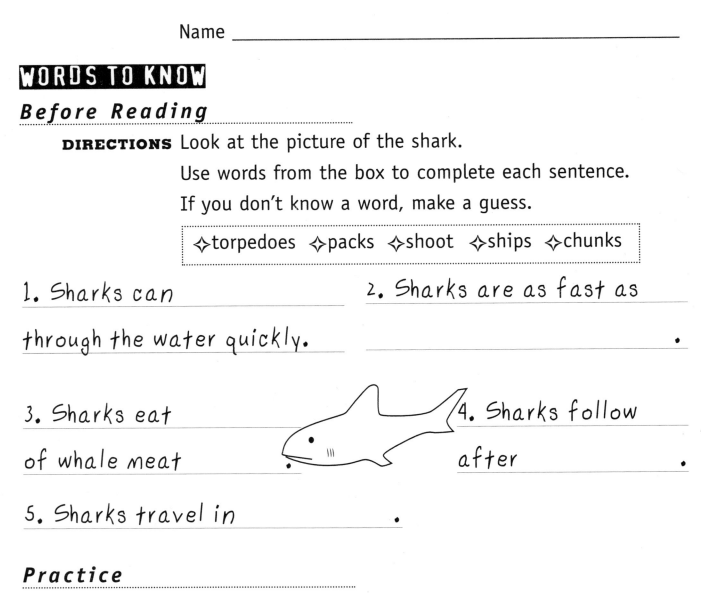

1. Sharks can _____

through the water quickly.

2. Sharks are as fast as

_____ .

3. Sharks eat _____

of whale meat _____ .

4. Sharks follow _____

after _____ .

5. Sharks travel in _____ .

Practice

Use the word *chunks* in a sentence of your own. Your sentence should show you know what the word means.

_____

_____

_____

_____

Name _____

BEFORE YOU READ

Quickwrite

DIRECTIONS Think of what you know about sharks.

Write everything that comes to mind on the lines below.

Write for 1 minute without stopping.

1-minute Quickwrite: Sharks

_____

_____

_____

_____

_____

_____

_____

_____

Name _____

COMPREHENSION

Double-entry Journal

DIRECTIONS Read the quotations from the article in the left-hand column. Say what you think they mean in the right-hand column.

Quotation	What I Think It Means
"If one shark gets hurt, the others turn on it."	
"Now the water is full of biting sharks."	
"Blue sharks are often called the wolves of the sea."	

Name _____

WORD WORK

After Reading

DIRECTIONS Change the beginning consonants and consonant clusters in the numbered words. Replace them with a new consonant or consonant cluster from the box below.

b d gr p fl pl

1. shark   dark

2. swim

3. deep

4. shoot

5. grown

Practice

DIRECTIONS Write a list of words that use the consonant clusters in the box. Write as many as you can think of.

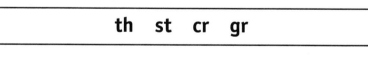

th st cr gr

_____   _____

_____   _____

_____   _____

_____   _____

Name _____

GET READY TO WRITE

Graphic Organizer

DIRECTIONS Use this chart to describe blue sharks.

Write words that show how they look and how they sound.

Then, in preparation for your paragraph, write a topic sentence.

How they look	How they sound
smooth	

My topic sentence: _____

_____

Name _____

LESSON TEST

Multiple-Choice

DIRECTIONS On the lines, write the letter of the best answer for each question.

_____ 1. Blue sharks are . . .
A. friendly.   C. easily scared.
B. dangerous.   D. lonely.

_____ 2. Blue sharks go after the smell of blood because . . .
A. it leads them to food.   C. they like the color red.
B. they want to drink it.   D. None of these answers

_____ 3. Sharks turn on each other when . . .
A. one shark gets hurt.   C. they follow a ship.
B. they swim too fast.   D. they are done eating whales.

_____ 4. Why are blue sharks like wolves?
A. They make funny noises.   C. They travel in packs.
B. They eat for fun.   D. They have furry tails.

_____ 5. An important idea in *Hungry, Hungry Sharks* is:
A. Sharks are blue.   C. Sharks are interesting.
B. Sharks can swim.   D. Sharks swim slowly.

Short Answer

Should you swim in the same water as blue sharks? Why or why not?

_____

_____

BACKGROUND

Eleanor Coerr's *Buffalo Bill and the Pony Express* is a fact-based novel about the exciting life and times of the legendary Buffalo Bill. Among other amazing feats, Buffalo Bill took a fourteen-hour Pony Express ride over 150 miles of dangerous Old West territory. Along the way, he escaped a wolf pack and outwitted a group of dangerous outlaws.

Coerr's humorous writing style and clearly rendered descriptions give readers a taste of what life was really like on the Pony Express trail. In addition, she offers young readers a valuable introduction to pioneer life in the mid- to late-1800s.

If you feel students would benefit, you might offer this background information about the Pony Express: The Pony Express was a mail service that operated between Saint Joseph, Missouri, and Sacramento, California. Service began on April 3, 1860. Prior to the Pony Express, regular mail took up to three weeks to cross the country. Pony Express carriers were able to make the 2000-mile trip in close to ten days. Stations were approximately 25 miles apart. Each rider was expected to cover 75 miles in a day.

BIBLIOGRAPHY Students might enjoy reading another book by the award-winning author, Eleanor Coerr. Read aloud her beautiful story *Sadako and the Thousand Paper Cranes,* or have students read one of these titles on their own:

(Lexile 440)   (Lexile 420)   (Lexile 400)

How to Introduce the Reading

Offer background information on Buffalo Bill and the Pony Express as needed. Explain that Buffalo Bill was the nickname of William Frederick Cody (1846–1917). Cody was an American guide, scout, and showman. He was born in Scott County, Iowa. At the age of 14, he became a rider with the newly established Pony Express. In 1865, he contracted with the Kansas Pacific Railroad to furnish buffalo meat to workers on the line. His claim of killing more than 4,000 buffalo earned him the name of Buffalo Bill.

In 1883, Cody organized a Wild West Show, which toured extensively in Europe and the United States. The Native American chief Sitting Bull and the sharpshooter Annie Oakley were both a part of the show.

Other Reading

Generate interest in the genre of biography by assigning a high-interest biography or autobiography for students to read on their own. Choose from one of these titles:

VINCENT VAN GOGH by Sean Connolly

(Lexile 440)

FREDERICK DOUGLASS FIGHTS FOR FREEDOM by Margaret Davidson

(Lexile 440)

A BOY NAMED BOOMER by Boomer Esiason

(Lexile 440)

Buffalo Bill and the Pony Express

STUDENT PAGES 125–134

Skills and Strategies Overview

PREREADING anticipation guide

READING LEVEL Lexile 430

RESPONSE question

VOCABULARY ◆fellows ◆spunk ◆station ◆shelter

COMPREHENSION story frame

WORD WORK base words

PREWRITING character map

WRITING letter / commas with dates and place names

ASSESSMENT ease

OTHER RESOURCES

The first **four** pages of this teacher's lesson describe Parts I–V of the lesson. Also included are **six** blackline masters. Use them to reinforce key elements of the lesson.

Vocabulary

Prereading

Comprehension

Assessment

Word Work

Prewriting

BEFORE YOU READ

Ask students to discuss books they've read or movies they've seen about pioneer life. What was life like for Americans in the 1800s? What challenges did pioneers face? What did people do for fun? When you feel they are ready to begin the lesson, assign the prereading activity, an **anticipation guide**. (Refer to the Strategy Handbook on page 48 for more help.)

Motivation Strategy

MOTIVATING STUDENTS   Put together a classroom library of pioneer books that students can thumb through or read during their free time. Look for books about Buffalo Bill and his Wild West show, along with fiction and nonfiction accounts of family life on the prairie. Use the art from these books to give students some background information on the time period.

Words to Know

CONTEXT CLUES   Use the **Words to Know** blackline master on page 202 to troubleshoot vocabulary problems. After working through the page, you might decide to teach a short vocabulary lesson on using **context clues.**

To begin, show students the key vocabulary words in *Buffalo Bill and the Pony Express: fellows, spunk, station,* and *shelter.* Model using context clues by saying: "I see the word *spunk,* but I'm not sure what it means. I'll reread the sentence in which it appears. I'll also pay attention to surrounding sentences. I see that it's Mr. Majors who uses the word. He describes what kind of person you need to be to be a Pony Express rider. I know that the job takes courage. Could *spunk* mean "courage"? I'll check the footnote definition to see if I'm correct."

Prereading Strategies

ANTICIPATION GUIDE   As a prereading activity, students will complete an **anticipation guide.** Read aloud the five statements on page 126 of the student book. Point out the "Before" column and ask students to mark whether they agree or disagree with each. Then call on volunteers to explain their answers. If they disagreed with a statement, find out why. This quick oral activity will help you assess the level of students' prior knowledge about the topic. If you think they could use more information, offer additional background on the time period.

PREDICTION   As a further prereading activity, ask students to make **predictions** about the reading. Remind the class that they can use the title, art, and first sentence of the work to help them form their predictions. Give students a moment or two to look at these elements. Then have them fill out the prediction organizer on the **Before You Read** blackline master on page 203. For additional help with this activity, see page 12 of the *Amelia Bedelia* lesson.

MY PURPOSE   Read aloud students' purpose for reading *Buffalo Bill*: *What kind of person is Buffalo Bill, and how did he get to be a rider on the Pony Express?* Point out that students' purpose is twofold for this reading. It may help to list the two parts of the purpose statement on the board:

1. Find out what kind of person Buffalo Bill was.

2. Find out how he got to be a rider on the Pony Express.

READ

Response Strategy

FIRST READING As students are settling down to read, discuss the strategy of **questioning** and the purpose it serves. Explain to the class that, as they read, questions will naturally occur to them. An excellent strategy they can use to improve their reading comprehension is to note questions *as they occur,* instead of waiting until they've finished reading. Each time they think of a question, have them note it in the Response Notes, even if they think it will be answered later. Questions that remain unanswered at the end should be addressed by the group.

Comprehension Strategy

SECOND READING As they're reading Coerr's story, students will stop three separate times to fill in **story frames** that help them track the essentials of a story: setting, character, conflict, and resolution. Help students understand the importance of these elements and how they can affect the story as a whole.

For more help with **Comprehension,** assign the blackline master on page 204.

Discussion Questions

COMPREHENSION 1. What do you know about Buffalo Bill? *(Encourage students to tell about Bill's appearance, personality, attitude toward others, and so on.)*

2. Why was he so determined to be a Pony Express rider? *(Answers will vary. Possible: He thought it would be exciting.)*

CRITICAL THINKING 3. How did the Pony Express work? *(Have students explain the job of individual riders and how they relied on teamwork to get the mail from one side of the country to the other.)*

4. Why do you think Mr. Murphy chose Bill as a Pony Express Rider? *(Possible: He liked Bill's spunk and considered him trustworthy. This answer is supportable with evidence from the text.)*

Reread

THIRD READING Before students return to the selection for an additional reading, have them mark the "After" column of the anticipation guide on page 126. This quick activity will show students how much they learned from their initial reading of Coerr's story. Then ask them to go back to the first page of the selection and begin rereading. Remind them of their reading purpose and have them concentrate on finding important details about Buffalo Bill. Any additional notes they make about Bill will come in handy when they create their character map, on page 132.

Word Work

BASE WORDS The Word Work lesson on page 131 extends students' knowledge of **base words**, especially base words that end with a silent *e*. Students need pratice reading words with silent *e*. It is sometimes hard to comprehend words where the silent *e* is dropped and a suffix that begins with a vowel is added (bake-baking).

For additional practice with suffixes, see the **Word Work** blackline master on page 205.

III. GET READY TO WRITE

Prewriting Strategies

CHARACTER MAPS As a prewriting activity, students will create a **character map** that explores four traits of Buffalo Bill. In each case, students will need to back up their assertions with evidence from the story. Model this for students by saying, "To find evidence that Bill was a hard worker, I'll return to the story and look for the part in which Bill says that he roped cattle when he was nine. I'll skim the text until I come to the bottom of page 128 and then use this quotation as proof that he was a hard worker: 'I roped cattle when I was nine, and I can ride like the wind.'" Have students follow your model as they look for proof for the other three blanks on the web.

Have students use the **Get Ready to Write** blackline master on page 206.

IV. WRITE

Students' assignment is to imagine they are Mr. Majors and write a **letter** to a friend that explains why Buffalo Bill will make a good Pony Express rider. Remind students to stay in character throughout their letters. They'll need to think of themselves as Mr. Majors and try to imagine the type of letter he might have written. They'll use the pronouns *I* and *we* throughout.

After students have drafted their letters, have them check to be sure they offered two or three interesting details to support the assertion that Buffalo Bill will be a good Pony Express rider.

WRITING RUBRIC Use this rubric to help with a quick assessment of students' writing.

Do students' letters

• open with a topic sentence about Buffalo Bill and his ability to ride in the Pony Express?

• offer two or more details about Bill to support the claim that he'll be a good rider?

• read as if they were written by Mr. Majors?

Grammar, Usage, and Mechanics

When students are ready to proofread, teach a brief lesson on **commas.** Remind them that commas are used in a series of three or more. In addition, they are used to separate the day from the year in a date and the city from the state when naming a location. Refer students to the **Writers' Checklist.** Have them read the example and then apply the lesson to their own writing.

V. LOOK BACK

Reflect with students on the **ease** with which they read Coerr's story. If they found the reading difficult, have them say why. Point out the **Readers' Checklist** and explain that good readers ask these two questions of themselves each time they finish a reading.

To test students' comprehension, use the **Lesson Test** blackline master on page 207.

Name _____

WORDS TO KNOW

Before Reading

DIRECTIONS Read each sentence.

Then say what you think the underlined words mean. Use the rest of the sentence to help you.

1. The sign asked for young <u>fellows</u>, not girls, for the job.

I think fellows *means* _____

2. You need to have a lot of <u>spunk,</u> or courage, to travel seventy-five miles by pony.

I think spunk *means* _____

3. Bill's home <u>station</u> where he returned after each ride, was a town called Red Buttes.

I think station *means* _____

4. Bill was able to stop for food and <u>shelter</u> along the journey.

I think shelter *means* _____

Practice

Use *shelter* in a sentence about a trip you took. Your sentence should give clues about what *shelter* means.

_____

_____

_____

Name _____

BEFORE YOU READ

Predictions

When you think about what happens next in a story, you are making predictions.

DIRECTIONS Read the title of the story.

Look at the pictures. Then read the first sentence.

Use these to predict what the story will be about.

Clue	My prediction
Prediction clue #1: Title	
Prediction clue #2: Pictures	
Prediction clue #3: First sentence	

Name _____

COMPREHENSION

Story Frame

DIRECTIONS Put together what you know about Eleanor Coerr's story.

Fill out the details on this story frame.

Check the notes you made during reading if you need help.

Story Frame: Buffalo Bill and the Pony Express

Where the story takes place ⟹

When it takes place ⟹

These are the characters ⟹

The characters have these problems ⟹

This is how they solve the problems ⟹

The story ends when ⟹

Name _____

WORD WORK

After Reading

DIRECTIONS Put an X through the suffix of each word.

Then write the base word.

Word	Base word
1. mov~~ing~~	move
2. agreed	
3. safer	
4. roping	
5. coming	

Practice

DIRECTIONS Add a suffix from the box to these base words. Write the new word on the line.

-ed   *-ing*

6. make   making _____

7. care   _____

8. please   _____

9. score   _____

10. share   _____

Name _____

GET READY TO WRITE
Writing a Letter

DIRECTIONS Follow these steps to write your letter.

STEP 1 Choose the person you will write to.

I will write to: _____

STEP 2 Write your topic sentence.

I think Buffalo Bill will be a good Pony Express rider

because: _____

_____

STEP 3 Write 3 facts from the story that prove your topic
sentence is true.

fact #1 _____

_____

fact #2 _____

_____

fact #3 _____

_____

Name _____

LESSON TEST

Multiple-Choice

DIRECTIONS On the lines, write the letter of the best answer for each question.

_____ 1. Buffalo Bill was a . . .
   A. cowboy.   C. buffalo rancher.
   B. Pony Express Rider. D. writer.

_____ 2. Which of these sentences describes Buffalo Bill?
   A. He was young.   C. He was skinny.
   B. He was eager.   D. All of these answers

_____ 3. Bill wanted to be a Pony Express rider because . . .
   A. he wanted excitement.   C. he hated school.
   B. he was hungry.   D. his friend was joining too.

_____ 4. Mr. Majors said the job was . . .
   A. fun.   C. dangerous.
   B. boring.   D. scary.

_____ 5. This story takes place . . .
   A. in the past.   C. in the future.
   B. right now.   D. None of these answers

Short Answer

Explain the job of the Pony Express rider.

_____

_____

_____

_____

BACKGROUND

Pat Mora's *Tomás and the Library Lady* tells the true story of a nationally known educator, Tomás Rivera, and the kind-hearted librarian who instilled in him a love of books that stayed with him for his entire life.

Far from his home in Texas, young Tomás visits the library in the hopes that he'll find a story to tell Papá Grande, his grandfather. The librarian welcomes him into the reading room, offers him a cold drink of water, and gives him a book to read. Tomás stays in the reading room the entire first day, and then returns again and again over the course of a long, hot summer.

On his visits to the library, Tomás practices speaking English and teaches the kindly librarian some Spanish words, including "adiós," a word he must use when it is time for his family to return to Texas. Thanks to the kindness of this librarian, however, young Tomás (who grew up to become chancellor of the University of California, Riverside) would never be without stories again.

BIBLIOGRAPHY Students might enjoy reading another book by the critically acclaimed author, Pat Mora. Do a search in your library's online catalog or have students choose from among the following:

(Lexile 410)   (Lexile 440)   (no Lexile score)

How to Introduce the Reading

Read the introduction to the lesson on page 135. Ask students to imagine a life without computers, TV, video games, and so on. How would their lives be different? What would they do after school and on the weekends? Explain that the boy in the story they're about to read chooses to spend his time talking to his grandfather and begging him to tell one of his fantastic tales.

As they read *Tomás and the Library Lady,* have students think about favorite family stories they've heard. Which of these is as memorable as the story Papá Grande tells Tomás?

Other Reading

Read aloud other high-interest books that have a Lexile score close to that of *Tomás and the Library Lady* (Lexile 440). Do a search at the Lexile website (www.Lexile.com), or suggest one of these titles:

(Lexile 400)   (Lexile 460)   (Lexile 410)

Tomás and the Library Lady

Skills and Strategies Overview

PREREADING	think-pair-and-share
READING LEVEL	Lexile 440
RESPONSE	draw
VOCABULARY	◇cot ◇sewn ◇howled ◇chattered ◇thorny
COMPREHENSION	Double-entry journal
WORD WORK	compound words
PREWRITING	story chart
WRITING	story ending / apostrophes with possessives
ASSESSMENT	enjoyment

OTHER RESOURCES

The first **four** pages of this teacher's lesson describe Parts I–V of the lesson. Also included are these **six** blackline masters. Use them to reinforce key elements of the lesson.

Vocabulary

Prereading

Comprehension

Word Work

Prewriting

Assessment

BEFORE YOU READ

As a warm-up to the topic of Mora's story, have students make a list of their all-time favorite family stories. Even if they don't share their list with anyone else, this short project will help students begin thinking about the theme of storytelling. Remind the class that anyone can be a storyteller, and just about any event or experience can become a story if the storyteller gives the subject a little thought. When students are ready to begin the lesson, assign the prereading activity, a **think-pair-and-share**. (Refer to the Strategy Handbook on page 50 for more help.)

Motivation Strategy

MOTIVATING STUDENTS Tell the story of Tomás Rivera and explain his inspiring struggle to overcome the difficulties of a migrant childhood. (Eventually Rivera became chancellor of one of the most prestigious universities in the United States.) Before you begin, borrow a copy of Mora's book to learn more about Rivera, or try an Internet search using Tomás Rivera as your key words.

Words to Know

CONTEXT CLUES Use the **Words to Know** blackline master on page 214 as a way to troubleshoot vocabulary problems. After working through the page, you might decide to teach a short vocabulary lesson on **context clues**.

To begin, show students the key vocabulary words for the reading: *cot, sewn, howled, chattered,* and *thorny*. Explain that these and other words are defined at the bottom of the story pages, but that you'd like students to try and figure out definitions for the words on their own. They can check the footnoted definitions later, to see if they are correct. Help students use context clues to figure out the meaning of each word. Later, help them use each word in a sentence of their own.

Prereading Strategies

THINK-PAIR-AND-SHARE The purpose of a **think-pair-and-share** is to pique students' interest in the story to come while at the same time help them do a little advance thinking about the theme. The quotations on page 136 have been chosen with the aim of offering clues about the topic and theme of Mora's story. Ask students to put the quotes in an order that makes sense to them. Be aware that "right" or "wrong" does not apply here. What's important is for students to take a quick taste of Mora's story before they actually begin reading. After they've finished ordering the quotes, have them make a prediction about the topic of the reading.

PREVIEW As an additional prereading activity, have students do a **preview** of *Tomás and the Library Lady*. What other predictions can they make about the story after they preview the art and text?

Have students keep track of what they find on the **Before You Read** blackline master on page 215.

MY PURPOSE Always establish a reading purpose for students before they begin an assignment. Move beyond the overly general "read to find out what happens" and create a purpose that gives students something to look for or think about as they read.

II. READ

Response Strategy

FIRST READING An excellent option is to have students stay with their reading partners and do a shared reading of *Tomás and the Library Lady*. Invite partners to read one page at a time, trading jobs at the end of every page. Students who are reading aloud should read with expression. Students who are listening should make a concerted effort to imagine people and places the reader tells about. Each time they "see" something new, they should **draw** in the Response Notes. When they do their second readings, students can add sketches or make notes about things they missed the first time around.

Comprehension Strategy

SECOND READING As they are reading Mora's story, students should think carefully about the connections they can make to the people and action described. To help, have students stop and reflect on what they're reading by using the **Double-entry journals** that are scattered throughout the text. Point out the first journal entry on page 138. Explain that students need to read the quote in the left-hand column and then respond to it in the right-hand column. Emphasize that their responses should be in the form of their thoughts and feelings.

For more help with **Comprehension,** assign the blackline master on page 216.

Discussion Questions

COMPREHENSION 1. Why are Tomás and his family in Iowa? (*They are migrant farm workers who have come from Texas to pick crops.*)

2. What story does Papá Grande tell Tomás? (*Ask students to retell Papá Grande's story in their own words. Have them check the book as needed for details.*)

CRITICAL THINKING 3. What difficulties do Tomás and his family face as migrant farm workers? (*Possible answer: They must move back and forth across the country following crops. This is hard on everyone.*)

4. What do you know about Tomás from reading this story? (*Possible answer: He is a bright, friendly, and good boy who loves to listen to stories.*)

Reread

THIRD READING The directions on page 142 ask students to reread the story and review the sketches they made during their first readings. They'll also need to pay particular attention to the story Papá Grande tells Tomás. Before they begin, read aloud the reading purpose on page 136. Encourage students to make inferences about Tomás as they read.

Word Work

COMPOUND WORDS The Word Work lesson offers a review of **compound words** and how they are formed. Give students a set of compounds and have them divide the words. Help students to see the smaller words that make up the compound word.

For additional practice, see the **Word Work** blackline master on page 217.

III. GET READY TO WRITE

Prewriting Strategies

STORY CHART Students will complete a **story chart** on page 144 in anticipation of writing a new ending for *Tomás and the Library Lady*. If you like, have students stay with their reading partners and ask them to complete the prewriting activity together. Have them begin by brainstorming possible new endings to Mora's text. When they have an idea they'd like to work on, they can fill out the story chart provided. Remind students that the central conflict, or problem, in their stories should be resolved at the end.

Have students use the **Get Ready to Write** blackline master on page 218.

IV. WRITE

Read aloud the directions at the top of page 145. Be sure students understand that they are to write a brand new **story ending** for *Tomás and the Library Lady*. (Review Mora's ending if necessary.) Have students use the story planner they created on page 144 to help. Notice the starter sentence that students should use as an opening for their stories.

When they've finished, have each student read what he or she has written to be sure it makes sense and meets the requirements of the rubric below. Encourage students to watch for poor word choices and problematic sequencing. Help students see that their endings should present a conflict and a resolution to that conflict.

WRITING RUBRIC Use this rubric to help with a quick assessment of students' writing.

Do students' story endings

• relate to the story they read in the *Sourcebook?*

• contain details about character, setting, conflict, and resolution?

• show they understood the characters and actions of Mora's original story?

Grammar, Usage, and Mechanics

When students are ready to proofread, refer them to the **Writer's Checklist** and teach a short lesson on using **apostrophes** to show possession. Explain that to form possessives of most singular words, students need to add an apostrophe and an *s*. This is also true for proper nouns that end in s, such as *Tomás*.

V. LOOK BACK

Point out the **Readers' Checklist** and reflect with students on their **enjoyment** of Mora's story. Have students discuss the highlights of the reading and explain what they did and did not like. Would they be interested in reading more from Mora's book? Why or why not?

To test students' comprehension, use the **Lesson Test** blackline master on page 219.

Name _____

WORDS TO KNOW

Before Reading

DIRECTIONS Answer each question with a word from the word box. Use the rest of the question to help you.

> ◇cot ◇sewn ◇howled ◇chattered ◇thorny

1. What did the wolf do in the middle of the night?

The wolf

2. What can you sleep on?

You can sleep on a

3. When you were cold last winter, what did your teeth do?

Last winter, my teeth

4. How is material put together to make a shirt?

The material is

5. How does a rosebush feel?

A rosebush feels

Practice

Write a sentence asking a friend to sleep over. Use the word *cot* in your note.

Name _____

BEFORE YOU READ

Preview

DIRECTIONS Preview *Tomás and the Library Lady*. Look quickly at every page.

Underline 2 or 3 key words in the first paragraph and the last.

Then fill out the preview guide.

Preview Guide

1. What do you think <u>Tomás and the Library Lady</u> is about?

2. What is the setting of the story?

Time:

Place:

3. Who are the characters?

Name _____

COMPREHENSION

Reader Response

DIRECTIONS Read the sentence starters below. Use your own thoughts and feelings about the story to complete each sentence.

Tomás makes me feel _____ because

_____

_____

_____ •

Papá Grande reminds me of _____ because

_____

_____

_____ •

(circle one)
I liked / didn't like this story because _____

_____

_____

_____ •

Name _____

WORD WORK

After Reading

DIRECTIONS Read the short words in the box. Put the words together to form compound words. Make as many compound words as you can.

time	table	out	sea	food	saw
field	over	line	look	come	

My Compound Words

1. _____

2. _____

3. _____

4. _____

5. _____

6. _____

7. _____

8. _____

9. _____

10. _____

Practice

DIRECTIONS Read these compound words. Put a line between the two small words. One is done for you.

11. every/body

12. buttermilk

13. background

14. somehow

15. grandfather

16. cardboard

Name _____

GET READY TO WRITE

Writing a Story Ending

DIRECTIONS Use this storyboard to plan what will happen in your story about Tomás.

Draw a picture in every box.

Below each picture, explain what happens.

Storyboard: What Happens Next

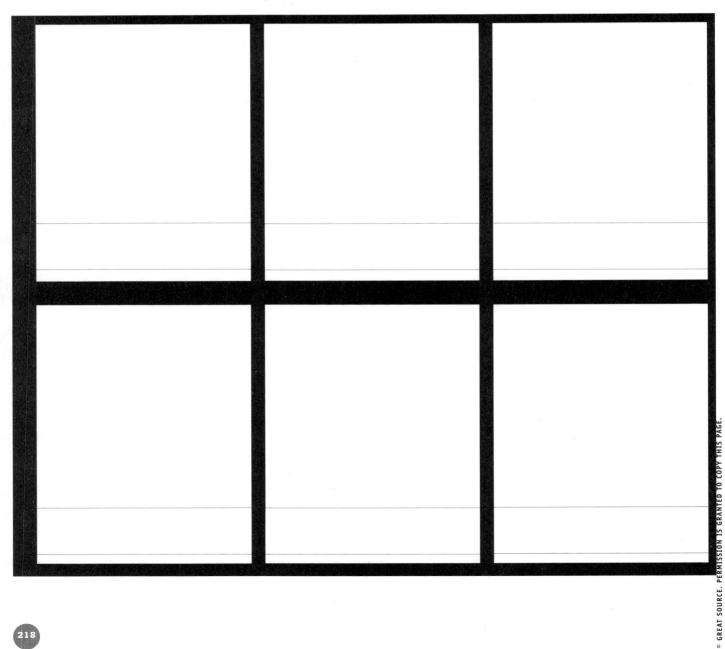

Name _____

LESSON TEST

Multiple-Choice

DIRECTIONS On the lines, write the letter of the best answer for each question.

_____ 1. How does Tomás feel during the trip to Iowa?
A. hot and tired   C. sad and upset
B. excited and happy   D. scared and confused

_____ 2. Tomás's parents are . . .
A. doctors.   C. teachers.
B. farm workers.   D. home builders.

_____ 3. Papá Grande is . . .
A. the farm owner.   C. Tomás's grandfather.
B. the librarian.   D. the mailman.

_____ 4. How does Tomás feel about Papá Grande's stories?
A. He loves them.   C. He thinks they are boring.
B. He hates them.   D. None of these answers

_____ 5. What lesson does Papá Grande try to teach Tomás?
A. Always look behind you.   C. Don't ride by yourself.
B. Reading is very   D. Drink a lot of water.
   important.

Short Answer

What kind of a person do you think is Tomás? Support your answer with facts from the story.

_____

_____

_____

Going Home

BACKGROUND

Eve Bunting's *Going Home* tells the story of a Mexican family who goes to the United States in the hopes of earning a better living. Working as farm laborers, the parents believe they can provide more for their children in the United States than they can in Mexico. Despite their faith in America, however, the parents consider Mexico their home.

The excerpt reprinted in the **Sourcebook** comes from the first part of Bunting's book, *Going Home*. Young Carlos narrates the story and describes his family's road trip to La Perla, the village where his parents grew up. Carlos and his siblings regard the United States as their home, even though they were born in Mexico. Carlos even encourages his parents to learn English. On the road to Mexico, all of the children struggle to understand their parents' strong ties to their native land.

Eve Bunting has written more than 150 children's books. She often writes about socially conscious issues that she discovered growing up in Northern Ireland. "I was aware that there was discrimination, although I didn't know there was anything to be done about it," Bunting said. Among her many awards are: the Caldecott Award for Smoky Night (1994) the School Library Journal Best Book of the Year Award for Dandelions (1995), and the 1997 Regina medal for "continued distinguished contribution to children's literature.

BIBLIOGRAPHY Students might enjoy reading another book by Eve Bunting. Recommend one of these titles:

SUPER-FINE VALENTINE

(Lexile 430)

THE DAY I WAS RICH

(Lexile 490)

SHIPWRECK SATURDAY

(Lexile 430)

How to Introduce the Reading

Have a volunteer read aloud the introduction to the lesson on page 147. Ask students to tell about a time they took a trip. Where did they go? With whom did they go? As they read, students can compare their experiences to Carlos's and his family's. As you know, the personal connections readers make to a text can make the reading process easier and more enjoyable.

Other Reading

Read aloud other high-interest books at this same reading level. The following titles all have Lexile scores close to that of Going Home (Lexile 480):

(Lexile 450)   (Lexile 480)   (Lexile 480)

Going Home

(STUDENT PAGES 147–156)

Skills and Strategies Overview

PREREADING prediction

READING LEVEL Lexile 480

RESPONSE connect

VOCABULARY

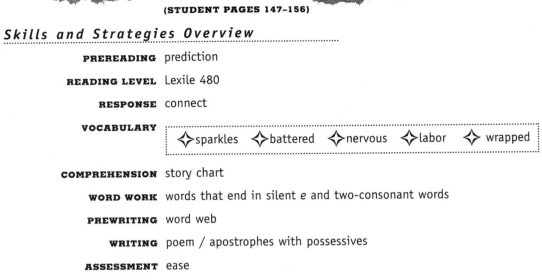

◇ sparkles ◇ battered ◇ nervous ◇ labor ◇ wrapped

COMPREHENSION story chart

WORD WORK words that end in silent *e* and two-consonant words

PREWRITING word web

WRITING poem / apostrophes with possessives

ASSESSMENT ease

OTHER RESOURCES

The first **four** pages of this teacher's lesson describe Parts I–V of the lesson. Also included are these **six** blackline masters. Use them to reinforce key elements of the lesson.

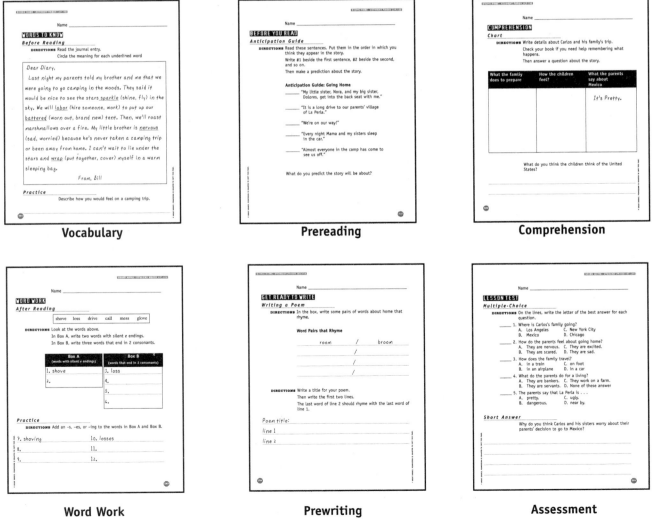

Vocabulary

Prereading

Comprehension

Word Work

Prewriting

Assessment

1. BEFORE YOU READ

Continue your discussion with students about taking a trip. What would they say to a younger sibling if he or she were going away for a little while? What advice do they have for children who get homesick? When you've finished the warm-up discussion, assign the prereading activity, a **prediction**. (Refer to the Strategy Handbook on page 48 for more help.)

Motivation Strategies

MOTIVATING STUDENTS Get a map of North America. Point out Mexico to students and show where Carlos and his family are traveling. Track the route to Mexico from your location. Talk about what you would see traveling from your home to Mexico.

CONNECTING WITH STUDENTS Ask students to do a to quickwrite about a time they took a trip. Have them describe the place they visited, why and when they went there, and who was along. A short writing activity like this one will serve as an excellent warm-up to the topic and theme of Bunting's book.

Words to Know

CONTEXT CLUES Use the **Words to Know** blackline master on page 226 to troubleshoot vocabulary problems. After working through the page, you might decide to teach a short vocabulary lesson on using **context clues**.

To begin, show students the key vocabulary words for the lesson: *sparkles, battered, nervous, labor,* and *wrapped*. Explain that four of the five words are footnoted at the bottom of the page, but that you'd like them to try to predict the meaning of the words first, before checking the footnoted definitions. Tell the class: "For example, I see the word *sparkles* on page 149. I don't know this word, so I'll look for context clues. I see that Carlos's mother is excited, and that she and Papa are happy. Could *sparkles* mean "shines"? I'll check the footnoted definition and refine my definition as needed."

Prereading Strategies

PREDICTION As a prereading activity, students are asked to make **predictions** about the story. Making predictions about a text can help generate student interest while at the same time give readers a purpose for reading. Students will want to continue reading to find out if their predictions come true.

ANTICIPATION GUIDE As an additional prereading activity, have students complete an **anticipation guide.** Choose four or more quotations from the text and ask students to order them in a way that makes sense. Then have them make a prediction about the topic of the story. This activity also will help create student interest in the reading.

For more help, see the **Before You Read** blackline master on page 227.

MY PURPOSE Students' purpose for reading the story is to find out where the family is going and what happens on the way there. Have them keep track of their during-reading predictions in the margins.

II. READ

Response Strategy

FIRST READING As they read *Going Home* students should note details that help them meet their reading purpose. Each time they see an important phrase or sentence, they should underline it and then **connect** what is described to their own lives. In addition, have them react to parts that they think are interesting or important. Later, they'll be asked to think about sensory language and how it can affect a piece of writing.

Comprehension Strategy

SECOND READING To aid in their comprehension of the reading (and the genre), students will fill out three separate story charts that challenge their comprehension and analytical skills. Remind students that the setting of a work is where and when the story takes place.

For more help with **Comprehension**, assign the blackline master on page 228.

Discussion Questions

COMPREHENSION 1. Where and when does this story take place? *(in the family's car on the way to Mexico; present day)*

2. Why is Nora sad to leave her home in the camp? *(She will miss her friend Maria.)*

CRITICAL THINKING 3. Why is Carlos nervous about going to Mexico? *(Possible: He worries that he and his family will not be allowed to return to the United States, even though they have the appropriate papers.)*

4. Why do you think Carlos wants his parents to learn English *(Possible: It's difficult to live and succeed in a country where one doesn't speak the language.)*

5. Do you think it's possible for one to feel as though he or she has two homes? *(Encourage students to discuss the parents' feelings for both Mexico and the United States. What does each country mean to them?)*

Reread

THIRD READING Be sure students reread the text at least once before they begin the prewriting activity. Ask them to look carefully at the details they marked and the connections they noted in the Response Notes. Also have them return to the predictions they completed on page 148. Which of their predictions came true? Which were way off the mark? Show students that making and checking predictions can be a fun way of thinking critically about a text.

Word Work

WORD ENDINGS The Word Work lesson on page 152 offers some review work on words with silent *e* endings. In addition, it explores words that end in two consonants. First, students will sort the words in the box into the two categories. Then they'll add –*s*/-*es* or –*ing* to these words. Remind the class of the rule for adding a suffix to a word that ends in a silent *e*.

For additional practice, see the **Word Work** blackline master on page 229.

GET READY TO WRITE

Prewriting Strategies

WORD WEB  The directions on page 154 ask students to plan a poem about home. Once they've settled on a topic, they'll complete a **web** using sensory language. Explain to the class that writers use sensory words to help readers feel more involved in the story. Sensory language helps the reader "see," "hear," "smell," "taste," and "feel" the things the writer describes.

Have students brainstorm words for another of the sense areas. As another option, give examples of sensory language from Bunting's writing, such as, "She sparkles with excitement."

For additional help, have students use the **Get Ready to Write** blackline master on page 230.

IV. WRITE

To complete Part IV, students will need to write a **poem** that uses sensory language. If you feel they will benefit, have students look at the poems they wrote after reading the selections in Lesson 2. Remind students that poetry does not have to rhyme, although you may want to have some students brainstorm some rhyming pairs they can use in their poetry.

After students have written a first draft, have them stop and think about the poem they've written. Are there lines or words they'd like to change? Is it clear that this is a poem about home?

WRITING RUBRIC Use this rubric to help with a quick assessment of students' writing.

Do the students' poems

- explore the subject of home?

- contain words that appeal to the five senses?

- follow the usual form for poetry: appropriate line breaks, first word of every line capitalized, and so on?

Grammar, Usage, and Mechanics

Refer the class to the **Writers' Checklist** and then teach a brief lesson on using **apostrophes** when forming possessives. Remind students that an apostrophe and a *s* are used together to form the possessive of most singular words. An apostrophe alone is used to form the possessive of plural words that end in *s*: the bees' hive.

V. LOOK BACK

Point out the **Readers' Checklist** at the bottom of page 156. Discuss the **ease** or difficulty with which students read Bunting's story. Most will say that the story was easy to read. Ask them to explain what about it was simple: the language, the subject, or something else?

To test students' comprehension, use the **Lesson Test** blackline master on page 231.

Name _____

Before Reading

DIRECTIONS Read the journal entry.

Circle the meaning for each underlined word.

Dear Diary,

Last night my parents told my brother and me that we were going to go camping in the woods. They said it would be nice to see the stars <u>sparkle</u> (shine, fly) in the sky. We will <u>labor</u> (hire someone, work) to put up our <u>battered</u> (worn out, brand new) tent. Then, we'll roast marshmallows over a fire. My little brother is <u>nervous</u> (sad, worried) because he's never taken a camping trip or been away from home. I can't wait to lie under the stars and <u>wrap</u> (put together, cover) myself in a warm sleeping bag.

From, Bill

Practice

Describe how you would feel on a camping trip.

Name _____

BEFORE YOU READ

Anticipation Guide

DIRECTIONS Read these sentences. Put them in the order in which you think they appear in the story.

Write #1 beside the first sentence, #2 beside the second, and so on.

Then make a prediction about the story.

Anticipation Guide: Going Home

_____ "My little sister, Nora, and my big sister, Dolores, get into the back seat with me."

_____ "It is a long drive to our parents' village of La Perla."

_____ "We're on our way!"

_____ "Every night Mama and my sisters sleep in the car."

_____ "Almost everyone in the camp has come to see us off."

What do you predict the story will be about?

_____

_____

_____

Name _____

COMPREHENSION

Chart

DIRECTIONS Write details about Carlos and his family's trip.

Check your book if you need help remembering what happens.

Then answer a question about the story.

What the famliy does to prepare	How the children feel?	What the parents say about Mexico
		It's Pretty.

What do you think the children think of the United States?

_____

_____

Name _____

WORD WORK

After Reading

| shove | loss | drive | call | mess | glove |

DIRECTIONS Look at the words above.

In Box A, write two words with silent *e* endings.

In Box B, write three words that end in 2 consonants.

Box A (words with silent *e* endings)	Box B (words that end in 2 consonants)
1. shove	3. loss
2.	4.
	5.
	6.

Practice

DIRECTIONS Add an –s, –es, or –ing to the words in Box A and Box B.

7. shoving   10. losses

8. _____   11. _____

9. _____   12. _____

Name _____

GET READY TO WRITE

Writing a Poem

DIRECTIONS In the box, write some pairs of words about home that rhyme.

Word Pairs that Rhyme

room	/	broom
	/	
	/	
	/	

DIRECTIONS Write a title for your poem.

Then write the first two lines.

The last word of line 2 should rhyme with the last word of line 1.

Poem title: _____

line 1 _____

line 2 _____

Name _____

LESSON TEST

Multiple-Choice

DIRECTIONS On the lines, write the letter of the best answer for each question.

_____ 1. Where is Carlos's family going?
A. Los Angeles   C. New York City
B. Mexico   D. Chicago

_____ 2. How do the parents feel about going home?
A. They are nervous.   C. They are excited.
B. They are scared.   D. They are sad.

_____ 3. How does the family travel?
A. in a train   C. on foot
B. in an airplane   D. in a car

_____ 4. What do the parents do for a living?
A. They are bankers.   C. They work on a farm.
B. They are servants. D. None of these answers

_____ 5. The parents say that La Perla is . . .
A. pretty.   C. ugly.
B. dangerous.   D. near by.

Short Answer

Why do you think Carlos and his sisters worry about their parents' decision to go to Mexico?

_____

_____

_____

_____

Fox and Crane

BACKGROUND

In the introductory note to her book *Babushka's Mother Goose,* Patricia Polacco explains that she first heard many of the stories she included when she was a child sitting on her babushka's (grandmother's) lap. One of the stories from Polacco's book is a retelling of Aesop's fable "Fox and the Crane."

Polacco is an author, an illustrator, and a storyteller who grew up in Oakland, California. As a child, Patricia had trouble reading because of dyslexia. She preferred drawing to writing. Even when she was quite young, she showed remarkable artistic talent. Along with several other titles, Polacco is the best-selling author/illustrator of *Rechenka's Eggs,* a modern-day children's classic.

BIBLIOGRAPHY Students might enjoy reading another story by Patricia Polacco. Read aloud *Rechenka's Eggs* (which may be too advanced for students to read on their own), or recommend one of these titles for independent reading:

BABUSHKA BABY YAGA

(Lexile 570)

BABUSHKA AND THE THREE KINGS

(Lexile 580)

BABUSHKA'S DOLL

(Lexile 360)

How to Introduce the Reading

Ask the class if anyone has heard Aesop's fable "Fox and Crane." If someone knows the story, ask for a brief summary. If not, read aloud the introduction to the lesson on page 157. Ask students to imagine themselves in this situation: They've invited a friend to dinner and served something the friend cannot or will not eat. What should they say? What should they do? Would this change the way they felt about their friend?

Other Reading

Spend a class period reading aloud fairy tales, folktales, fables, and myths. Choose stories from around the world in order to give students a taste of many different cultures. Three good anthologies are listed below.

"Fox and Crane"

STUDENT PAGES 157–166

Skills and Strategies Overview

PREREADING	think-pair-and-share
READING LEVEL	Lexile NP*
RESPONSE	question
VOCABULARY	◇invited ◇accepted ◇porridge ◇pleased ◇arrived
COMPREHENSION	retell
WORD WORK	suffixes and base words
PREWRITING	story chart
WRITING	story ending / apostrophes with possessives
ASSESSMENT	understanding

*NP = Not Prose and cannot be Lexiled.

OTHER RESOURCES

The first **four** pages of this teacher's lesson describe Parts I–V of the lesson. Also included are these **six** blackline masters. Use them to reinforce key elements of the lesson.

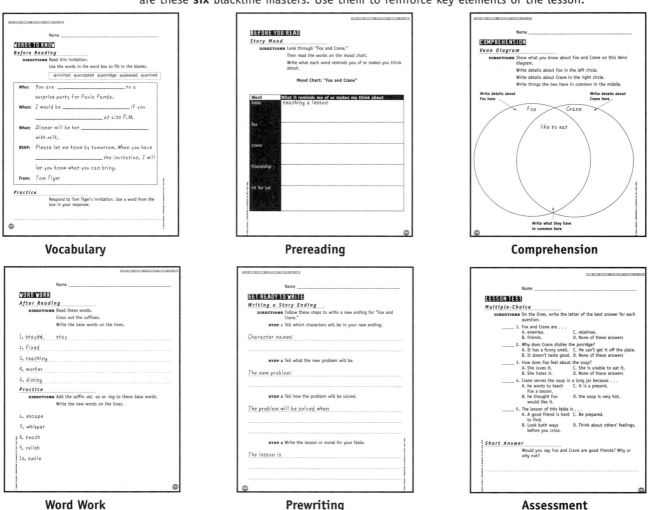

Vocabulary   **Prereading**   **Comprehension**

Word Work   **Prewriting**   **Assessment**

⊥. BEFORE YOU READ

Read the directions at the top of page 158. Explain to students that you'd like them to complete a **think-pair-and-share** before they begin reading "Fox and Crane." Divide the class into pairs and ask them to work together on the activity. Remind students that they'll work on the first part alone and *then* join with their partner to share answers. (Refer to the Strategy Handbook on page 50 for more help.)

Motivation Strategy

MOTIVATING STUDENTS   Ask students to plan a menu for a dinner party with a friend. Have them choose foods they know their friend will like. Ask them to make a menu on a piece of cardboard and then illustrate the edges so that it looks like something you'd find in a restaurant. Remind students that they'll want to serve things they know their friend will enjoy. What they themselves would like to eat should be of secondary importance.

Words to Know

SYNONYMS   Use the **Words to Know** blackline master on page 238 as a way to troubleshoot vocabulary problems. Several of the words in Polacco's story may be unfamiliar to students. Assess what words they do and do not know and then concentrate on helping them learn to pronounce, spell, and use the unfamiliar words. After working through the page, you might decide to teach a short vocabulary lesson on **synonyms.**

To begin, show students the five key vocabulary words in "Fox and Crane"*: invited, accepted, porridge, pleased,* and *arrived.* Ask students to say which words they've heard before, and in what context. Create a synonym chart on the board and ask students to suggest synonyms for each of the words. As you know, learning the synonym for a word can be a shortcut to learning the word's full definition. Your chart might look something like this:

Word	Where I've heard it before	Synonym
porridge	"The Three Bears"	oatmeal

Prereading Strategies

THINK-PAIR-AND-SHARE   The **think-pair-and-share** on page 158 should be fun for students. Many of them will know enough of this tale that they'll be able to put the sentences in the correct order. Others will enjoy guessing what happens next in the story. Encourage students to discuss their numbering with their reading partners. Explain that there are no wrong answers at this point, but that you'd like them to be able to tell why they made the choices they did.

STORY IMPRESSION   As an additional prereading activity, explain to students that the impression a story gives readers, or the atmosphere a writer establishes, is called the story's **mood.** Some stories (like "Fox and Crane") have a lighthearted but instructive mood. Ask students to read a list of words related to the story. What do these words remind them of? How do they make them feel? These questions will help students consider the mood of Polacco's story.

See the **Before you Read** blackline master on page 239 to extend the activity.

MY PURPOSE   Review with students the characteristics of a fable. A fable is a short, simple story that teaches a lesson. It usually includes animals that act and talk like people. Then read aloud the purpose statement on page 158. Students should keep this purpose in mind as they read.

II. READ

Response Strategy

FIRST READING Before students begin their first readings, remind them of the response strategy of asking during-reading **questions.** They should make a note of their questions in the Response Notes even if they think the question will be answered later on. When everyone has finished, discuss as a class any questions that remain. Some of their questions may point them toward a discussion of the main idea, or lesson, of this fable.

Comprehension Strategy

SECOND READING As they read Polacco's fable, students will need to stop at two different points and **retell** the action of the story. Remind them that when they retell, they need to use their own words, not the author's words. Their retellings should be brief and to the point. You don't want them to interrupt their reading for any longer than just a minute or two.

For more help with **Comprehension,** assign the blackline master on page 240.

Discussion Questions

COMPREHENSION 1. What is the relationship between Fox and Crane? *(They are friends.)*

2. What "mistake" does Fox make at her dinner party? What "mistake" does Crane make? *(They both serve food in such a way that their guest cannot eat it.)*

CRITICAL THINKING 3. What does the author mean when she says, "Crane had given [Fox] tit for tat"? *(Fox got what she deserved since she too had served a meal that a friend could not eat.)*

4. Do Fox and Crane stay angry with each other? Explain why or why not. *(No. They both value the other's friendship too much and now serve food that can be eaten by either.)*

5. What is the lesson of this fable? *(Ask students to explain in their own words the moral and what it means. Have them support what they say with evidence from the story.)*

Reread

THIRD READING The directions on page 162 ask students to reread Polacco's fable from start to finish. On their second readings, they should look for details that reveal the lesson of the story. Have them review the questions they wrote in the Response Notes to see which they're now able to answer.

Word Work

SUFFIXES AND BASE WORDS Use the Word Work lesson on page 163 as a review of **suffixes** and **base words**. Help students get into the habit of checking for suffixes when they come across a word they don't know. In some cases, the suffix can offer a clue about the word's meaning or at the very least show how the word should be used in a sentence. Begin with the common suffixes *-ed, -ing*, and *-s/-es*. Add to the suffix list when students have mastered these four endings.

For additional practice, see the **Word Work** blackline master on page 241.

III. GET READY TO WRITE

Prewriting Strategies

STORY CHART In **Part IV**, students will write a new story ending for "Fox and Crane." In preparation for this writing assignment, students will fill out a **story chart** that explores their understanding of these important elements: setting, conflict, and resolution. If you feel students will benefit, post the chart on page 164 on the board and discuss possible answers as a class. Be sure students fully understand each story element so that they can incorporate the essential ones in their own version of "Fox and Crane."

Have students use the **Get Ready to Write** blackline master on page 242.

IV. WRITE

The directions at the top of page 165 instruct students to write a new **story ending** for "Fox and Crane." Before students begin writing, ask a volunteer to retell Polacco's ending. Then have students work in small groups to brainstorm endings they'd like to tell. Other students in the group might have suggestions or ideas that the writer can use to refine what he or she plans to write. Remind the class to use ideas from the story chart when writing.

After students have written a first draft, have them exchange papers and read each other's work. Ask student editors to check to be sure that the new ending makes sense. Does it use some elements from the original? If not, editors should make suggestions for revisions.

WRITING RUBRIC Use this rubric to help with a quick assessment of students' writing.

Do students' story endings

• use some elements (such as setting and characters) from the original?

• present a new conflict for Fox and Crane?

• offer a resolution to that conflict by the end?

Grammar, Usage, and Mechanics

When students are ready to proofread their work, refer them to the **Writers' Checklist.** Read aloud the information about using **apostrophes** to forming possessives for plural nouns that do not end in *s*. For practice, put some words on the board and have students make possessives out of each. These words might work well:

children   deer   ox   women

V. LOOK BACK

Point out the **Readers' Checklist** and reflect with students on their **understanding** of Polacco's tale. Are they able to state the moral of the fable? Can they retell what it was about?

To test students' comprehension, use the **Lesson Test** blackline master on page 243.

Name _____

WORDS TO KNOW

Before Reading

DIRECTIONS Read this invitation.

Use the words in the word box to fill in the blanks.

⟡invited ⟡accepted ⟡porridge ⟡pleased ⟡arrived

Who: You are _____ to a
surprise party for Paula Panda.

When: I would be _____ if you
_____ at 6:00 P.M.

What: Dinner will be hot _____
with milk.

RSVP: Please let me know by tomorrow. When you have
_____ the invitation, I will
let you know what you can bring.

From: Tom Tiger

Practice

Respond to Tom Tiger's invitation. Use a word from the
box in your response.

Name _____

BEFORE YOU READ

Story Mood

DIRECTIONS Look through "Fox and Crane."

Then read the words on the mood chart.

Write what each word reminds you of or makes you think about.

Mood Chart: "Fox and Crane"

Word	What it reminds me of or makes me think about
fable	*teaching a lesson*
fox	
crane	
friendship	
tit for tat	

Name _____

COMPREHENSION

Venn Diagram

DIRECTIONS Show what you know about Fox and Crane on this Venn diagram.

Write details about Fox in the left circle.

Write details about Crane in the right circle.

Write things the two have in common in the middle.

Write details about Fox here

Write details about Crane here

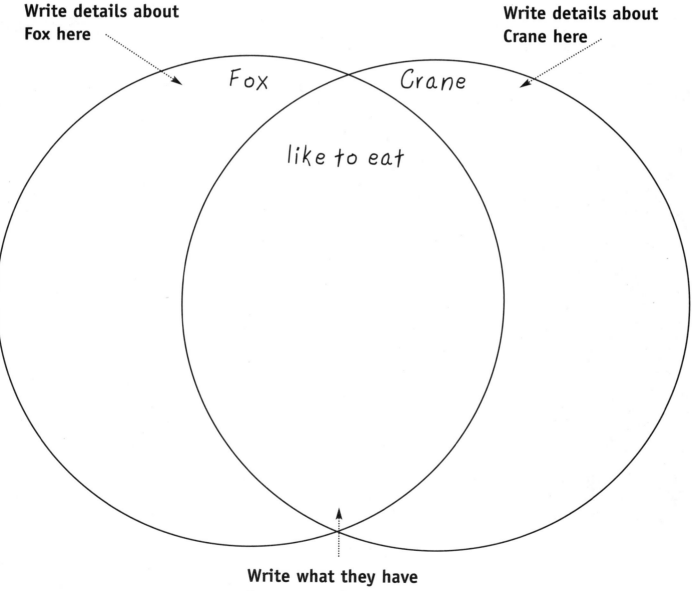

Fox   Crane

like to eat

Write what they have in common here

Name _____

WORD WORK

After Reading

DIRECTIONS Read these words.

Cross out the suffixes.

Write the base words on the lines.

1. stayed   stay

2. fixed

3. reaching

4. worker

5. dining

Practice

DIRECTIONS Add the suffix *-ed, -es,* or *-ing* to these base words.

Write the new words on the lines.

6. escape

7. whisper

8. teach

9. relish

10. smile

Name _____

GET READY TO WRITE

Writing a Story Ending

DIRECTIONS Follow these steps to write a new ending for "Fox and Crane."

STEP 1 Tell which characters will be in your new ending.

Character names: _____

_____

STEP 2 Tell what the new problem will be.

The new problem: _____

_____

STEP 3 Tell how the problem will be solved.

The problem will be solved when _____

_____

_____

STEP 4 Write the lesson or moral for your fable.

The lesson is _____

_____

_____

Name _____

LESSON TEST

Multiple-Choice

DIRECTIONS On the lines, write the letter of the best answer for each question.

_____ 1. Fox and Crane are . . .
A. enemies.   C. relatives.
B. friends.   D. None of these answers

_____ 2. Why does Crane dislike the porridge?
A. It has a funny smell.   C. He can't get it off the plate.
B. It doesn't taste good.   D. None of these answers

_____ 3. How does Fox feel about the soup?
A. She loves it.   C. She is unable to eat it.
B. She hates it.   D. None of these answers

_____ 4. Crane serves the soup in a long jar because . . .
A. he wants to teach   C. it is a present.
   Fox a lesson.
B. he thought Fox   D. the soup is very hot.
   would like it.

_____ 5. The lesson of this fable is . . .
A. A good friend is hard   C. Be prepared.
   to find.
B. Look both ways   D. Think about others' feelings.
   before you cross.

Short Answer

Would you say Fox and Crane are good friends? Why or why not?

_____

_____

Abuela

BACKGROUND

Arthur Dorros's award-winning *Abuela* is a celebration of the relationship between grandparents and grandchildren. The story is told through the eyes of a young child who takes her beloved Abuela on a walk through the park. Since Abuela speaks mostly Spanish, the narrator trades back and forth between English and Spanish as she recounts their adventure.

The narrator of the story is Rosalba, a joyful little girl who imagines possibilities in all things. Rosalba wonders what it would be like to fly like the birds. She also wonders whether or not she can get her Abuela to fly with her. Then the two could soar together, she says, which would make her day wonderfully complete.

In the second half of the book, Rosalba does indeed convince her grandmother to take an imaginary trip above the Manhattan rooftops. Along the way, Abuela points out the places she grew up and parts of the city that are important to their family's heritage.

Reprinted in the ***Sourcebook*** is the first half of *Abuela*. If students enjoy the story, be sure to recommend that they look for the book on their next trip to the library.

BIBLIOGRAPHY Students might enjoy reading another book by the talented Arthur Dorros. Suggest they choose one of these books to read during their free time:

(Lexile 540)   (Lexile 560)   (Lexile 550)

How to Introduce the Reading

Introduce the lesson by reading aloud the opening paragraph on page 167. The questions on this page are intended to pique students' interest in the reading to come. They will also help students make an initial connection to the topic of the reading: grandmothers.

Ask students to think for a moment about a person in their family who is important to them, such as a grandmother, an aunt, or a sibling. Then have volunteers name the person and tell a little about him or her. If students are reluctant to volunteer, have them all draw a picture of their important person and then write a sentence explaining what they have learned from this person.

Other Reading

The following three books all have a Lexile score similar to that of *Abuela* (Lexile 510). Recommend one of these or do a search of your own on the Lexile website (www.Lexile.com):

THIS FOR THAT: A TONGA TALE by Verna Aardema

NINE DAYS TO CHRISTMAS: A STORY OF MEXICO by Marie Hall Ets and Aurora La Bastida

THE BEST OLDER SISTER by Sook Nyull Choi

(Lexile 500)   (Lexile 510)   (Lexile 520)

Abuela

Skills and Strategies Overview

PREREADING word web

READING LEVEL Lexile 510

RESPONSE draw

VOCABULARY ✦abuela ✦flock ✦reply ✦leaped ✦flapping

COMPREHENSION Double-entry journal

WORD WORK prefixes and suffixes

PREWRITING character map

WRITING descriptive paragraph / capitalizing proper names

ASSESSMENT meaning

OTHER RESOURCES

The first **four** pages of this teacher's lesson describe Parts I–V of the lesson. Also included are these **six** blackline masters. Use them to reinforce key elements of the lesson.

Vocabulary

Prereading

Comprehension

Word Work

Prewriting

Assessment

BEFORE YOU READ

> After students have finished their discussion (or drawing) of an important family member, explain that they are about to read a story about a little girl named Rosalba and her abuela, or grandmother. Then assign the prereading activity, a **word web**. (Refer to the Strategy Handbook on page 51 for more help.)

Motivation Strategy

CONNECTING WITH STUDENTS
Ask students to tell the Spanish words they know, or words they know from another language. See if you can find several different ways to say such common words as *hello*, *goodbye*, and *thank-you*. Then ask which students speak a language other than English at home. What advantages are there to knowing more than one language?

MOTIVATING STUDENTS
Have students imagine they could fly like a bird. Where would they want to fly to if they had just one day to do it in? Would they fly above their houses, or would they take a trip far away? Invite students to explain their choices. Establish an imaginative mood in your classroom that matches the mood of Dorros's mood in the story.

Words to Know

CONTEXT CLUES
Use the **Words to Know** blackline master on page 250 as a way to troubleshoot vocabulary problems. After working through the page, you might decide to teach a short vocabulary lesson on using **context clues.**

To begin, show students the key vocabulary words in *Abuela*: *abuela, flock* (as a noun), *reply, leaped,* and *flapping.* Remind students that writers often place clues about a word's meaning within the same sentence or in nearby sentences. (This is particularly important for students to know before they read *Abuela,* since Dorros defines each Spanish phrase Rosalba uses in a nearby phrase or sentence.) Read the first few sentences of the second paragraph aloud to students. What context clues can they find for the word *abuela?*

Prereading Strategies

WORD WEB
As a prereading activity, students are asked to make a **word web** for the word *grandma* or the word *older woman*. Have students call on their own thoughts and feelings when creating the web. This prereading activity will help you create another valuable link between student and text.

PICTURE WALK
As a further prereading activity, take a **picture walk** of *Abuela*. Remind the class that during a picture walk, they look carefully at the art (and captions) and then say what these elements remind them of. Have them consider how the pictures make them feel and what they think the selection will be about. Doing a picture walk beforehand can make the text seem more familiar and less intimidating when it comes time to read.

To extend the activity, use the **Before You Read** blackline master on page 251.

MY PURPOSE
Students' purpose for reading *Abuela* will be to find out what the grandmother in the story is like. Be sure they note their inferences about Abuela as they read. In particular, they should watch for clues about her personality and how she feels about her granddaughter.

II. READ

Response Strategy

FIRST READING When students are ready to read, remind them of the importance of the response strategy, **draw**. Have the class supplement the art on the page with their own pictures that capture the actions and feelings described. Each time students make a picture, they'll need to think carefully about what's happening in the text. This can greatly improve their comprehension of the story.

Comprehension Strategy

SECOND READING During their reading of *Abuela*, students will need to pause and fill in a **Double-entry journal** that asks them to respond to a quotation with their own thoughts and feelings. Once again, your purpose here is to help students make a personal connection to the reading. Students will find it easier to understand Abuela (and what motivates her as a character) if they've made connections to their own lives along the way.

For more help with **Comprehension,** assign the blackline master on page 252.

Discussion Questions

COMPREHENSION 1. Who narrates this story? *(a little girl named Rosalba)*

2. Where do Rosalba and Abuela live? *(in a city. The art shows that the city is Manhattan, although students should not be expected to know that.)*

CRITICAL THINKING 3. How does Rosalba feel about her grandmother? *(She adores her. Rosalba's tone in describing her grandmother is respectful, admiring, and joyful.)*

4. Why do you think Rosalba would like to fly? *(She'd like to swoop above the park and call down to her grandmother. She'd like to "leap" and "flap" in the wind.)*

5. What kind of a person is Abuela? *(She is observant and appreciative of the sights around her. She clearly takes as much pleasure in her granddaughter as her granddaughter does in her.)*

Reread

THIRD READING Instead of having students reread all of *Abuela*, ask them to skim the pages of the story, paying careful attention to the art printed there and the art they created in the margins. What clues about Abuela does this art reveal? Students will need to collect as many character clues about Abuela as they can in order to make a thorough character description of her in **Part IV**.

Word Work

PREFIXES AND SUFFIXES Use the Word Work lesson on page 171 as a review of **prefixes** and **suffixes**. Remind students that the prefixes and suffixes listed on page 171 are just a few of the ones that are commonly used in English. Other common suffixes include *-able, -ible, -en, -ess,* and *-ly*. Other common prefixes include *ex-, im-, in-, mis-, pre-,* and *pro-*. If you have time, build lists of words that contain these prefixes and suffixes.

For additional practice, see the **Word Work** blackline master on page 253.

III. GET READY TO WRITE

Prewriting Strategies

CHARACTER MAP Use the prewriting activity on page 172 to help prepare students to write a descriptive paragraph about Abuela. Remind the class that good writers never tell everything you need to know about a character. They offer clues, and then leave it up to the reader to decide what they mean. This is called *making inferences,* and it's something good readers do when they read.

The **character map** on the prewriting page asks students to look in the text for proof of four inferences about Abuela: she likes to have fun, she is thoughtful, she enjoys nature, and she loves her granddaughter. Encourage students to use direct quotes when supplying proof. Show them how to make quotation marks and explain that they need to use these marks of punctuation each time they quote directly from a text.

Have students use the **Get Ready to Write** blackline master on page 254.

IV. WRITE

The directions at the top of page 173 instruct students to write a **descriptive paragraph** about Abuela. Remind the class of the rule that a paragraph has a beginning (the introduction, which includes the topic sentence), middle (body) and end (concluding sentence).

WRITING RUBRIC Use this rubric to help with a quick assessment of students' writing.

Do students' descriptive paragraphs

• open with a topic sentence that names Abuela and says what she is like?

• offer three or more pieces of proof from the story to support the topic sentence?

• include a closing sentence that is a restatement of the topic sentence, or that says how the writer feels about Abuela?

• stay focused on the topic of Abuela throughout?

Grammar, Usage, and Mechanics

When students are ready to proofread their work, refer them to the **Writers' Checklist.** Be sure they know that **proper nouns** require **capital letters**, while common nouns do not. Explain the difference between "Abuela" and "my abuela."

V. LOOK BACK

Refer students to the **Readers' Checklist.** Reflect with students on the **meaning** of *Abuela*. Help them express the connections they were able to make to the text as they were reading.

To test students' comprehension, use the **Lesson Test** blackline master on page 255.

Name _____

WORDS TO KNOW

Before Reading

DIRECTIONS Read each sentence.

Then say what you think the underlined words mean.

Use the rest of the sentence to help you.

1. My Abuela is my mother's mother.

I think Abuela *means* _____

2. The <u>flock</u> of hundreds of seagulls flew over our heads.

I think flock *means* _____

3. The puppy <u>leaped</u> into the little girl's lap.

I think leaped *means* _____

4. My grandmother was <u>flapping</u> her fan up and down to cool herself.

I think flapping *means* _____

5. When I asked my brother a question, he did not <u>reply</u>.

I think reply *means* _____

Practice

Use the word <u>flock</u> in a sentence to show what it means.

_____

_____

Name _____

BEFORE YOU READ

Picture Walk

DIRECTIONS Take a picture walk through *Abuela*.

Look at every picture. Think about how they make you feel.

Then answer these questions.

My Picture Walk of *Abuela*

The pictures make me feel . . .	They make me think about . . . .

My favorite picture is . . .

because . . .

What do you predict *Abuela* is about?

_____

_____

Name _____

COMPREHENSION

Storyboard

DIRECTIONS Retell what happens in *Abuela*. Draw pictures of the action. Write sentences that explain each picture.

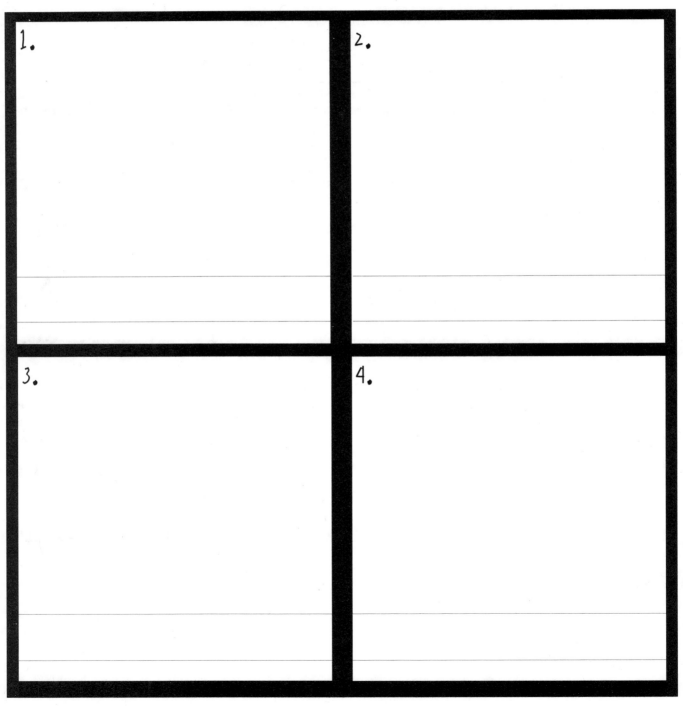

1.

2.

3.

4.

Name _____

WORD WORK

After Reading

DIRECTIONS Look at the prefixes and suffixes in the box.

Add a prefix or suffix to each of the words. Choose the prefix or suffix that makes the most sense.

prefixes: *re-, un-*	**suffixes:** *-ing, -ed, -ful, -er*

Small word	**Bigger word**
1. prefix + do =	
2. fly + suffix =	
3. prefix + appear =	
4. wonder + suffix =	
5. prefix + able =	
6. soar + suffix =	

Practice

DIRECTIONS Add a suffix or prefix to each word in the box.

write	tear	act	dance

7. _____

8. _____

9. _____

10. _____

Name _____

GET READY TO WRITE

Writing a Descriptive Paragraph

DIRECTIONS Follow these steps to write your paragraph about Abuela.

STEP 1 Write your topic sentence.

Abuela is _____ .

STEP 2 Then write 3 words in the Word Bank that describe her.

Word Bank
kind

STEP 3 Now write details that prove your topic sentence is true.

proof #1 _____

proof #2 _____

proof #3 _____

Name _____

LESSON TEST

Multiple-Choice

DIRECTIONS On the lines, write the letter of the best answer for each question.

_____ 1. Who is Abuela?
   A. the bus driver   C. the grandfather
   B. the grandmother   D. the park ranger

_____ 2. What do Abuela and Rosalba (the narrator) do together?
   A. They go to the park.   C. They drive out of town.
   B. They go for a swim.   D. They watch a race.

_____ 3. What is the mood of the story?
   A. angry   C. joyful
   B. sad   D. quiet

_____ 4. How does Rosalba feel about Abuela?
   A. She is angry with her. C. She is frightened of her.
   B. She doesn't know her.   D. She loves her.

_____ 5. An important idea in _Abuela_ is . . .
   A. Grandmothers are special. C. We can't fly.
   B. A park is a fun place.   D. All of these answers

Short Answer

Why does the author imagine she is flying with Abuela?

_____

_____

PLAY BALL, AMELIA BEDELIA

II. Read

(Students' answers will vary.)

What do you remember about Amelia Bedelia so far?
(She misses the first two balls that she tries to hit. She hits the third one really hard.)

What is the story about?
(Amelia Bedelia plays baseball with the Grizzlies. After she hits the ball, she starts running. When the other players tell her to steal the bases, she thinks she has to pick them up.)

Word Work

jumping
leaped
reading
mixes
spending
waiting
smelled

III. Get Ready to Write

(Students' answers will vary.)

Make a List
1. She took the first base.
2. She took second and third bases.
3. She took home plate.
4. She ran all the way to her house.

TEACHER'S GUIDE ANSWERS

Words to Know

1. full
2. nervous
3. picked up
4. confused

Word Work

1. going
2. fixes
3. reaches
4. loaded
5. missed
6. stealing
7. loaded
8. shouted
9. mixes
10. starting

Assessment

1. C
2. A
3. C
4. C
5. D

POEMS ABOUT THE WEATHER

II. Read

What You Think This Means
(The snow makes the world look like it has white icing on it.)

What You Think This Means
(The wind can push anything until it pushes the speaker around. Then he/she doesn't like it anymore.)

What You Think This Means
(When the sun goes down, it looks like it pulls down a dark shade because all the light goes away.)

Word Work

possible answers:
takes, fakes, makes, stakes, snakes, shakes, lakes
fun, bun, spun, stun, shun

TEACHER'S GUIDE ANSWERS

Words to Know

1. putting, laying out
2. wet and icy
3. throw
4. exchanging, swapping

Comprehension

(Students' answers will vary.)
1. "Winter Morning" by Ogden Nash is about the great beauty and fun of winter. Snow covers the ground like icing on a cake and people enjoy making snowmen.
2. "Go Wind" by Lilian Moore is about the sounds and effects of wind.
3. "Mister Sun" by J. Patrick Lewis is about the sun. It describes its changing color at different times of day and its ultimate disappearance at night.

Word Work

(Students' answers will vary.)
2. clay
3. free
4. snip
5. from
6. climb
7. glimmer
8. stop

Assessment

1. A
2. C
3. B
4. A
5. D

FROGS

II. Read

(Students' answers will vary.)

Why do frogs feel at home in ponds?

(They start their lives in the water when they are eggs.)

What are 2 ways the tadpole changes at it grows?

1. It gets bigger.
2. It grows little legs.
   or
3. Its tail disappears.

Word Work

possible answers:

COMPOUND WORD	SMALL WORD	SMALL WORD
underwater	under	water
into	in	to
anymore	any	more
inside	in	side

III. Get Ready to Write

(Students' answers will vary.)

From Egg to Frog

1. Frog babies hatch from eggs as tadpoles.
2. Tadpoles get bigger.
3. Tadpoles grow legs.
4. Tadpoles lose their tails.
5. Baby frogs can now breathe out of water.

TEACHER'S GUIDE ANSWERS

Words to Know

1. hatch
2. shrink
3. disappear
4. webbed
5. breathe

Comprehension

1. After a frog hatches, frog babies swim out into the water like fish. They are tadpoles.
2. As tadpoles get bigger they grow little back legs, then front legs, and then their tails shrink and disappear.
3. When the baby frogs breathe out of water, they are land animals. They can still swim.

Word Work

2. waterfall
3. sunlight
4. sometimes
5. school teacher
6. anybody
7. sandpaper
8. teardrop
9. without

Assessment

1. B
2. D
3. A
4. D
5. A

I'LL CATCH THE MOON

II. Read

(Students' answers will vary.)

What things does the girl see and feel?
(She sees the city and the sky. She looks at the traffic moving below and the tall buildings and moon above her. She wishes she could put the moon in her pocket. She thinks of the pictures that she's seen of the moon.)

In your own words, predict what she will do with the moon.
(She will travel around with the moon and see the earth from far away like the moon does.)

What will the girl and moon do together?
(She will not be able to travel up to it, but she can see it every night and wave to it.)

Word Work

possible answers:
catch, scratch, patch, match, latch, batch
night, slight, fright, might, tight, light, sight
round, ground, pound, mound, bound, sound, found

III. Get Ready to Write

TEACHER'S GUIDE ANSWERS

Words to Know

1. away from the earth
2. flying machines with a propeller on top
3. sits
4. bright flying objects made of ice and gases
5. going

Comprehension

sees — city, sky, buildings, helicopters, airplanes, clouds

hears — sounds of the city, like honking of cars

On her journey to the moon, the little girl . . .

feels — excited, energetic

plays — hide-and-seek

Word Work

2. slump
3. bladder
4. far, car, par, bar, mar
5. coats, moats, boats
6. growl.
7. frown.
8. smart.

Assessment

1. C
2. B
3. D
4. C
5. D

VOLCANOES

II. Read

(Students' answers will vary.)

How is the earth like an orange?

(The earth is round. Its top layer is like the skin of an orange.)

How does a volcano start?

(Melted rock under the surface pushes up on the top layers of the earth. When it finds a crack between plates, it pushes up and out.)

Word Work

Silent e words + ing	Other words + ed
1. moving	1. seemed
2. liking	2. melted
3. living	3. pushed

III. Get Ready to Write

Detail 2 When the magma finds a crack between plates, it pushes up through the earth.

Detail 3 The magma bubbles up a tube to a hole called a crater.

Detail 4 The magma spills out of the crater.

Detail 5 This lava sometimes turns into sharp rocks and ash in the sky.

TEACHER'S GUIDE ANSWERS

Words to Know

1. b
2. e
3. a
4. c
5. d

Comprehension

First, magma pushes on the plates and moves up through a crack.

Next, the magma bubbles up toward the hole at the top.

Then, the magma spills out of the hole, called a crater.

After that, the spilled magma is called lava.

Finally, the lava either sprays out of the crater into the sky and hardens into ash.

Word Work

1. baking
2. scooped
3. computing
4. saved
5. statement
6. careful
7. filled
8. seemed
9. hiding
10. smiled
11. tasteless
12. grateful

Assessment

1. B
2. C
3. D
4. D
5. A

CAVE PEOPLE

II. Read

(Students' answers will vary.)

How are Neanderthals like people today?

(They sometimes had to hunt for their food. They hid from big animals.)

Word Work

Same consonants	Different consonants
mam/moth	hun/ter
sum/mers	rein/deer
bet/ter	win/ters
	shor/ter

III. Get Ready to Write

(Students' answers will vary.)

Who: Neanderthals were the people who lived here a long time ago.

When: It was the Ice Age, a time when it was much colder than it is now.

Where: The Neanderthals are ouside of their caves, where they live.

Why: The people are hungry and need to hunt some kind of animal.

Closing: (Answers will vary.)

TEACHER'S GUIDE ANSWERS

Words to Know

1. a large animal with curved tusks and thick hair
2. marked in a different color
3. deer with antlers
4. a sharp and pointed stick
5. grooves

Comprehension

1. The Neanderthals were hunters who had big teeth and low foreheads.
2. They ate reindeer and other animals.
3. They lived in caves.
4. Their lives were difficult because they had to search for food and avoid dangerous animals.
5. Answers will vary.

Word Work

1. dan/ger
2. spot/ted
3. fif/ty
4. num/ber
5. bum/mer in left-hand column
6. smel/ly in left-hand column
7. let/ter in left-hand column
8. ab/le in right-hand column
9. war/mer in right-hand column
10. far/mer in right-hand column

Assessment

1. A
2. B
3. C
4. B
5. D

LOOK AT YOUR EYES

II. Read

(Students' answers will vary.)

What is the effect (or result) of the cause below?
Effect: Your pupil gets smaller.

Word Work

smallish	darkest
relighted	widen
looking	growth
	counter

III. Get Ready to Write

What do you want to say about your eyes?
(Answers will vary.)

What causes your eyes to change?
(Sometimes your eye needs a lot of light, but other times, it needs only a little light.)

What happens when your eyes change?
(In dark places, your pupil gets bigger. In bright areas, it gets smaller.)

What do you think about how your eyes change?
(Answers will vary.)

TEACHER'S GUIDE ANSWERS

Words to Know

1. pupil
2. smaller
3. window, light
4. bigger

Comprehension

When you close your eyes, the pupil becomes bigger and the pupil takes in less light.

When you open your eyes in bright light, the pupil becomes smaller and the pupil takes in more light.

Word Work

1. returns, returning, returned
2. tallest, taller
3. revisiting
4. faster
5. re-froze
6. widen, widest
7-10. (Answers will vary.)
8. helped, helping
9. slow, slower, slowest
10. taller, tallest

Assessment

1. C
2. A
3. B
4. A
5. D

JUST A FEW WORDS, MR. LINCOLN

II. Read

(Students' answers will vary.)

Why did Lincoln not want to leave?
(His son Tad was sick.)

What happened on the train?
(Lincoln talked with the important people on the car and finished writing his speech.)

What happened when the singers asked Lincoln to give them a speech?
(Lincoln didn't want to because he didn't have anything to say and didn't want to sound silly.)

How do you know Abraham Lincoln really loved his son, Tad?
(He kept thinking and worrying about Tad when he was away from home.)

Word Work

Base word
b. sound
c. talk
d. sing
e. crowd
f. do
g. think
h. able

TEACHER'S GUIDE ANSWERS

Words to Know

1. filled
2. respect, praise
3. people in attendance
4. silly
5. letter

Comprehension

Setting
Where the story takes place: The story takes place on the way to and in Gettysburg.
When it takes place: The story takes place in 1863.

Character names

Tad	President Lincoln	Mrs. Lincoln
sickly	committed	supportive

Problem
Tad is ill and the president is not focused enough to deliver a speech in Gettysburg.

How the problem is solved
The president concentrates on writing his speech and then receives word that Tad has recovered.

Word Work

1. crying cry
2. unmade made
3. retry try
4. walked walk
5. undo do
6. remarkable mark
7. untie
8. falling
9. unwinding
10. reread

Assessment

1. B
2. C
3. D
4. C
5. D

WHY I SNEEZE, SHIVER, HICCUP, AND YAWN

II. Read

(Students' answers will vary.)

What would you tell a friend about sneezes?
(You can't control a sneeze. It is a reflex.)

What have you learned about nerves?
(Nerves look like threads and are all over your body, including your brain and spine. They are like telephone wires and carry messages from your brain to the rest of your body.)

What do nerves do?
(Nerves in your hand sense the stove is hot, and they send a message to your spine. The spine signals the muscle that can move your arm.)

What is one important fact you learned about why people sneeze, shiver, hiccup, and yawn?
(People do those things whether they want to or not.)

Word Work

Same Consonants	Different Consonants
hic/cup	un/der
mid/dle	sig/nal
sud/den	ner/vous
hap/pen	sys/tem
mes/sage	mus/cle
up/per	re/flex
car/ry	
swal/low	

III. Get Ready to Write

Possible details:
(Nerves control reflexes. They send signals from body parts to the brain and spine, which control muscles. You cannot control the message that your nerves send your brain and spine.)

TEACHER'S GUIDE ANSWERS

Words to Know

1. bunch
2. feel
3. without a lot of thought
4. quickly moves
5. all the way

Comprehension

1. A reflex is something that happens without your thinking about it or making it happen.
2. sneezes, hiccups, belches
3. Nerves carry messages back and forth, telling your muscles how to react.
4. A signal from your nerves tells your muscles to move your hand quickly away.

Word Work

1. fic/tion
2. jum/ping
3. trou/ble
4. hel/met
5. mil/lion
6. ner/vous
7. cot/ton

Assessment

1. A
2. C
3. C
4. B
5. C

MARVIN REDPOST: ALONE IN HIS TEACHER'S HOUSE

II. Read

(Students' answers will vary.)

What This Tells You About Marvin
(He will do anything to get the dog to eat. He is not scared of doing something strange.)

What This Tells You About Marvin
(He is sad that his friends are mad at him. He doesn't want them to be angry just because he got to do a job at his teacher's house.)

Word Work

	+ed	+ing
2. promise	promised	promising
3. stroke (to pet)	stroked	stroking
4. rinse	rinsed	rinsing
5. taste	tasted	tasting
6. smile	smiled	smiling

III. Get Ready to Write

Description: patient
Proof: (Marvin eats the dog food in front of Waldo.)

Description: caring
Proof: (When Waldo won't eat the dog food, Marvin buys and cooks him liver.)

Description: funny
Proof: (Marvin acts like a dog to get Waldo to eat.)

TEACHER'S GUIDE ANSWERS

Words to Know

1. grainy
2. interested, positive
3. have a strong effect on the minds and feelings of, affect in a positive way
4. volunteered

Comprehension

What he does	
Marvin acts responsibly by taking care of the dog any way he can.	

Why he acts this way	How others feel about him
Marvin feels lucky and proud that his teacher entrusted him with caring for the dog. He doesn't want to let the teacher down.	His classmates, Nick and Stuart, dislike him. They say Marvin thinks he's better than everyone.

Word Work

1. fined
2. shaping
3. basted
4. taking
5. guided
6. smile
7. like
8. have
9. write
10. stay

Assessment

1. D
2. A
3. A
4. C
5. B

HUNGRY, HUNGRY SHARKS

II. Read

(Students' answers will vary.)

How do blue sharks eat?
(They tear off big chunks of meat from a dead animal.)

Why do blue sharks follow ships?
(They hear noises from the ship and then eat the garbage that the people throw off board.)

Word Work

possible answers:
speed: (deed, feed, greed, heed, need, reed, seed, weed)
blow: (bow, cow, grow, how, brow, chow, crow, now, row, sow, show, tow, vow)
stay: (bay, clay, day, bray, hay, jay, lay, may, pay, say, stay, way)
call: (ball, fall, hall, gall, mall, wall)

III. Get Ready to Write

(Students' answers will vary.)

How blue sharks swim
(They move through the water very quickly.)

How blue sharks eat
(They eat big chunks off of dead animals. They even eat other sharks.)

What sharks are called
(They're called the wolves of the sea.)

How blue sharks know food is near
(They smell blood.)

What I think about sharks
(Answers will vary.)

TEACHER'S GUIDE ANSWERS

Words to Know

1. shoot
2. torpedoes
3. chunks
4. ships
5. packs

Word Work

(Students' answers will vary.)
1. dark
2. grim
3. peep
4. boot
5. flown

Assessment

1. B
2. A
3. A
4. C
5. C

BUFFALO BILL AND THE PONY EXPRESS

II. Read

(Students' answers will vary.)

Where does the story Happens:
Fort Laramie

When does the story take place:
spring, 1860

Why is riding the Pony Express hard work?

Reason #1
(Bill might have to ride 70 or more miles each day.)

Reason #2
(Bill might run into trouble.)

What is Buffalo Bill's Problem?
He is young and inexperienced.

Word Work

Base Word
b. close
c. rope
d. promise
e. ride
f. chase
g. take
h. show

III. Get Ready to Write

How Was He Bold?
Bill asks Mr. Majors for the job even though he is young.

How Was He a Hard Worker?
He roped cattle when he was only nine and now wants to do this job.

How Was He Daring?
Bill wants to do the job even though it is hard and dangerous.

How Was He Honest?
He tells Mr. Majors his real age.

TEACHER'S GUIDE ANSWERS

Words to Know

1. boys
2. spirit, courage
3. base
4. a place to rest

Comprehension

Where the story takes place: Fort Laramie

When it takes place: 1860

These are the characters: Buffalo Bill, Mr. Majors

The characters have these problems: Bill is too young to join the Pony Express. Mr. Majors has to know he can trust Bill to do the job.

This is how they solve the problems: Bill proves he has spunk and Mr. Majors knows he's the right person for the job.

The story ends when: Mr. Majors assigns Bill his home station and tells him when to come back for more mail.

Word Work

1. move
2. agreed agree
3. safer safe
4. roping rope
5. coming come
6. making
7. cared, caring
8. pleased, pleasing
9. scored, scoring
10. shared, sharing

Assessment

1. B
2. D
3. A
4. C
5. A

TOMÁS AND THE LIBRARY LADY

II. Read

(Students' answers will vary.)

What I Think About It
(Tomás's family works hard and has to travel all the time. They make the trip between different farms every year though, which must be difficult.)

What I Think About It
(The family members work in difficult conditions every day. They must be brave.)

What I Think About It
(The man was so scared he didn't want to move.)

What I Think About It
(Tomás wants to hear many stories and would enjoy reading books.)

Word Work

Compound Word	Small Word	Small Word
yourself	your	self
grandfather	grand	father
storyteller	story	teller

1. bookcase
2. hilltop
3. snowboard

III. Get Ready to Write

Where and when the story takes place
(The story takes place at an Iowa farm.)
Who the character is
(Tomás is a young boy who moves from farm to farm with his family.)
What problem the character has
(Tomás wants to hear more stories than his grandfather can tell.)
How the character solves the problem
(Tomás's grandfather tells him that he should go to the library.)

TEACHER'S GUIDE ANSWERS

Words to Know

1. howled
2. cot
3. chattered
4. sewn
5. thorny

Word Work

1. timetable
2. timeout
3. timeline
4. tablesaw
5. outfield
6. outline
7. outlook
8. outcome
9. seafood
10. lookout
11. every/body
12. butter/milk
13. back/ground
14. some/how
15. grand/father
16. card/board

Assessment

1. A
2. B
3. C
4. A
5. B

GOING HOME

II. Read

Where is the family going?
(to the parents' village of La Perla in Mexico)

How do the parents feel about Mexico?
(They love Mexico. They still regard it as home. La Perla is nice and pretty.)

Word Work

Silent _e_ Words   **Words Ending in 2 Consonants**

Silent _e_ Words	Words Ending in 2 Consonants
home	crops
drive	work
smile	ground

Words	Add _–s_ or _–es_	Add _–ing_
home	homes	
work	works	working
drive	drives	driving
smile	smiles	smiling

TEACHER'S GUIDE ANSWERS

Words to Know

1. shine
2. work
3. worn out
4. worried
5. cover

Comprehension

What the family does to prepare	How the children feel	What the parents say about Mexico
They load the car, lock the house, and say goodbye to friends.	nervous, curious about La Perla; Nora is sad to leave home at first.	It's pretty. It's nice. Their village is small.

Word Work

1. shove
2. drive
3. glove
4. loss
5. call
6. mess
7. shoves, shoving
8. drives, driving
9. gloves
10. losses
11. calls, calling
12. messes, messing

Assessment

1. B
2. C
3. D
4. C
5. A

FOX AND CRANE

II. Read

(Students' answers will vary.)
What happened at Fox's dinner?
(Crane couldn't get the food off of his plate because of his long beak.)
What happened at Crane's dinner?
(Fox couldn't get the soup out of the narrow jar because of her big head.)

Word Work

Base Word
2. value
3. sniff
4. relish
5. answer

III. Get Ready to Write

Where and when does the fable take place?
(Fox's and Crane's houses during two dinners)
What is Fox's problem?
(She cannot get the soup out of the narrow jar.)
What is Crane's problem?
(He cannot eat the porridge off the flat plate.)
How does the fable end?
(Both characters learn to make it easy for a friend to eat.)
What did you learn?
(Friends should always think about each other's feelings.)
What are some ideas for your new ending?
(Answers will vary.)

TEACHER'S GUIDE ANSWERS

Words to Know

1. invited
2. pleased, arrived
3. porridge
4. accepted

Comprehension

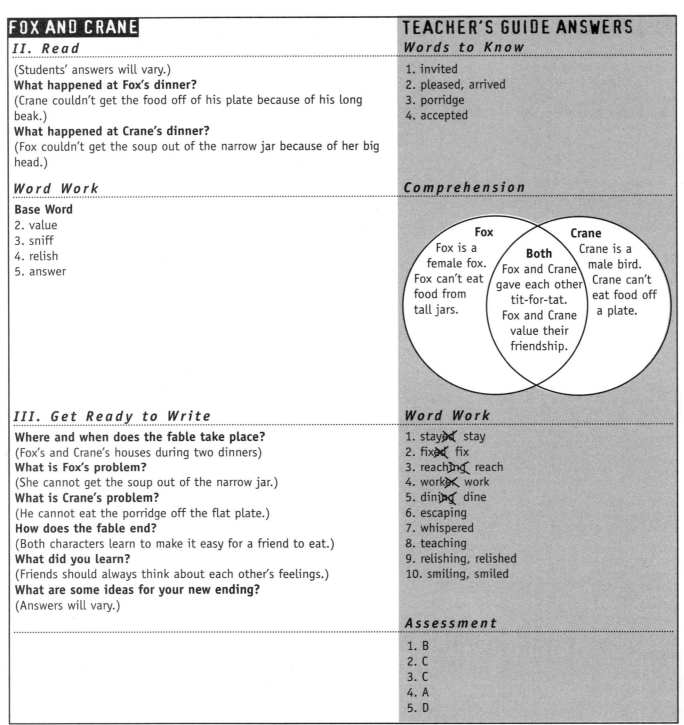

Word Work

1. stayed stay
2. fixed fix
3. reaching reach
4. worked work
5. dining dine
6. escaping
7. whispered
8. teaching
9. relishing, relished
10. smiling, smiled

Assessment

1. B
2. C
3. C
4. A
5. D